D0050009

OTHER VOLUMES IN THIS SERIES

THE

BEST OF

THE BEST

AMERICAN

POETRY

25TH ANNIVERSARY EDITION

◊ ◊ ◊

Robert Pinsky, Editor

David Lehman, Series Editor

SCRIBNER POETRY
NEW YORK   LONDON   TORONTO   SYDNEY   NEW DELHI

SCRIBNER POETRY
A Division of Simon & Schuster, Inc.
1230 Avenue of the Americas
New York, NY 10020

First Scribner edition April 2013

For information about special discounts for bulk purchases,
please contact Simon & Schuster Special Sales at 1-866-506-1949
or business@simonandschuster.com.

The Simon & Schuster Speakers Bureau can bring authors to your live event.
For more information or to book an event contact the Simon & Schuster Speakers
Bureau at 1-866-248-3049 or visit our website at www.simonspeakers.com.

Manufactured in the United States of America

3   5   7   9   10   8   6   4   2

Library of Congress Control Number: 88644281

ISBN 978-1-4516-5887-3
ISBN 978-1-4516-5888-0 (pbk)
ISBN 978-1-4516-5889-7 (ebook)

CONTENTS

For Glen Hartley

David Lehman was born in New York City in 1948, the son of refugees from Nazi Germany and Austria. Educated at Stuyvesant High School and Columbia University, he went to Clare College, Cambridge, on a two-year Kellett Fellowship and worked as Lionel Trilling's research assistant on his return to New York. He is the author of eight books of poetry, including *Yeshiva Boys* (2009), *When a Woman Loves a Man* (2005), *The Daily Mirror* (2000), and *Valentine Place* (1996), from Scribner, and *Operation Memory* (1990) and *An Alternative to Speech* (1986), from Princeton University Press. He is the editor of *The Oxford Book of American Poetry* (Oxford University Press, 2006) and *Great American Prose Poems: From Poe to the Present* (Scribner, 2003). *A Fine Romance: Jewish Songwriters, American Songs* (Nextbook/Schocken), his most recent nonfiction book, won the Deems Taylor Award from the American Society of Composers, Authors and Publishers (ASCAP) in 2010. Among Lehman's other books are a study in detective novels (*The Perfect Murder*), a group portrait of the New York School of poets (*The Last Avant-Garde*), and an account of the scandal sparked by the revelation that a Yale University eminence had written for a collaborationist newspaper in his native Belgium (*Signs of the Times: Deconstruction and the Fall of Paul de Man*). Lehman initiated *The Best American Poetry* series in 1988. He teaches in the graduate writing program of The New School and lives in New York City and in Ithaca, New York.

FOREWORD

by David Lehman

◊   ◊   ◊

Forty years ago, two professors working independently—Harvard's Walter Jackson Bate and Yale's Harold Bloom—changed the way we think about literary tradition. In *The Burden of the Past and the English Poet* (1970), Bate challenged the idea that literary influence was a largely benign activity on the model of mentor and sometimes rebellious pupil. In *The Anxiety of Influence* (1973), Bloom went further and propounded a compelling new theory, which quickly caught on. Students today learn that poets labor under the weight of their self-chosen masters—that, for example, the Romantic poets had Milton on the brain or that James Merrill in the United States and James Fenton in Britain illustrate two rival ways of absorbing the masterly influence of the transatlantic W. H. Auden. The encounter with the master is bound to provoke anxiety. What the latecomer does with that anxiety determines his or her chances at originality.

Anxiety can certainly prove a source for poetry. When, for a commemorative volume, Bloom selected poems from the first ten years of *The Best American Poetry,* it is telling that he chose two poems that are not about anxiety as much as they appear to spring from it: "Anxiety's Prosody" by A. R. Ammons from the 1989 volume (ed. Donald Hall) and John Ashbery's "The Problem of Anxiety" from that of 1997 (ed. James Tate). Bloom's theory may help us practically in our confrontations with such works and their authors. His love of poetry, the passion on display when he quotes touchstone passages from his prodigious memory, make an essay of his, whether on Hamlet or the King James Bible, Walter Pater or Walt Whitman, a profound and at times sublime experience.

Yet I contend that the process by which one poet assimilates the influence of another is not always quite so joyless, anxiety-ridden, or bereft of affection, as the theory would seem to imply. The pugilistic metaphors that appealed to Hemingway and Norman Mailer don't quite fit. The competition between and among poets is more like a team sport—you have teammates as well as opponents, you play for a chance at postseason glory (the sportswriters call it "immortality"), but you also play the occasional "exhibition game" (U.S.) or "friendly" (Britain). The best poetry anthologies demonstrate that there is often an element of sport and gamesmanship in the way that a poet can take note of an ancestor, an ally, or a rival. And in consequence, it's as though the poems they write are engaged in a dialogue.

To one who loves poetry and teaches Marvell's "The Garden" in relation to the first three chapters of Genesis, or William Carlos Williams's *Pictures from Brueghel* in relation to poems by W. H. Auden and John Berryman on the same paintings, it seems a self-evident proposition that poems partner with other poems. E. M. Forster's metaphor in *Aspects of the Novel* applies to poems—he imagines a timeless British Museum Reading Room where the books of any and all eras may converse among themselves, sharing secrets and trading intimacies. I love the metaphor but would amend it to say that favorite poems have a way of pairing off, like the characters of certain books—like Don Quixote and Sancho Panza, say, or Holmes and Watson, or Beatrice and Benedick in *Much Ado About Nothing*—that continue to live after the reader has returned them to the shelf.

Looking over the poems published in *The Best American Poetry* over the last twenty-five years, I am struck by the number of such poem pairings. In *The Best American Poetry 2012* (ed. Mark Doty), Jennifer Chang and Angelo Nikolopoulos react to Wordsworth's daffodils just as Billy Collins, back in the 1998 edition (ed. John Hollander), responded to the same poet's "Tintern Abbey." Also in the 2012 volume, Amy Glynn Greacen confronts William Blake on the matter of the sunflower ("and fie, / By the way, on any and all, who'd think to call / You weary of time"), and David Mason addresses the gap between Shelley's life and his ideals—the subject of a poem by Galway Kinnell that Paul Muldoon chose for *The Best American Poetry 2005*. In 1999 (ed. Robert Bly), John Brehm's "Sea of Faith" ponders Matthew Arnold's "Dover Beach"; in 2001 (ed. Robert Hass), Alan Feldman's "Contemporary American Poetry" struggles with Donald Hall's "Kicking the Leaves"; in 2008 (ed. Charles Wright), Ron Padgett's "Method, or Kenneth Koch" pays homage to a mentor; in 2007 (ed. Heather McHugh), Albert Goldbarth's poem takes its title from Robert Frost's "Stopping by Woods on a Snowy Evening," with which it has a lover's quarrel. Of "The Rose Has Teeth," Terrance Hayes's poem in the 2012 volume, its author writes, "My poem found its bones after I read Matthew Zapruder's marvelous poem, 'Never to Return,' in the 2009 edition of *The Best American Poetry*."

Let me linger over another example or two. Julie Sheehan's poem in *The Best American Poetry 2005* confronts the problem of writing a contemporary love poem. How do you avoid the clichés or the embarrassment of either purple patches or pink ones? Sheehan expresses the emotion by turning it on its head. Where the word "love" would ordinarily be found, she substitutes *hate*: "I hate you. Truly I do. / Everything about me hates everything about you." The poem ends with this crescendo:

> My breasts relaxing in their holster from morning till night
>   hate you
> Layers of hate, a parfait.
> Hours after our last row, brandishing the sharp glee of hate,
> I dissect you cell by cell, so that I may hate each one
>   individually and at leisure.
> My lungs, duplicitous twins, expand with the utter validity
>   of my hate, which can never have enough of you,
> Breathlessly, like two idealists in a broken submarine.

Sheehan may have inaugurated a new subgenre. Go to *The Best American Poetry 2009* (ed. David Wagoner) and you will find Martha Silano's riff ("Love") on Sheehan's "Hate Poem." In her note on "Love," Silano acknowledges the debt. She had, in fact, given herself and her students the "assignment" to "write a poem of address" modeled on "Hate Poem."

The desire of poems to link themselves explicitly to others can cross cultural boundaries of time and space. Walt Whitman's poems achieve such an immediacy of effect upon readers that many find themselves adopting his signature characteristics—the use of anaphora, long lines, extended arias, an imperial *I* that insists on its egolessness, and a penchant for making inclusive lists that substitute simultaneity for hierarchy as a governing principle. Among the writers of many nationalities who have given in to the impulse to talk back to Whitman, the Portuguese poet Fernando Pessoa (1888–1935) holds a prominent place. Pessoa, who was born in Lisbon, lived there, and infused a strong flavor of the city and the river Tagus in his poems, adopted heteronyms—like pseudonyms, except that each is outfitted with an identity and life story. One of them writes an ecstatic "Salutation to Walt Whitman": "I salute you, Walt, I salute you my brother in the Universe." In accents that recall "Crossing Brooklyn Ferry," he adds, "And just as you felt everything, so I feel everything, and so here we are clasping hands, / Clasping hands, Walt, clasping hands, with the universe doing a dance in our soul."* It

---

* Fernando Pessoa, *Poems of Fernando Pessoa*, trans. by Edwin Honig and Susan M. Brown (San Francisco: City Lights Books, 1998).

is as if the very form of the writing constituted an expression of affection and praise.

Now the lovely unexpected thing about these literary partnerships is that they have a way of doubling back to the source. Pessoa's "Salutation to Walt Whitman" has stimulated not one but two rather different responses from American poets, and both have been anthologized in *The Best American Poetry*. "Salutation to Fernando Pessoa" by Allen Ginsberg was chosen by Richard Howard for the 1995 volume, was reprinted in Harold Bloom's selection, and appears again here. Catching the spirit of extravagant self-celebration undermined by shrewd irony at the expense of the self, Ginsberg conceives his poem as a challenge to Pessoa—or, rather, as a statement of his own superiority. Here is how his poem opens:

> Everytime I read Pessoa I think
> I'm better than he is I do the same thing
> more extravagantly—he's only from Portugal,
> I'm American greatest Country in the world
> right now End of XX Century tho Portugal
> had a big empire in the 15th century never mind
> now shrunk to a Corner of Iberian peninsula
> whereas New York take New York for instance
> tho Mexico City's bigger N.Y.'s richer think of Empire State
> Building not long ago world empire's biggest skyscraper—

The writer goes on to observe that Pessoa lived "only till 1936" whereas he is still alive nearly sixty years later. The odd logic is part of the poem's charm, as is our knowledge that Ginsberg's braggadocio is meant only half-seriously—it is his means of laying claim to the spirit that animates Whitman and Pessoa alike, which involves a huge assertion of self but also a dissolution of the ordinary barriers between self and other. With cheerful immodesty Ginsberg tells us that at five feet seven and a half inches he is taller than Pessoa and that his "celebrated 'Howl'" has "already [been] translated into 24 languages," a boast Pessoa could not make.

In *The Best American Poetry 2000* (ed. Rita Dove), a second poem provoked by Pessoa's appeared. Lynn Emanuel's "Walt, I Salute You!" directly addresses Whitman, as Pessoa's "Salutation" does. The poem annotates its excitement with a liberal use of exclamation points that signify not only passion but the equally needed undercutting irony. The union of identity the speaker celebrates is so strong that it blurs ordinary gender differences:

You have been women! Women with white legs, women
        with black mustaches,
waitresses with their hands glued to their rags on the counter,
waitresses in Dacron who light up the room with their serious
        wattage.
Yes! You are magically filling up, like milk in a glass, the white
nylon uniform, the blocky shoes with their slab of rubber sole!
Your hair is a platinum helmet. At your breast, a bouquet of
        rayon violets.

The poem reaches its climax when the barrier between the female self
and the male other breaks down completely:

                                    Walt, I salute you!
And therefore myself! In our enormous hats! In our huge
        mustaches!
We can't hide! We recognize ourselves!

Acts of adulation, these poems—Ginsberg's, Emanuel's, and the Pessoa
poem behind them—were quickened into existence by the large-souled
poet reaching out to "men and women of a generation, or ever so many
generations hence."

Alexis de Tocqueville wrote *Democracy in America* before Whitman mate-
rialized as that previously absent being, a poet of the democratic repub-
lic. Tocqueville envisaged the problems that an aristocratic art form
must endure in a populist culture based on equality. In a democracy,
he wrote, "the number of works grows rapidly, while the merit of each
diminishes," and some will see in American poetry today a fulfillment of
the vision Tocqueville recorded in the fourth decade of the nineteenth
century: "Form will usually be neglected and occasionally scorned. Style
will frequently seem bizarre, incorrect, exaggerated, or flaccid and almost
always seem brazen and vehement. Authors will aim for rapidity of exe-
cution rather than perfection of detail. Short texts will be more common
than long books, wit more common than erudition, and imagination
more common than depth."★ There is truth to this, and critics of the
MFA degree, the writing workshop as a pedagogical model, the prolif-
eration of small presses, and the idea of teaching poetry writing to school

★ Tocqueville, *Democracy in America,* trans. Arthur Goldhammer (New York:
Library of America, 2004), pp. 533, 542.

children, will find much in Tocqueville to comfort them, though it is possible to rebut or modify any of the specific charges brought against contemporary poetry. Take, for example, the accusation that our poets neglect form. While free verse and colloquial idioms characterize much of the poetry of our moment, it is not as though the formal dimensions of poetry have gone unexamined. Our scribes have given us examples galore of exotic verse forms. The sonnet sequence, the haiku sequence, the sestina, the cento, the dialogue, the crown of sonnets, the pantoum, the villanelle, the prose poem, the abecedarius and even a double abecedarius: all have put in appearances in this anthology series. It may also be said that groups of American poets have been and continue to be almost obsessively committed to formal causes: the revival of past models of rhyme and meter, or the search for a measure to take the place of iambic pentameter, or the development of new constrictive verse forms like those generated by the Oulipo, or the relentless impulse to foreground language as the medium of communication and distortion.

The more significant of the problems Tocqueville predicted for the fine arts in a democratic state is a tendency to widen the aesthetic impulse but weaken its quality. It cannot be denied that we no longer conceive of lyric poetry as strictly a solitary and self-taught act but rather as one that can be taught, encouraged, quickened into being, a collaborative and even group activity. Poetry serves self-expression, narcissistic and otherwise; it also has a therapeutic application. The notion that anyone can be a poet may have a leveling effect on the art, and that is why we need not critics but editors to help us by discriminating among the contending voices and insisting on the genuine article. About critics many of us agree with Hemingway, who defined the species as "men who watch a battle from a high place, then come down and shoot the survivors." But about the need to make choices, to discriminate among the poems set before us, there can be no doubt. And I believe that the best choosers come from the ranks of the poets themselves.

This seems the right moment to acknowledge the efforts of the twenty-five poets who, in their year as guest editor, read poems by the score on an almost daily basis. Picking the seventy-five poems of "your" year is a demanding task, even if you don't stumble over the idea of hierarchies. You need reserves of generosity and goodwill and a feeling for the idea of community. It is possible, and the editors proved it, to be loyal to an aesthetic position and, at the same time, to strive to be ecumenical; to include your favorites but also to be able to recognize quality in a style unlike your own, from an unfamiliar voice, speaking an alien dialect.

Glen Hartley has been my literary agent since I began writing books. A lover of poetry and literature, he advised me on *The Best American Poetry* when it was little more than an idea that popped into my head as I drove on a country road between Ludlowville and Ithaca, New York, one Sunday in August 1987. This volume is dedicated to Glen, without whose advocacy and support the series would neither have come into existence nor fared so well as it has. I am fortunate, too, to have worked with talented editors at Scribner: John Glusman, who signed the book in 1987 when nobody else but Glen and I thought it had a snowball's chance in Hades; Erika Goldman; Hamilton Cain; Gillian Blake; and, since 2004, Alexis Gargagliano. One thing we learned early on was that the sheer number of poems that get published in the United States is overwhelming. In our fourth year we made the decision to exclude poems published in individual poetry collections and to choose only poems that appear in periodicals. Some great magazines ended their distinguished runs: *Partisan Review, Antæus.* New magazines sprung up: poems in the 2010 and 2011 volumes of this series were printed originally in *Conduit, Court Green, The Hat, jubilat, LIT, New Ohio Review, Open City, A Public Space, Post Road, Sentence, The Sienese Shredder,* and *Vanitas,* to cite just some that didn't exist twenty-five years ago. The perennially unsung editors of these magazines continue to be our front line; I thank them and honor them. Little has been as important in my own evolution as a poet than the friendly, attentive, and frank responses that my work has elicited from magazine editors.

The abundance and variety of the poems we have published in our twenty-five years led us to suspend our usual practice of limiting each book in the series to seventy-five poems. There are an even hundred poems in this volume. Each has the distinction of having been picked twice. The year beneath the poem designates the volume in which it originally appeared. In the back of the book, after updated biographical notes, we print the original comment, if any, that the poet made in response to my plea for some words about the composition of the chosen poem.

Robert Pinsky comes from the generation of American poets that earned the PhD rather than the MFA degree if they went to graduate school. He studied at Stanford, where he absorbed the lessons of Yvor Winters; wrote a book on Landor, another one on the situation of poetry in the year of our nation's bicentennial; and taught at Wellesley, Berkeley, and Boston University. He wrote plain-style poems, acts of moral attention devoted to subjects as vast and complicated as America, psychiatry, sadness, happiness, the design of a shirt, the human heart. When *The Figured Wheel,* comprising new and collected poems, appeared from Farrar, Straus and Giroux in 1996, the poet and critic James Longenbach said it constituted "the most scrupulously intelligent body of work produced by an American poet in the past twenty-five years." A new *Selected Poems* came out from the same publisher in 2011. Pinsky has written autobiographical poems, lyrics, intellectual investigations ("Ode to Meaning"), and poems endowed with the purpose of explaining ourselves to us. But he has not eschewed the sheer pleasure of wordplay, as in his abecedarian poems that consist of exactly twenty-six words. In the variousness of his pursuits, he has done much to challenge any limiting notion of what a serious modern poet can be and do. In addition to his poems and his essays on poetry, he produced a widely acclaimed translation of Dante's *Inferno,* wrote a book on the Bible's King David, and devised a computer interactive novel (*Mindwheel*) when the personal computer was in its infancy. He plays the saxophone, loves jazz, and has recently been collaborating with jazz musicians in the presentation of his poems. On the CD *PoemJazz* Pinsky reads thirteen of his own poems plus one by Ben Jonson while Laurence Hobgood improvises on the piano. A reviewer in the *JazzTimes* wrote that Pinsky's "performances" of his poems are, in keeping with the dictates of jazz, "rich with spontaneous touches."*

When he served as United States Poet Laureate for two terms during the Clinton administration, that office reached the peak of its prestige. Pinsky launched the Favorite Poem Project, which proved immensely popular. He made frequent appearances reading poems on television on the *PBS NewsHour.* In 2001 he delivered The Tanner Lectures on Human Values at Princeton University, later published under the title *Democracy, Culture and the Voice of Poetry,* a defense of poetry as a living art whose importance will always surpass its popularity. "Poetry reflects, perhaps concentrates, the American idea of individualism as it encounters the American experience of the mass," Pinsky writes, as neat a statement as you will find of the central paradox of our culture.

The poets assembled in this volume have written about matters of public concern: "the war," whether that means Vietnam or "Bush's War"; suicide bombers, murderous explosions, a terrorist act, a deadly oil spill, the death of the shah of Iran, the videotaped assassination of an American journalist in Pakistan. The poets have accepted the challenge to write about history in the making. To be sure, they also like to tell a story or make a prophecy, to sing the blues or a sad ballad, to

---

* Christopher Loudon, *jazztimes.com.* June 2012.

contemplate desire, love, loss, nostalgia, garbage, pornography, married life, Wagner at the Met, lunch, childhood, dogs, paranoia, fathers, the end of a love affair, forgiveness, poison pen letters, and the letter "Q."

Among the miraculous inventions in Raymond Roussel's *Locus Solus* are the *tableaux vivants* featuring figures immobile as wax dummies in a huge glass case. The figures turn out to be dead people who revive when injected with a substance called "resurrectine," at which time they act out the greatest event in their lives. Poems are a little like that. An excellent poem of any vintage returns to life the moment somebody reads it. What we can do, in a retrospective anthology, is to bring back poems that have given pleasure to more than a few discerning readers—poems that prove, in Tocqueville's terms, that an aristocratic art form can thrive in a democratic culture.

Robert Pinsky was born in 1940 in Long Branch, New Jersey, graduating from Long Branch High School, as did his parents, who met there. Also in Long Branch, his paternal grandfather ran a bar, the Broadway Tavern, and his maternal grandfather washed the windows of stores on Broadway. The town appears in his prose book, *Thousands of Broadways*. He attended Rutgers and Stanford, where he held a Stegner Fellowship, and has taught at the University of Chicago and the University of California, Berkeley. His *Selected Poems* was published in paperback in March 2012 by Farrar, Straus and Giroux. His CD *PoemJazz*, a collaboration with the pianist Laurence Hobgood, was released in 2012 by Circumstantial Productions. He has won the Italian Premio Capri, the Korean Manhae Prize, and the Howard Washington Award of the City of Chicago. His bestselling translation *The Inferno of Dante* was awarded the *Los Angeles Times* Book Prize. As Poet Laureate of the United States from 1997 until 2000, he launched the Favorite Poem Project, which now includes the videos at www.favoritepoem.org and an annual summer Poetry Institute for K-12 educators. Pinsky is the author of *The Situation of Poetry* (1977) and *The Sounds of Poetry: A Brief Guide* (1998). He also has written an interactive computer game (*Mindwheel*, 1984), a prose book about King David (*The Life of David*, 2006), and a verse adaptation of Schiller's *Wallenstein* (premiere performance in March 2013). He lives in Cambridge, Massachusetts, and teaches in the MFA program at Boston University.

INTRODUCTION
The Centrality of Poetry

by *Robert Pinsky*

◊   ◊   ◊

My assignment has been to choose one hundred poems from the nearly two thousand selected by the poets who edited the annual *Best American Poetry* volumes over the past twenty-five years. An intimidating task: just look at the anthologies of even a generation or two ago, with their surprising omissions and mistaken inclusions—in hindsight. See, too, the lists of prizewinners and poets laureate.

William Shakespeare, John Donne, John Keats, Emily Dickinson, and Gerard Manley Hopkins were ignored or underestimated by experts of their times. Present-day scholars and critics, the equivalents of those experts, now write books about those poets.

On the other hand, I have the encouraging thought that the editors of the annual volumes in the series, from John Ashbery in 1988 to Mark Doty in 2012, are poets. And poets, though certainly not infallible in judgment, have a stringent, in a way ruthless motive or framework for judgment, distinct from the more curatorial role of scholars and critics. Actual composition, the effort to make something new, is a fiery, inherently disruptive form of criticism.

Who, after all, called attention to the once-neglected work of Donne and Hopkins? Mainly, subsequent generations of poets. More recently, Elizabeth Bishop and George Oppen, during their lives, were not as widely celebrated as James Dickey and Archibald MacLeish. But in time, young poets decided they needed to learn from Bishop and Oppen.

"What's posterity ever done for me?" Groucho Marx is said to have asked. In poetry, the answer is clear: posterity chooses. The new poets to come are the arbiters of what is best, or at least what is recognized as best in their time. Even their mistakes may be illuminating, because of the energy that drives them. The maker's pressure, the craving to make something new and good, exerts a greater force for the artist than schools, categories, expectations—greater, and sometimes in an opposite direction, toward surprise or defiance. In each generation, the practitioners for their own purposes revise that forever shape-shifting and evolving organism, the canon.

What has been my basis for choosing the poems in this book? A short answer would be: ear and imagination. Those are the prerequisites. But beyond that, there is—not subject matter, exactly, but a large and adventuresome sense of subject matter: in one form or another, an implicit idea of poetry, the art of the individual human voice, as central and fundamental: like singing, dancing, cuisine, ceremony. In a word, culture.

By "ear" I mean the way poetry's medium is breath: the art is rooted in the human-scale, extremely intimate yet social medium of each reader's actual or imagined voice. The reader imagines what it might feel like to need to say the poem. By "imagination" I mean an act of mind that is similarly individual, on a human scale. At the juncture of imagination and body, poetry like dance and song is central to human culture, in the mysterious fusion at the core of mind and body. With imagination, mind expresses itself in gesture and sound. Breath, the medium (for me) of poetry, is literally at the center of the human body, inhaling and exhaling. As speech is a fundamental social means, poetry based on speech is a fundamental art.

By "culture" I mean something distinct from the two realms that are sometimes assumed to encompass all of culture: the entertainment industry and the academic industry. Both are constituent parts of something larger and deeper, and yet often—maybe because it is less visible than the curriculum or the *TV Guide*—underestimated. Culture generates the curriculum and the *TV Guide,* and incorporates elements of them, and shrugs them aside, like the god Kronos eating his children. The underestimation of culture may have roots in the fearsome truth that culture is not ornamental and static; that it is an unsettling, tectonic force, not always benign. Sometimes it is sinister or appalling. It cannot reliably be predicted or manipulated.

In February 2007, in the state of Qatar, I attended a Brookings Institution conference, the U.S.-Islamic World Forum: "Confronting What Divides Us." Along with people from the media, politics, science, and business there were some representatives from the arts, religion, and media, designated under the rubric of "Culture." A session of our cultural group included an Arabic pop singer, a comedian, and a graphic-novel artist, along with on-air and online journalists and—notably—experts in the world of the Internet: social media and digital entertainment, and the merging of the two. Our seminar's moderator emphasized demographic facts, in particular that the median age throughout the Arab world was very young and getting younger. Combined with the surge in computer skills and access, this demographic change would become increasingly determinative. That was the recurring theme.

But an Egyptian playwright protested against this emphasis on demographics. As I remember, she argued passionately that demographics and technology, though significant, should not lead us to neglect the immense force of culture, and of art within culture. The cultural forces within particular nations, religions, and religious groups, she declared, were organic, various, and enduring, as well as constantly evolving. An Egyptian thirteen-year-old and a Kurdish thirteen-year-old were in certain ways profoundly different from each other and from their Bosnian, Iranian, and Yemeni contemporaries, though they might have similar T-shirts and computer games. Culture, she argued, trumps demographics.

Against a general, polite tide away from the playwright's viewpoint, I and a few others were moved by her argument. Notably, a Palestinian filmmaker observed that the Koran's power came largely from a matter of art: the fact that it was composed in verses, making it both magnetic and memorizable. I had never thought about this fact, a refutation of the tag from W. H. Auden that "poetry makes nothing happen." The Koran has made many things happen.

Then, a moment later, an American entrepreneur, representing a website where people engage in alternate lives, said: "Everyone in this room is a dinosaur"—implying that in 2007 there might be something a bit outdated, or even extinct, about the playwright's notions regarding art.

Three years later, the Arab Spring uprisings indicated that both sides of that 2007 argument were onto something. Computer literacy among the young and their use of social media enabled large demonstrations, as in Tahrir Square. Regimes that had seemed invulnerable toppled. And though the means of the demonstrators were digital, the meanings they expressed were cultural.

The urgency of art, or the art of poetry, with its scale that is at once individual and immense, somehow both dreamy and fundamental, is not easy to formulate. But that urgency is a sense that the ancient art must strive to get to the bottom of things, that a lot is at stake. That implicit dimension of the art, a matter of intensity and scale, was a primary guide as I chose from among the selections made by the poets who preceded me as editors of the annual *Best American Poetry* volumes.

By urgency, I don't mean preaching or mere high-minded sentiments, but rather something like the role for art envisioned by the Modernist predecessors T. S. Eliot, James Joyce, Stéphane Mallarmé, and Ezra Pound. Their vision of art shaped my generation, but like others I have come to mistrust the Modernist saying that the poet's mission is to "purify the language of the tribe": the political history of the Modernist period and after suggests misgivings about both purity and tribalism as ideals.

Many poems honored by the annual volumes in the past twenty-five years seem to embrace that old Modernist largeness of vision, but sometimes in a way opposite to purifying the language of a tribe—expanding it and hybridizing it or even mongrelizing it. (In a separate discussion, it's more than arguable that Pound and Eliot in their best poems do the same.) Impurity—as variously and gloriously as in Dickinson, Twain, Melville, Whitman—has been an urgent, significant part of American writing, reflecting American experience. In a contemporary version of that urgency, poets in the *BAP* volumes find ways to extend that project: to tell some historical truth grounded in the unique evidence of American speech, and through the intimate, communal, profoundly vocal medium of poetry.

In 1994, for example, A. R. Ammons selected a passage from Harryette Mullen's *Muse & Drudge,* published the next year as a book-length poem. An epigraph from Callimachus (*"Fatten your animal for sacrifice, poet, / but keep your muse slender."*), precedes the first section, which orchestrates different kinds of language within the four athletic quatrains of the opening section, an example of expressive, improvisatory movement, more expressive than mere "purity":

1.

sapphire's lyre styles
plucked eyebrows
bow lips and legs
whose lives are lonely too

my last nerve's lucid music
sure chewed up the juicy fruit
you must don't like my peaches
there's some left on the tree

you've had my thrills
a reefer a tub of gin

don't mess with me I'm evil
I'm in your sin

clipped bird eclipsed moon
soon no memory of you
no drive or desire survives
you flutter invisible still

If the ancient poet's advice means for the poem to be quick and alert, it is fulfilled by the movement here among idioms, from the blues to the eclipsed moon and back, including points in between. Slavery, pop music, and plucked eyebrows do not preclude the more analytical language of "no drive or desire survives." The four syllables of the third line, with their comic double meaning heartbreaking for the character, establish a certain, requisite alertness: a music of Cupid's-bow lips and bowed legs, together, make a jagged chord. The peach-tree image of the blues lyric and the blues syntax, in a similar way, jostle and harmonize with the more literary, also rich music of vowel, consonant, and vocabulary in "my last nerve's lucid music," echoed in "juicy fruit."

That syncretic range of ear and of idea takes a quite different form, yet I think related, in Paul Violi's "Counterman" from the 2006 volume (ed. Billy Collins), which begins with a deceptive, reportorial meticulousness:

—What'll it be?

Roast beef on rye, with tomato and mayo.

—Whaddaya want on it?

A swipe of mayo.
Pepper but no salt.

—You got it. Roast beef on rye.
You want lettuce on that?

No. Just tomato and mayo.

—Tomato and mayo. You got it.
. . . Salt and pepper?

No salt, just a little pepper.

—You got it. No salt.
You want tomato.

Yes. Tomato. No lettuce.

—No lettuce. You got it.
. . . No salt, right?

Right. No salt.

—You got it.—Pickle?

This manic accuracy of dialogue, in itself engaging, turns out to be a slow curve, a deadpan setup for a left turn of the imagination:

Right. No pickle.

—You got it.
Next!

Roast beef on whole wheat, please,
With lettuce, mayonnaise, and a center slice
Of beefsteak tomato.
The lettuce splayed, if you will,
In a Beaux Arts derivative of classical acanthus,
And the roast beef, thinly sliced, folded
In a multifoil arrangement
That eschews Bragdonian pretensions
Or any idea of divine geometric projection
For that matter, but simply provides
A setting for the tomato
To form a medallion with a dab
Of mayonnaise as a fleuron.
And—as eclectic as this may sound—
If the mayonnaise can also be applied
Along the crust in a Vitruvian scroll
And as a festoon below the medallion,
That would be swell.

—You mean like in the Cathedral St. Pierre in Geneva?

Yes, but the swag more like the one below the rosette
At the Royal Palace in Amsterdam.

—You got it.
Next!

I think this fantastical dialogue—precise about Beaux Art acanthus deriv-
atives in the lettuce and equally precise in its rendering of New York
deli idiom—makes the scene not less real or abundantly rich, but more
so. As the two kinds of language intertwine and blend, absurdly yet
productively, language itself is not glibly dismissed or deprecated. The
enterprise of poetry, implicitly, has its weird majesty. In the meeting of
naturalistic speech and New York School elaboration, something large
and mysterious transpires.

The large reach and intense focus of these passages, embodied
vocally, exemplify a certain spirit, for me—the contrary of depreca-
tion. Deprecation may have as many modes and varieties as art itself.
In contemporary poetry, it can vary between opposites that meet: at
one pole, a bland, companionable chuckle that dismisses importance;
at the other, a complacent, arbitrary mash-up that dismisses meaning.
An easy middlebrow scoff and an easy postmodern smirk. For a keener,
more exacting and thrilling form of both comedy and skepticism, see
(for instance) Kenneth Koch's "Proverb," where the Proverb and the
proper names both have their significance, along with a cosmic absur-
dity. The language is plainer than Mullen's or Violi's, but the spirit is
wide-ranging.

"Les morts vont vite," Koch begins by quoting, "et les vivants sont dingues."
In his poem's translation, "The dead go fast, the next day absent!" and
"the living are haywire." The speed and ardor of his poem, with its
amazed, awed laughter, puts the human voice, hovering somewhere
between speech and song, at the center of things, evoking in the cadences
and patterns of speech the movement of life, encompassing "Alexander
of Macedon, on time! / Prudhomme on time, Gorbachev on time, the
beloved and the lover on time!"

The large, multiple vision called up by the single human voice feel-
ing the tides and currents of time, from amid them: that notion or force
has been a primary guide for me. I have tried to honor its variety. As a
closing example, partly for its contrast with Koch's poem, and partly for
its consonance, here are the closing lines—in a relatively "pure" idiom,
but intensely vocal—of Anne Winters's "The Mill-Race":

It's not a water mill really, work. It's like the nocturnal
paper-mill pulverizing, crushing each fiber of rag into atoms,
or the smooth-lipped workhouse
treadmill, that wore down a London of doxies and sharps,
or the paper-mill, faërique, that raised the cathedrals and
    wore out hosts of dust-demons,
but it's mostly the miller's curse-gift, forgotten of God yet
    still grinding, the salt-
mill, that makes the sea, salt.

I am glad to present the energy and variety of these one hundred poems,
culled from the choices of poets over twenty-five years.

THE
BEST OF
THE BEST
AMERICAN
POETRY

25TH ANNIVERSARY
EDITION

Terminal Nostalgia

◇   ◇   ◇

The music of my youth was much better
Than the music of yours. So was the weather.

Before Columbus came, eagle feathers
Detached themselves for us. So did the weather.

During war, the country fought together
Against all evil. So did the weather.

The cattle were happy to be leather
And made shoes that fit. So did the weather.

Before Columbus came, eagle feathers
Were larger than eagles. So was the weather.

Every ball game was a double-header.
Mickey Mantle was sober. So was the weather.

Before Adam and Eve, an Irish Setter
Played fetch with God. So did the weather.

Before Columbus came, eagle feathers
Married Indians. So did the weather.

Indians were neither loaners nor debtors.
Salmon was our money. So was the weather.

Back then, people wrote gorgeous letters
And read more poetry. So did the weather.

On all issues, there was only one dissenter,
But we loved him, too. So did the weather.

Before Columbus came, eagle feathers
Gave birth to eagles. So did the weather.

We all apprenticed to wise old mentors
And meditated for days. So did the weather.

We were guitar-players and inventors
Of minor chords and antibiotics. So was the weather.

Every person lived near the city center
And had the same income. So did the weather.

Before Columbus, eagle feathers
Lived in the moment. So did the weather.

2012

Garbage

◇ ◇ ◇

I

Creepy little creepers are insinuatingly
curling up my spine (bringing the message)

saying, Boy!, are you writing that great poem
the world's waiting for: don't you know you

have an unaccomplished mission unaccomplished;
someone somewhere may be at this very moment

dying for the lack of what W. C. Williams says
you could (or somebody could) be giving: yeah?

so, these messengers say, what do you
mean teaching school (teaching *poetry* and

poetry writing and wasting your time painting
sober little organic, meaningful pictures)

when values thought lost (but only scrambled into
disengagement) lie around demolished

and centerless because you (that's me, boy)
haven't elaborated everything in everybody's

face, yet: on the other hand (I say to myself,
receiving the messengers and cutting them down)

who has done anything or am I likely to do
anything the world won't twirl without: and

since SS's enough money (I hope) to live
from now on on in elegance and simplicity—

or, maybe, just simplicity—why shouldn't I
at my age (63) concentrate on chucking the

advancements and rehearsing the sweetnesses of
leisure, nonchalance, and small-time byways: couple

months ago, for example, I went all the way
from soy flakes (already roasted and pressed

and in need of an hour's simmering boil
to be cooked) all the way to soybeans, the

pure golden pearls themselves, 65¢ lb. dry: they
have to be soaked overnight in water and they

have to be boiled slowly for six hours—but
they're welfare cheap, are a complete protein,

more protein by weight than meat, more
calcium than milk, more lecithin than eggs,

and somewhere in there the oil that smoothes
stools, a great virtue: I need time and verve

to find out, now, about medicare/medicaid,
national osteoporosis week, gadabout tours,

hearing loss, homesharing programs, and choosing
good nutrition! for starters! why should I

be trying to write my flattest poem, now, for
whom, not for myself, for others?, posh, as I

have never said: Social Security can provide
the beans, soys enough: my house, paid for for

twenty years, is paid for: my young'un
is raised: nothing one can pay cash for seems

very valuable: that reaches a high enough
benchmark for me—high enough that I wouldn't

know what to do with anything beyond that, no
place to house it, park it, dock it, let it drift

down to: elegance and simplicity: I wonder
if we need those celestial guidance systems

striking mountaintops or if we need fuzzy
philosophy's abstruse failed reasonings: isn't

it simple and elegant enough to believe in
qualities, simplicity and elegance, pitch in a

little courage and generosity, a touch of
commitment, enough asceticism to prevent

fattening: moderation: elegant and simple
moderation: trees defined themselves (into

various definitions) through a dynamics of
struggle (hey, is the palaver rapping, yet?)

and so it is as if there were a genetic
recognition that a young tree would get up and

through only through taken space (parental
space not yielding at all, either) and, further:

so, trunks, accommodated to rising, to reaching
the high light and deep water, were slender

and fast moving, and this was okay because
one good thing about dense competition is that

if one succeeds with it one is buttressed by
crowding competitors; that is, there was little

room for branches, and just a tuft of green
possibility at the forest's roof: but, now,

I mean, take my yard maple—put out in the free
and open—has overgrown, its trunk

split down from a high fork: wind has
twisted off the biggest, bottom branch: there

was, in fact, hardly any crowding and competition,
and the fat tree, unable to stop pouring it on,

overfed and overgrew and, now, again, its skin's
broken into and disease may find it and bores

of one kind or another, and fungus: it just
goes to show you: moderation imposed is better

than no moderation at all: we tie into the
lives of those we love and our lives, then, go

as theirs go; their pain we can't shake off;
their choices, often harming to themselves,

pour through our agitated sleep, swirl up as
no-nos in our dreams; we rise several times

in a night to walk about; we rise in the morning
to a crusty world headed nowhere, doorless:

our chests burn with anxiety and a river of
anguish defines rapids and straits in the pit of

our stomachs: how can we intercede and not
interfere: how can our love move more surroundingly,

convincingly than our premonitory advice

II

garbage has to be the poem of our time because
garbage is spiritual, believable enough

to get our attention, getting in the way, piling
up, stinking, turning brooks brownish and

creamy white: what else deflects us from the
errors of our illusionary ways, not a temptation

to trashlessness, that is too far off, and,
anyway, unimaginable, unrealistic: I'm a

hole puncher or hole plugger: stick a finger
in the dame (*dam,* damn, dike), hold back the issue

of creativity's flood, the forthcoming, futuristic,
the origins feeding trash: down by I-95 in

Florida where flat land's ocean- and gulf-flat,
mounds of disposal rise (for if you dug

something up to make room for something to put
in, what about the something dug up, as with graves:)

the garbage trucks crawl as if in obeisance,
as if up ziggurats toward the high places gulls

and garbage keep alive, offerings to the gods
of garbage, of retribution, of realistic

expectation, the deities of unpleasant
necessities: refined, young earthworms,

drowned up in macadam pools by spring rains, moisten
out white in a day or so and, round spots,

look like sputum or creamy-rich, broken-up cold
clams: if this is not the best poem of the

century, can it be about the worst poem of the
century: it comes, at least, toward the end,

so a long tracing of bad stuff can swell
under its measure: but there on the heights

a small smoke wafts the sacrificial bounty
day and night to layer the sky brown, shut us

in as into a lidded kettle, the everlasting
flame these acres-deep of tendance keep: a

free offering of a crippled plastic chair:
a played-out sports outfit: a hill-myna

print stained with jelly: how to write this
poem, should it be short, a small popping of

duplexes, or long, hunting wide, coming home
late, losing the trail and recovering it:

should it act itself out, illustrations,
examples, colors, clothes or intensify

reductively into statement, bones any corpus
would do to surround, or should it be nothing

at all unless it finds itself: the poem,
which is about the pre-socratic idea of the

dispositional axis from stone to wind, wind
to stone (with my elaborations, if any)

is complete before it begins, so I needn't
myself hurry into brevity, though a weary reader

might briefly be done: the axis will be clear
enough daubed here and there with a little ink

or fined out into every shade and form of its
revelation: this is a scientific poem,

asserting that nature models values, that we
have invented little (copied), reflections of

possibilities already here, this where we came
to and how we came: a priestly director behind the

black-chuffing dozer leans the gleanings and
reads the birds, millions of loners circling

a common height, alighting to the meaty steaks
and puffy muffins (puffins?): there is a mound

too, in the poet's mind dead language is hauled
off to and burned down on, the energy held and

shaped into new turns and clusters, the mind
strengthened by what it strengthens for

where but in the very asshole of come-down is
redemption: as where but brought low, where

but in the grief of failure, loss, error do we
discern the savage afflictions that turn us around:

where but in the arrangements love crawls us
through, not a thing left in our self-display

unhumiliated, do we find the sweet seed of
new routes: but we are natural: nature, not

we, gave rise to us: we are not, though, though
natural, divorced from higher, finer configurations:

tissues and holograms and energy circulate in
us and seek and find representations of themselves

outside us, so that we can participate in
celebrations high and know reaches of feeling

and sight and thought that penetrate (really
penetrate) far, far beyond these our wet cells,

right on up past our stories, the planets, moons,
and other bodies locally to the other end of

the pole where matter's forms diffuse and
energy loses all means to express itself except

as spirit, there, oh, yes, in the abiding where
mind but nothing else abides, the eternal,

until it turns into another pear or sunfish,
that momentary glint in the fisheye having

been there so long, coming and going, it's
eternity's glint: it all wraps back round,

into and out of form, palpable and impalpable,
and in one phase, the one of grief and love,

we know the other, where everlastingness comes to
sway, okay and smooth: the heaven we mostly

want, though, is this jet-hoveled hell back,
heaven's daunting asshole: one must write and

rewrite till one writes it right: if I'm in
touch, she said, then I've got an edge: what

the hell kind of talk is that: I can't believe
I'm merely an old person: whose mother is dead,

whose father is gone and many of whose
friends and associates have wended away to the

ground, which is only heavy wind, or to ashes,
a lighter breeze: but it was all quite frankly

to be expected and not looked forward to: even
old trees, I remember some of them, where they

used to stand: pictures taken by some of them:
and old dogs, specially one imperial black one,

quad dogs with their hier*archies* (another *archie*)
one succeeding another, the barking and romping

sliding away like slides from a projector: what
were they then that are what they are now:

III

toxic waste, poison air, beach goo, eroded
roads draw nations together, whereas magnanimous

platitude and sweet semblance ease each nation
back into its comfort or despair: global crises

promote internationalist gettings-together,
problems the best procedure, whether they be in the

poet warps whose energy must be found and let
work or in the high windings of sulfur dioxide:

I say to my writing students—prize your flaws,
defects, behold your accidents, engage your

negative criticisms—these are the materials
of your ongoing—from these places you imagine,

find, or make the ways back to all of us, the figure,
keeping the aberrant periphery worked

clear so the central current may shift or slow
or rouse adjusting to the necessary dynamic:

in our error the defining energies of cure
errancy finds: suffering otherwises: but

no use to linger over beauty or simple effect:
this is just a poem with a job to do: and that

is to declare, however roundabout, sideways,
or meanderingly (or in those ways) the perfect

scientific and materialistic notion of the
spindle of energy: when energy is gross,

rocklike, it resembles the gross, and when
fine it mists away into mystical refinements,

sometimes passes right out of material
recognizability and becomes, what?, motion,

spirit, all forms translated into energy, as at
the bottom of Dante's hell all motion is

translated into form: so, in value systems,
physical systems, artistic systems, always this

same disposition from the heavy to the light,
and then the returns from the light downward

to the staid gross: stone to wind, wind to
stone: there is no need for "outside," hegemonic

derivations of value: nothing need be invented
or imposed: the aesthetic, scientific, moral

are organized like a muff along this spindle,
might as well relax: thus, the job done, the

mind having found its way through and marked
out the course, the intellect can be put by:

one can turn to tongue, crotch, boob, navel,
armpit, rock, slit, roseate rearend and

consider the perfumeries of slick exchange,
heaving breath, slouchy mouth, the mixed

means by which we stay attentive and keep to
the round of our ongoing: you wake up thrown

away and accommodation becomes the name of your
game: getting back, back into the structure

of protection, caring, warmth, numbers: one
and many, singles and groups, dissensions and

cooperations, takings and givings—the dynamic
of survival, still the same: but why thrown

out in the first place: because while the
prodigal stamps off and returns, the father goes

from iron directives that drove the son away
to rejoicing tears at his return: the safe

world of community, not safe, still needs
feelers sent out to test the environment, to

bring back news or no news; the central
mover, the huge river, needs, too, to bend,

and the son sent away is doubly welcomed home:
we deprive ourselves of, renounce, safety to seek

greater safety: but if we furnish a divine
sanction or theology to the disposition, we

must not think when the divine sanction shifts
that there is any alteration in the disposition:

the new's an angle of emphasis on the old:
new religions are surfaces, beliefs the shadows

of images trying to construe what needs no
belief: only born die, and if something is

born or new, then that is not it, that is not
the it: the it is the indifference of all the

differences, the nothingness of all the poised
somethings, the finest issue of energy in which

boulders and dead stars float: for what
if it were otherwise and the it turned out to

be *something,* damning and demanding, strict and
fierce, preventing and seizing: what range of

choice would be given up then and what value
could our partial, remnant choices acquire then:

with a high whine the garbage trucks slowly
circling the pyramid rising intone the morning

and atop the mound's plateau birds circling
hear and roil alive in winklings of wings

denser than windy forest shelves: and meanwhile
a truck already arrived spills its goods from

the back hatch and the birds as in a single computer
formed net plunge in celebrations, hallelujahs

of rejoicing: the driver gets out of his truck
and wanders over to the cliff on the spill and

looks off from the high point into the rosy-fine
rising of day, the air pure, the wings of the

birds white and clean as angel-food cake: holy, holy,
holy, the driver cries and flicks his cigarette

in a spiritual swoop that floats and floats before
it touches ground: here, the driver knows,

where the consummations gather, where the disposal
flows out of form, where the last translations

cast away their immutable bits and scraps,
flits of steel, shivers of bottle and tumbler,

here is the gateway to beginning, here the portal
of renewing change, the birdshit, even, melding

enrichingly in with debris, a loam for the roots
of placenta: oh, nature, the man on the edge

of the cardboard-laced cliff exclaims, that there
could be a straightaway from the toxic past into

the fusion-lit reaches of a coming time! our
sins are so many, here heaped, shapes given to

false matter, hamburger meat left out

IV

scientists plunge into matter looking for the
matter but the matter lessens and, looked too

far into, expands away: it was insubstantial all
along: that is, boulders bestir; they

are "alive" with motion and space: there is a
riddling reality where real hands grasp each

other in the muff but toward both extremes the
reality wears out, wears thin, becomes a reality

"realityless": this is satisfactory, providing
permanent movement and staying, providing the

stratum essential with an essential air, the
poles thick and thin, the middles, at interchange:

the spreader rakes a furrow open and lights a
drying edge: a priestly plume rises, a signal, smoke

like flies intermediating between orange peel
and buzzing blur: is a poem about garbage garbage

or will this abstract, hollow junk seem beautiful
and necessary as just another offering to the

high assimilations: (that means up on top where
the smoke is; the incinerations of sin,

corruption, misconstruction pass through the
purification of flame:) old deck chairs,

crippled aluminum lawn chairs, lemon crates
with busted slats or hinges, strollers with

whacking or spinningly idle wheels: stub ends
of hot dogs: clumps go out; rain sulls deep

coals; wind slams flickers so flat they lose
the upstanding of updraft and stifle to white

lingo—but oh, oh, in a sense, and in an
intention, the burning's forever, O eternal

flame, principle of the universe, without which
mere heaviness and gray rust prevail: dance

peopling the centers and distances, the faraway
galactic slurs even, luminescences, plasmas,

those burns, the same principle: but here on
the heights, terns and flies avoid the closest

precincts of flame, the terrifying transformations,
the disappearances of anything of interest,

morsel, gobbet, trace of maple syrup, fat
worm: addling intensity at the center

where only special clothes and designated
offices allay the risk, the pure center: but

down, down on the lowest appropinquations, the
laborsome, loaded vessels whine like sails in

too much wind up the long ledges, the whines
a harmony, singing away the end of the world

or spelling it in, a monstrous surrounding of
gathering—the putrid, the castoff, the used,

the mucked up—all arriving for final assessment,
for the toting up in tonnage, the separations

of wet and dry, returnable and gone for good:
the sanctifications, the burn-throughs, ash free

merely a permanent twang of light, a dwelling
music, remaining: how to be blessed are mechanisms,

procedures that carry such changes! the
garbage spreader gets off his bulldozer and

approaches the fire: he stares into it as into
eternity, the burning edge of beginning and

ending, the catalyst of going and becoming,
and all thoughts of his paycheck and beerbelly,

even all thoughts of his house and family and
the long way he has come to be worthy of his

watch, fall away, and he stands in the presence
of the momentarily everlasting, the air about

him sacrosanct, purged of the crawling vines
and dense vegetation of desire, nothing between

perception and consequence here: the arctic
terns move away from the still machine and

light strikes their wings in round, a fluttering,
a whirling rose of wings, and it seems that

terns' slender wings and finely tipped
tails look so airy and yet so capable that they

must have been designed after angels or angels
after them: the lizard family produced man in

the winged air! man as what he might be or might
have been, neuter, guileless, a feathery hymn:

the bulldozer man picks up a red bottle that
turns purple and green in the light and pours

out a few drops of stale wine, and yellow jackets
burr in the bottle, sung drunk, the singing

not even puzzled when he tosses the bottle way
down the slopes, the still air being flown in

in the bottle even as the bottle dives through
the air! the bulldozer man thinks about that

and concludes that everything is marvelous, what
he should conclude and what everything is: on

the deepdown slopes, he realizes, the light
inside the bottle will, over the weeks, change

the yellow jackets, unharmed, having left lost,
not an aromatic vapor of wine left, the air

percolating into and out of the neck as the sun's
heat rises and falls: all is one, one all:

hallelujah: he gets back up on his bulldozer
and shaking his locks backs the bulldozer up

V

dew shatters into rivulets on crunched cellophane
as the newly started bulldozer jars a furrow

off the mesa, smoothing and packing down:
flattening, the way combers break flat into

speed up the strand: unpleasant food strings down
the slopes and rats' hard tails whirl whacking

trash: I don't know anything much about garbage
dumps: I mean, I've never climbed one: I

don't know about the smells: do masks mask
scent: or is there a deodorizing mask: the

Commissioner of Sanitation in a bug-black caddy
hearse-long glisters creepy up the ziggurat: at

the top his chauffeur pops out and opens the
big back door for him: he goes over a few feet

away, puts a stiff, salute-hand to his forehead
and surveys the distances in all depths: the

birds' shadows lace his white sleeve: he
rises to his toes as a lifting zephyr from the

sea lofts a salt-shelf of scent: he approves: he
extends his arm in salute to the noisy dozer's

operator, waves back and forth canceling out
any intention to speak, re-beholds Florida's

longest vistas, gets back into the big buggy
and runs up all the windows, trapping, though,

a nuisance of flies: (or, would he have run
the windows down: or would anyone else have:

not out there: strike that:) rightness, at
any rate, like a benediction, settles on the

ambiance: all is proceeding: funding will be
continued: this work will not be abandoned:

this mound can rise higher: things are in order
when heights are acknowledged; the lows

ease into place; the wives get back from the laundromat,
the husbands hose down the hubcaps; and the

seeringly blank pressures of weekends crack
away hour by hour in established time: in your

end is my beginning: the operator waves back
to the Commissioner, acknowledging his understanding

and his submission to benign authority, and falls
to thinking of his wife, née Minnie Furher, a woman

of abrupt appetites and strict morals, a woman
who wants what she wants legally, largely as a

function of her husband's particulars: a closet
queen, Minnie hides her cardboard, gold-foiled

crown to wear in parade about the house when
nobody's home: she is so fat, fat people

like to be near her: and her husband loves
every bit of her, every bite (bit) round enough to get

to: and wherever his dinky won't reach, he finds
something else that will: I went up the road

a piece this morning at ten to Pleasant Grove
for the burial of Ted's ashes: those above

ground care; those below don't: the sun was
terribly hot, and the words of poems read out

loud settled down like minnows in a shallows
for the moment of silence and had their gaps

and fractures filled up and healed quiet: into
the posthole went the irises and hand-holds of dirt:

spring brings thaw and thaw brings the counterforce
of planted ashes which may not rise again,

not as anything recognizable as what they leach
away from: oh, yes, yes, the matter goes on,

turning into this and that, never the same thing
twice: but what about the spirit, does it die

in an instant, being nothing in an instant out of
matter, or does it hold on to some measure of

time, not just the eternity in which it is not,
but does death go on being death for a billion

years: this one fact put down is put down
forever, is it, or forever, forever to be a

part of the changes about it, switches in the
earth's magnetic field, asteroid collisions,

tectonic underplays, to be molten and then not
molten, again and again: when does a fact end:

what does one do with this gap from just yesterday
or just this morning to fifty-five billion

years—to infinity: the spirit was forever
and is forever, the residual and informing

energy, but here what concerns us is this
manifestation, this man, this incredible flavoring and

building up of character and éclat, gone,
though forever, in a moment only, a local

event, infinitely unrepeatable: the song of
the words subsides, the shallows drift away,

the people turn to each other and away: motors
start and the driveways clear, and the single

fact is left alone to itself to have its first
night under the stars but to be there now

for every star that comes: we go away who must
ourselves come back, at last to stay: tears

when we are helpless are our only joy: but
while I was away this morning, Mike, the young

kid who does things for us, cut down the
thrift with his weedeater, those little white

flowers more like weedsize more than likely:
sometimes called cliff rose: also got the grass

out of the front ditch now too wet to mow, slashed:
the dispositional axis is not supreme (how tedious)

and not a fiction (how clever) but plain (greatness
flows through the lowly) and a fact (like as not)

1993

Soft Money

◇   ◇   ◇

They're sexy
because they're needy,
which degrades them.

They're sexy because
they don't need you.

They're sexy because they pretend
not to need you,

but they're lying,
which degrades them.

They're beneath you
and it's hot.

They're across the border,
rhymes with dancer—

they don't need
to understand.

They're content to be
(not *mean*),

which degrades them
and is sweet.

They want to be
the thing-in-itself

and the thing-for-you—

Miss Thing—

but can't.

They want to be you,
but can't,

which is so hot.

2011

Wakefulness

◇　◇　◇

An immodest little white wine, some scattered seraphs,
recollections of the Fall—tell me,
has anyone made a spongier representation, chased
fewer demons out of the parking lot
where we all held hands?

Little by little the idea of the true way returned to me.
I was touched by your care,
reduced to fawning excuses.
Everything was spotless in the little house of our desire,
the clock ticked on and on, happy about
being apprenticed to eternity. A gavotte of dust motes
came to replace my seeing. Everything was as though
it had happened long ago
in ancient peach-colored funny papers
wherein the law of true opposites was ordained
casually. Then the book opened by itself
and read to us: "You pack of liars,
of course tempted by the crossroads, but I like each
and every one of you with a peculiar sapphire intensity.
Look, here is where I failed at first.
The client leaves. History matters on,
rolling distractedly on these shores. Each day, dawn
condenses like a very large star, bakes no bread,
shoes the faithless. How convenient if it's a dream."

In the next sleeping car was madness.
An urgent languor installed itself
as far as the cabbage-hemmed horizons. And if I put a little

bit of myself in this time, stoppered the liquor that is our selves'
truant exchanges, brandished my intentions
for once? But only I get
something out of this memory.
A kindly gnome
of fear perched on my dashboard once, but we had all been instructed
to ignore the conditions of the chase. Here, it
seems to grow lighter with each passing century. No matter how you
             twist it,
life stays frozen in the headlights.
Funny, none of us heard the roar.

1998

Bored

◊   ◊   ◊

All those times I was bored
out of my mind. Holding the log
while he sawed it. Holding
the string while he measured, boards,
distances between things, or pounded
stakes into the ground for rows and rows
of lettuces and beets, which I then (bored)
weeded. Or sat in the back
of the car, or sat still in boats,
sat, sat, while at the prow, stern, wheel
he drove, steered, paddled. It
wasn't even boredom, it was looking,
looking hard and up close at the small
details. Myopia. The worn gunwales,
the intricate twill of the seat
cover. The acid crumbs of loam, the granular
pink rock, its igneous veins, the sea-fans
of dry moss, the blackish and then the greying
bristles on the back of his neck.
Sometimes he would whistle, sometimes
I would. The boring rhythm of doing
things over and over, carrying
the wood, drying
the dishes. Such minutiae. It's what
the animals spend most of their time at,
ferrying the sand, grain by grain, from their tunnels,
shuffling the leaves in their burrows. He pointed
such things out, and I would look
at the whorled texture of his square finger, earth under
the nail. Why do I remember it as sunnier

all the time then, although it more often
rained, and more birdsong?
I could hardly wait to get
the hell out of there to
anywhere else. Perhaps though
boredom is happier. It is for dogs or
groundhogs. Now I wouldn't be bored.
Now I would know too much.
Now I would know.

1995

FRANK BIDART

Injunction

◊   ◊   ◊

As if the names we use to name the uses of buildings
x-ray our souls, war without end:

Palace. Prison. Temple. School.
Market. Theater. Brothel. Bank.

War without end. Because to name is to possess
the dreams of strangers, the temple

is offended by, demands the abolition of brothel, now theater, now
school; the school despises temple, palace, market, bank; the bank by

refusing to name depositors welcomes all, though in rage prisoners each
night gnaw to dust another stone piling under the palace.

War without end. Therefore time past time:

Rip through the fabric. Nail it. Not
to the wall. Rip through

the wall. Outside

time. Nail it.

2002

Feminine Intuition

◇   ◇   ◇

I. LITTLE RED RIDING HOOD

Astrid comes from upstate New York.
She comes from distress.
She's enthusiastic about it.
She doesn't belong, but she tries hard.
Her husband hurts her, but they have a drug-free life.
They roller skate and take up fads enthusiastically,
Neon clothing and the like.
He's an air traffic controller, so they move constantly.
This time it's California. After the picnic
I said, "She reminds me of Little Red Riding Hood."
My husband said, "Yeah."
We were doing the dishes.
I can't say some other things, so I say this.

II. PLASTIC SURGERY, SKIPPED DESSERT

That simple woman thought I was simple, but I was not.
I was never simple.
Not trees, stars, plot.
She smoked her fingers down to the yellow.
She had the harsh hearty laughter
Of the women who believe the men will leave them.
All the mothers I knew went nuts.
Hair the color of a screwdriver.
It's a cliché, but it's an altar.
Cotton candy spun into a knot.
Especially rich women, with art.

Kimono, muumuu.
Ice cubes.

But I was never simple. I was never simple.
The way I was raised, the men never leave a woman.
She was a woman: I could not trust her.

III. A Woman Clothed with the Sun

Imagine, all over America, women are losing bone mass.

Brittle old ladies: we create them.
Coiffured movie sirens lounging around the pool transmogrify
into brittle old sea hags.
(They don't know anything: they just nag.)
Let's let them swim out to sea.
Let's give them a spiny seahorse to ride on.
"Goodbye brittle old ladies, beautiful ones—
Ride out against the horizon and the orange sun!"

1997

Three Oranges

◊   ◊   ◊

first time my father overheard me listening to
this bit of music he asked me,
"what is it?"
"it's called Love for Three Oranges,"
I informed him.
"boy," he said, "that's getting it
cheap."
he meant sex.
listening to it
I always imagined three oranges
sitting there,
you know how orange they can
get,
so mightily orange.
maybe Prokofiev had meant
what my father
thought.
if so, I preferred it the
other way
the most horrible thing
I could think of
was part of me being
what ejaculated out of the
end of his
stupid penis.
I will never forgive him
for that,
his trick that I am stuck
with,

I find no nobility in
parenthood.
I say kill the Father
before he makes more
such as
I.

1993

The Life of Towns

◊   ◊   ◊

Towns are the illusion that things hang together somehow, my pear,
your winter. I am a scholar of towns, let God commend that. To explain
what I do is simple enough. A scholar is someone who takes a position.
From which position, certain lines become visible. You will at first
think I am painting the lines myself; it's not so. I merely know where
to stand to see the lines that are there. And the mysterious thing, it
seems a very mysterious thing, is how these lines do paint themselves.
Before there was any up or down, any bright or dark, any edges or
angles or virtue—who was there to ask the questions? Well, let's not
get carried away with exegesis. A scholar is someone who knows how
to limit oneself to the matter at hand. Matter which has painted itself
within lines constitutes a town. Viewed in this way the world is, as we
say, an open book. But what about variant readings? For example, con-
sider the town defined for us by Lao Tzu in the twenty-third chapter
of the Tao Te Ching:

> *A man of the way conforms to the way; a man of virtue*
> *conforms to virtue; a man of loss conforms to loss.*
> *He who conforms to the way is gladly accepted by the way;*
> *he who conforms to virtue is gladly accepted by virtue;*
> *he who conforms to loss is gladly accepted by loss.*

This sounds like a town of some importance, where a person could
reach beyond himself, or meet himself, as he chose. But another scholar
(Kao) takes a different position on the Town of Lao Tzu. "The word
translated 'loss' throughout this section does not make much sense,"
admonishes Kao. "It is possible that it is a graphic error for 'heaven.'"
Now, in order for you or I to quit living here and go there—either to
the Town of Lao Tzu or to the Town of Kao—we have to get certain

details clear, like Kao's tone. Is he impatient or deeply sad or merely droll? The position you take on this may pull you separate from me. Hence, towns. And then, scholars.

I am not being trivial. Your separateness could kill you unless I take it from you as a sickness. What if you get stranded in the town where pears and winter are variants for one another? Can you eat winter? No. Can you live six months inside a frozen pear? No. But there is a place, I know the place, where you will stand and see pear and winter side by side as walls stand by silence. Can you punctuate yourself as silence? You will see the edges cut away from you, back into a world of another kind—back into real emptiness, some would say. Well, we are objects in a wind that stopped, is my view. There are regular towns and irregular towns, there are wounded towns and sober towns and fiercely remembered towns, there are useless but passionate towns that battle on, there are towns where the snow slides from the roofs of the houses with such force that victims are killed, but there are no empty towns (just empty scholars) and there is no regret.

APOSTLE TOWN

After your death.
It was windy every day.
Every day.
Opposed us like a wall.
We went.
Shouting sideways at one another.
Along the road.
It was useless.
The spaces between us.
Got hard.
They are empty spaces.
And yet they are solid.
And black and grievous.
As gaps between the teeth.
Of an old woman.
You knew years ago.
When she was.
Beautiful the nerves pouring around in her like palace fire.

"Spring is always like what it used to be."
Said an old Chinese man.
Rain hissed down the windows.
Longings from a great distance.
Reached us.

LEAR TOWN

Clamor the bells falling bells.
Precede silence of bells.
As madness precedes.
Winter as childhood.
Precedes father.
Into the kill-hole.

DESERT TOWN

When the sage came back in.
From the desert.
He propped the disciples up again like sparrows.
On a clothesline.
Some had fallen into despair this puzzled him.
In the desert.
Where he baked his heart.
Were no shadows no up and down to remind him.
How they depended on him a boy died.
In his arms.
It is very expensive he thought.
To come back.
He began to conform.
To the cutting away ways.
Of this world a fire was roaring up.
Inside him his bones by now liquid and he saw.
Ahead of him.
Waiting nothing else.
Waiting itself.

HÖLDERLIN TOWN

You are mad to mourn alone.
With the wells gone dry.
Starlight lying at the bottom.
Like a piece of sound.
You are stranded.
Props hurtle past you.
One last thing you may believe.
Before the lights go out is.
That the mourning is at fault.
Then the sin of wishing to die.
Collapses behind you like a lung.
Night.
The night itself.

A TOWN I HAVE HEARD OF

"In the middle of nowhere."
Where.
Would that be?
Nice and quiet.
A rabbit.
Hopping across.
Nothing.
On the stove.

TOWN OF THE DEATH OF SIN

What is sin?
You asked.
The moon screamed past us.
All at once I saw you.
Just drop sin and go.
Flashing after the moon.
Black as a wind over the forests.

LOVE TOWN

She ran in.
Wet corn.
Yellow braid.
Down her back.

TOWN OF THE SOUND OF A TWIG BREAKING

Their faces I thought were knives.
The way they pointed them at me.
And waited.
A hunter is someone who listens.
So hard to his prey it pulls the weapon.
Out of his hand and impales.
Itself.

TOWN OF THE MAN IN THE MIND AT NIGHT

Twenty-five.
To four blackness no.
Waking thing no voice no wind huge.
Wads of silence stuff.
The air outside the room blackness.
Outside the streets blackness outside.
The world blackness outside blackness I wonder.
As hard as it can.
Press from deep.
In here to far.
Out there farther.
Farthest pressing out.
Where black.
Winds drop from star.
To star where the deep.
Tinkle of the moon grazes.
It knocks.
It.
Off.
The blade.

Of night like a.
Paring if a man.
Falls off the world in the dark.
Because he doesn't.
Know it is there does that mean it.
Is?

Town on the Way Through God's Woods

Tell me.
Have you ever seen woods so.
Deep so.
Every tree a word does your heart stop?
Once I saw a cloud over Bolivia so deep.
Mountains were cowering do you ever?
Look in so quick you see the secret.
Word inside the word?
As in an abandoned railway car.
One winter afternoon I saw.
The word for "God's woods."

Pushkin Town

When I live I live in the ancient future.
Deep rivers run to it angel pavements are in use.
It has rules.
And love.
And the first rule is.
The love of chance.
Some words of yours are very probably ore there.
Or will be by the time our eyes are ember.

Town of Finding Out About the Love of God

I had made a mistake.
Before this day.
Now my suitcase is ready.

Two hardboiled eggs.
For the journey are stored.
In the places where.
My eyes were.
How could it be otherwise?
Like a current.
Carrying a twig.
The sobbing made me.
Audible to you.

DEATH TOWN

This day.
Whenever I pause.
The noise of the town.

LUCK TOWN

Digging a hole.
To bury his child alive.
So that he could buy food for his aged mother.
One day.
A man struck gold.

MEMORY TOWN

In each one of you I paint.
I find.
A buried site of radioactive material.
You think 8 miles down is enough?
15 miles?
140 miles?

September Town

One fear is that.
The sound of the cicadas.
Out in the blackness zone is going to crush my head.
Flat as a piece of paper some night.
Then I'll be expected.
To go ahead with normal tasks anyway just because.
Your head is crushed flat.
As a piece of paper doesn't mean.
You can get out of going to work.
Mending the screen door hiding.
Your brother from the police.

Entgegenwärtigung Town

I heard you coming after me.
Like a lion through the underbrush.
And I was afraid.
I heard you.
Crashing down over flagpoles.
And I covered my ears.
I felt the walls of the buildings.
Sway once all along the street.
And I crouched low on my heels.
In the middle of the room.

Staring hard.
Then the stitches came open.
You went past.

Wolf Town

Let tigers.
Kill them let bears.
Kill them let tapeworms and roundworms and heartworms.
Kill them let them.
Kill each other let porcupine quills.

Kill them let salmon poisoning.
Kill them let them cut their tongue on a bone and bleed.
To death let them.
Freeze let them.
Starve let them get.
Rickets let them get.
Arthritis let them have.
Epilepsy let them get.
Cataracts and go blind let them.
Run themselves to death let eagles.
Snatch them when young let a windblown seed.
Bury itself in their inner ear destroying equilibrium let them have.
Very good ears let them yes.
Hear a cloud pass.
Overhead.

EMILY TOWN

"Riches in a little room."
Is a phrase that haunts.
Her since the voltage of you.
Left.
Snow or a library.
Or a band of angels.
With a message is.
Not what.
It meant to.
Her.

TOWN OF THE DRAGON VEIN

If you wake up too early listen for it.
A sort of inverted whistling the sound of sound.
Being withdrawn after all where?
Does all the sound in the world.
Come from day after day?
From mountains but.
They have to give it back.

At night just.
As your nightly dreams.
Are taps.
Open reversely.
In.
To.
Time.

Sylvia Town

The burners and the starvers.
Came green April.
Drank their hearts came.
Burning and starving her.
Eyes pulled up like roots.
Lay on the desk.

Town of My Farewell to You

Look what a thousand blue thousand white.
Thousand blue thousand white thousand.
Blue thousand white thousand blue thousand.
White thousand blue wind today and two arms.
Blowing down the road.

Town Just Before the Lightning Flash

"Nuances not effective in point form."
Wrote Paul Klee (1923).

Town Gone to Sleep

There was distant thunder that was its.
Voice there was blood.
Hitting the ground that was.
A Creature's life melting.

In its time there.
Was air forcing.
Out to the edges of that garden as.
Veins of a diver who.
Shoots toward the surface that was a Creature's.
Hope in it just before turning to see.
Ah there we lay.
There the desert.
Of the world immense and sad as hell.
That *was* hell that.
Was a Creature's heart.
Plunged.

TOWN OF BATHSHEBA'S CROSSING

Inside a room in Amsterdam.
Rembrandt painted a drop of life inside.
The drop he painted Rembrandt's stranger.
Dressed as a woman rippling.
With nakedness she has.
A letter in her hand she is.
Traveling.
Out of a thought toward us.
And has not yet.
Arrived even when he.
Paints Rembrandt's stranger.
As Rembrandt he shows.
Him bewildered and tousled.
As if just in.
From journeys.
On tracks and sideroads.

ANNA TOWN

What an anxious existence I led.
And it went on for years it was years.
Before I noticed the life of objects one day.
Anna gazed down at her.

Sword I saw the sword yield up.
To her all that had been accumulated.
Within it all that strange.
World where an apple weighs more.
Than a mountain then.
We set off.
For bitter warfare.
Is dear to us.

Town of the Wrong Questions

How.
Walls are built why.
I am in here what.
Pulleys and skin when.
The panels roll back what.
Aching what.
Do they eat—light?

Freud Town

Devil say I am an unlocated.
Window of myself devil.
Say nobody sit.
There nobody light.
The lamp devil.
Say one glimpse of it.
From outside do the trick do.
The trick devil.
Say smell this devil say.
Raw bones devil say the mind.
Is an alien guest I say.
Devil outlived devil in.

Town of the Little Mouthful

Without arrows how?
Do I know if I hit.
The target he said smiling from ear.
To cut.
Through by the bowstring.

Bride Town

Hanging on the daylight black.
As an overcoat with no man in it one cold bright.
Noon the Demander was waiting for me.

Judas Town

Not a late hour not unlit rows.
Not olive trees not locks not heart.
Not moon not dark wood.
Not morsel not I.

1990

Self-Portrait as Four Styles of Pompeian Wall Painting

◊　◊　◊

FIRST STYLE

To become oneself is so exhausting
that I am as others have made me,
imitating monumental Greek statuary
despite my own feminized way of being.
Like the empire, I was born of pain—
or like a boy, one might say, for I have
become my father, whom I cannot fathom;
the past is a fetish I disdain.
Since they found the bloodless little girl,
with voluptuous lips, buried in me,
I am unsentimental. I do not see
the gold sky at sunset but blackbirds hurled
like lava stones. I am like a severed
finger lost in the wreckage forever.

SECOND STYLE

Unable to care for people, I care
mostly for things. At my bitterest,
I see love as self-censorship.
My face is a little Roman theater
in perfect perspective—with colonnades
and landscapes—making illusionistic
reference to feelings I cannot admit.

Painted in Dionysiac yellows and reds,
my unconscious is a rocky grotto
where flies buzz like formalists.
Despite myself, I am not a composite
of signs to be deciphered. In the ghetto—
where Jews, prostitutes and sailors once lived—
I am happiest because I am undisguised.

THIRD STYLE

Tearing away at an old self to make
a new one, I am my most Augustan.
I grieve little. I try to accustom
myself to what is un-Hellenized and chaste.
I let my flat black dado assert itself
without ornament. Can it be, at last,
that I am I—accepting lice clasped
to me like a dirty Colosseum cat?
On a faded panel of Pompeian red,
there's an erotic x-ray of my soul:
a pale boy-girl figure is unconsoled,
pinned from behind at the farthest edge
of human love, where the conscience is not whole,
yet finely engraved like a snail's shell.

FOURTH STYLE

If great rooms declare themselves by the life
lived in them, each night I am reborn
as men and boys stroll among the ruins,
anonymously skirting the floodlights,
sinking into me tenderly, as they do
each other during their brief hungry acts.
"As brief as love," they used to say, Plato
and his kind, exiling man from happiness,
but I am more than a cave whose campfire,
swelling and contracting, is all that is real.
Tomorrow, when I am drunk on sunlight,

I will still feel the furtive glances,
the unchaste kisses and the wet skin
imprinting me until I am born again.

1998

Dharma

◇   ◇   ◇

The way the dog trots out the front door
every morning
without a hat or an umbrella,
without any money
or the keys to her dog house
never fails to fill the saucer of my heart
with milky admiration.

Who provides a finer example
of a life without encumbrance?
Thoreau in his curtainless hut
with a single plate, a single spoon?
Gandhi with his staff and his holy diapers?

Off she goes into the material world
with nothing but her brown coat
and her modest blue collar,
following only her wet nose,
the twin portals of her steady breathing,
followed only by the plume of her tail.

If only she did not shove the cat aside
every morning
and eat all his food
what a model of self-containment she would be,
what a paragon of earthly detachment.
If only she were not so eager

for a rub behind the ears,
so acrobatic in her welcomes,
if only I were not her god.

1999

ROBERT CREELEY

En Famille

◇   ◇   ◇

I wandered lonely as a cloud . . .
I'd seemingly lost the crowd
I'd come with, family—father, mother, sister and brothers—
fact of a common blood.

Now there was no one,
just my face in the mirror, coat on a single hook,
a bed I could make getting out of.
Where had they gone?

•

What was that vague determination
cut off the nurturing relation
with all the density, this given company—
what made one feel such desperation

to get away, get far from home, be gone from those
would know us even if they only saw our noses or our toes,
accept with joy our helpless mess,
taking for granted it was part of us?

•

My friends, hands on each other's shoulders,
holding on, keeping the pledge
to be for one, for all, a securing center,
no matter up or down, or right or left—

to keep the faith, keep happy, keep together,
keep at it, so keep on

despite the fact of necessary drift.
Home might be still the happiest place on earth?

•

You won't get far by yourself.
It's dark out there.
There's a long way to go.
The dog knows.

It's him loves us most,
or seems to, in dark nights of the soul.
Keep a tight hold.
Steady, we're not lost.

•

Despite the sad vagaries,
anchored in love, placed in the circle,
young and old, a round—
love's fact of this bond.

One day one will look back
and think of them—
where they were, now gone—
remember it all.

•

Turning inside as if in dream,
the twisting face I want to be my own,
the people loved and with me still,
I see their painful faith.

Grow, dears, then fly away!
But when the dark comes, then come home.
Light's in the window, heart stays true.
Call—and I'll come to you.

•

The wind blows through the shifting trees
outside the window, over the fields below.
Emblems of growth, of older, younger,
of towering size or all the vulnerable hope

as echoes in the images of these three
look out with such reflective pleasure,
so various and close. They stand there,
waiting to hear a music they will know.

•

I like the way you both look out at me.
Somehow it's sometimes hard to be a human.
Arms and legs get often in the way,
making oneself a bulky, awkward burden.

Tell me your happiness is simply true.
Tell me I can still learn to be like you.
Tell me the truth is what we do.
Tell me that care for one another is the clue.

•

We're here because there's nowhere else to go,
we've come in faith we learned as with all else.
Someone once told us and so it is we know.
No one is left outside such simple place.

No one's too late, no one can be too soon.
We comfort one another, making room.
We dream of heaven as a climbing stair.
We look at stars and wonder why and where.

•

Have we told you all you'd thought to know?
Is it really so quickly now the time to go?
Has anything happened you will not forget?
Is where you are enough for all to share?

Is wisdom just an empty word?
Is age a time one might finally well have missed?
Must humanness be its own reward?
Is happiness this?

2001

You Art A Scholar, Horatio, Speak To It

◇   ◇   ◇

You say you walk and sew alone?
I walk and sew alone.

You say you gape and waver?
I am mostly dizzy, most open-mouthed.

You say you taste it with each dish?
I drink it and I spit it up.

You say it lays you face-down?
I kiss the dirt.

Carved into your bone china?
Mine's more fine.

Folded into your laundry?
Dry. Dry. Dry.

Is it quite awful and unbearable?
Quite.

Is it sweet and gentle?
Most sweet, most gentle.

Does it make you retch?
I am wretched.

Do you write it poems?
I compose on it daily.

Is it epic?
In thought and in treatment.

Do you cry upon it?
It is flat and wet.

Will you humor it?
Forever.

Will you forsake it?
Never.

You say you keep it in a box?
I've Cornelled mine.

You say you call it soft names?
I call it softly. I name it.

Clipped of fledge?
Clipped of fledge.

You say it sits up on your soul?
It has it licked.

A new religion?
Nay, a faith.

Do you take it to bed?
I've pillowed and I've laid with it.

Does it propagate?
I sharpen my chastity upon it.

I belt it. I go down on it.
I keep it down.

Have you done your best to bury it?
I have dug.

With half a heart?
With dull spade, yea, half-heartedly.

Has it a sword?
A long-tailed lion on its crest.

Would you unknow it?
I've called it bastard.

Bastard!
Would you divorce it?

Untie it, would you?
Have you

Done with it?
No. I will have more.

2004

CARL DENNIS

Our Generation

◇   ◇   ◇

Whatever they say about us, they have to agree
We managed to bridge the gap between
Those who arrived before us and those who've followed.
We learned enough at the schools available
To fill the entry-level positions at the extant sawmills
Our elders managed, at banks, freight yards, and hospitals,
Then worked our way up to positions of trust.
There we were, down on the shop floor
Or up in the manager's office, or outside the office
On scaffolds, washing the windows.
Did we work with joy? With no less joy
Than people felt in the generations before us.
And on weekends and weekday evenings
We did our best to pursue the happiness
Our founders encouraged us to pursue,
And with equal gusto. Whatever they say about us,
They can't deny that we filled the concert halls,
Movie houses, malls, and late-night restaurants.
We took our bows onstage or waited on tables
Or manned the refreshment booths to earn a little extra
For the things we wanted, the very things
Pursued by the generations before us
And likely to be pursued by generations to come:
Children and lawns and cars and beach towels.
And now and then we stood back to admire
The colorful spectacle, the endless variety,
As others before us admired it, and then returned
To fill our picnic baskets, drive to the park,
And use the baseball diamonds just as their makers
Intended they should be used. And if we too

Crowded into the square to cheer the officials
Who proclaimed our country as fine in fact
As it is in theory, a few of us, confined to a side street,
Carried signs declaring a truth less fanciful.
A few unheeded, it's true, but no more unheeded
Than a similar few in generations before us
Who hoped that the truth in generations to come,
Though just as homely, would find more followers.

2006

Skin

◇　◇　◇

And what are they to do with pieces of it that lie in the grass
or waft down afterwards, floating through the atmosphere

like feathers from a featherbed in the tale about the girl
who disappears down a well and returns

in a shower of gold? What to do
with all the minute pieces, the shreds?

The air at times turns violet, the sun neglects
to warm the grainy strip of sand we lie on

waiting to be touched and transformed. And the body
falls apart like hair unloosed, returns element to element,

distills itself. We are only bone and water after all.
Skin covers the gray-tinged grass like the oldest balm

to heal sickness. The air corrupts, dries it,
breaks it down into its former life of cells

to join the inert world of soil and leaf.
They say Da Vinci's molecules

still orbit the globe, that the air he breathed,
we breathe today. So that when blood is spilled

when skin rains down on this dry earth, perhaps
somehow, the earth remembers.

Jerusalem bombing, February 1996

2003

Desire

◊   ◊   ◊

A woman in my class wrote that she is sick
of men wanting her body and when she reads
her poem out loud the other women all nod
and even some of the men lower their eyes

and look abashed as if ready to unscrew
their cocks and pound down their own dumb heads
with these innocent sausages of flesh, and none
would think of confessing his hunger

or admit how desire can ring like a constant
low note in the brain or grant how the sight
of a beautiful woman can make him groan
on those first spring days when the parkas

have been packed away and the bodies are staring
at the bodies and the eyes stare at the ground;
and there was a man I knew who even at ninety
swore that his desire had never diminished.

Is this simply the wish to procreate, the world
telling the cock to eat faster, while the cock
yearns for that moment when it forgets its loneliness
and the world flares up in an explosion of light?

Why have men been taught to feel ashamed
of their desire, as if each were a criminal
out on parole, a desperado with a long record
of muggings, rapes, such conduct as excludes

each one from all but the worst company,
and never to be trusted, no never to be trusted?
Why must men pretend to be indifferent as if each
were a happy eunuch engaged in spiritual thoughts?

But it's the glances that I like, the quick ones,
the unguarded ones, like a hand snatching a pie
from a window ledge and the feet pounding away;
eyes fastening on a leg, a breast, the curve

of a buttock, as the pulse takes an extra thunk
and the cock, that toothless worm, stirs in its sleep,
and fat possibility swaggers into the world
like a big spender entering a bar. And sometimes

the woman glances back. Oh, to disappear
in a tangle of fabric and flesh as the cock
sniffs out its little cave, and the body hungers
for closure, for the completion of the circle,

as if each of us were born only half a body
and we spend our lives searching for the rest.
What good does it do to deny desire, to chain
the cock to the leg and scrawl a black X

across its bald head, to hold out a hand
for each passing woman to slap? Better
to be bad and unrepentant, better to celebrate
each difference, not to be cruel or gluttonous

or overbearing, but full of hope and self-forgiving.
The flesh yearns to converse with other flesh.
Each pore loves to linger over its particular story.
Let these seconds not be full of self-recrimination

and apology. What is desire but the wish for some
relief from the self, the prisoner let out
into a small square of sunlight with a single
red flower and a bird crossing the sky, to lean back

against the bricks with the legs outstretched,
to feel the sun warming the brow, before returning
to one's mortal cage, steel doors slamming
in the cell block, steel bolts sliding shut?

1991

Difference

◇　◇　◇

The jellyfish
float in the bay shallows
like schools of clouds,

a dozen identical—is it right
to call them creatures,
these elaborate sacks

of nothing? All they seem
is shape, and shifting,
and though a whole troop

of undulant cousins
go about their business
within a single wave's span,

every one does something unlike:
this one a balloon
open on both ends

but swollen to its full expanse,
this one a breathing heart,
this a pulsing flower.

This one a rolled condom,
or a plastic purse swallowing itself,
that one a Tiffany shade,

this a troubled parasol.
This submarine opera's
all subterfuge and disguise,

its plot a fabulous tangle
of hiding and recognition:
nothing but trope,

nothing but something
forming itself into figures
then refiguring,

sheer ectoplasm
recognizable only as the stuff
of metaphor. What can words do

but link what we know
to what we don't,
and so form a shape?

Which shrinks or swells,
configures or collapses, blooms
even as it is described

into some unlikely
marine chiffon:
a gown for Isadora?

Nothing but style.
What binds
one shape to another

also sets them apart
—but what's lovelier
than the shapeshifting

transparence of *like* and *as:*
clear, undulant words?
We look at alien grace,

unfettered
by any determined form,
and we say: balloon, flower,

heart, condom, opera,
lampshade, parasol, ballet.
Hear how the mouth,

so full
of longing for the world,
changes its shape?

1994

All Souls'

◊   ◊   ◊

Starting up behind them,
all the voices of those they had named:
mink, gander, and marmoset,
crow and cockatiel.
Even the duck-billed platypus,
of late so quiet in its bed,
sent out a feeble cry signifying
grief and confusion, et cetera.

Of course the world had changed
for good. As it would from now on
every day, with every twitch and blink.
Now that change was de rigueur,
man would discover desire, then yearn
for what he would learn to call
distraction. This was the true loss.
And yet in that first

unchanging instant,
the two souls
standing outside the gates
(no more than a break in the hedge;
how had they missed it?) were not
thinking. Already the din was fading.
Before them, a silence
larger than all their ignorance

yawned, and this they walked into
until it was all they knew. In time

they hunkered down to business,
filling the world with sighs—
these anonymous, pompous creatures,
heads tilted as if straining
to make out the words to a song
played long ago, in a foreign land.

2004

How It Will End

◊   ◊   ◊

We're walking on the boardwalk
but stop when we see a lifeguard and his girlfriend
fighting. We can't hear what they're saying,
but it is as good as a movie. We sit on a bench to find out
how it will end. I can tell by her body language
he's done something really bad. She stands at the bottom
of the ramp that leads to his hut. He tries to walk halfway down
to meet her, but she keeps signaling *Don't come closer.*
My husband says, "Boy, he's sure in for it,"
and I say, "He deserves whatever's coming to him."
My husband thinks the lifeguard's cheated, but I think
she's sick of him only working part-time
or maybe he forgot to put the rent in the mail.
The lifeguard tries to reach out
and she holds her hand like Diana Ross
when she performed "Stop in the Name of Love."
The red flag that slaps against his station means strong currents.
"She has to just get it out of her system,"
my husband laughs, but I'm not laughing.
I start to coach the girl to leave the no-good lifeguard,
but my husband predicts she'll never leave.
I'm angry at him for seeing glee in their situation
and say, "That's your problem—you think every fight
is funny. You never take her seriously," and he says,
"You never even give the guy a chance and you're always nagging,
so how can he tell the real issues from the nitpicking?"
and I say, "She doesn't nitpick!" and he says, "Oh really?
Maybe he should start recording her tirades," and I say
"Maybe he should help out more," and he says
"Maybe she should be more supportive," and I say

"Do you mean supportive or do you mean support him?"
and my husband says that he's doing the best he can,
that he's a lifeguard for Christ's sake, and I say
that her job is much harder, that she's a waitress
who works nights carrying heavy trays and is hit on all the time
by creepy tourists and he just sits there most days napping
and listening to "Power 96" and then ooh
he gets to be the big hero blowing his whistle
and running into the water to save beach bunnies who flatter him
and my husband says it's not as though she's Miss Innocence
and what about the way she flirts, giving free refills
when her boss isn't looking or cutting extra large pieces of pie
to get bigger tips, oh no she wouldn't do that because she's a saint
and he's the devil, and I say, "I don't know why you can't just admit
he's a jerk," and my husband says, "I don't know why you can't admit
she's a killjoy," and then out of the blue the couple is making up.
The red flag flutters, then hangs limp.
She has her arms around his neck and is crying into his shoulder.
He whisks her up into his hut. We look around, but no one is watching us.

2009

STEPHEN DUNN

The Imagined

◇   ◇   ◇

If the imagined woman makes the real woman
seem bare-boned, hardly existent, lacking in
gracefulness and intellect and pulchritude,
and if you come to realize the imagined woman
can only satisfy your imagination, whereas
the real woman with all her limitations
can often make you feel good, how, in spite
of knowing this, does the imagined woman
keep getting into your bedroom, and joining you
at dinner, why is it that you always bring her along
on vacations when the real woman is shopping,
or figuring the best way to the museum?

                    And if the real woman

has an imagined man, as she must, someone
probably with her at this very moment, in fact
doing and saying everything she's ever wanted,
would you want to know that he slips in
to her life every day from a secret doorway
she's made for him, that he's present even when
you're eating your omelette at breakfast,
or do you prefer how she goes about the house
as she does, as if there were just the two of you?
Isn't her silence, finally, loving? And yours
not entirely self-serving? Hasn't the time come,

                    once again, not to talk about it?

2012

Powers of Congress

◇　◇　◇

How the lightstruck trees change sun
to flamepaths: veins, sap, stem, all
on brief loan, set to give all
their spooled, coded heat to stoves called
Resolute: wet steel diecast
by heat themselves. Tree, beast, bug—
the worldclass bit parts in this
world—flit and skid through it; the
powers of congress tax, spend, law
what lives to pure crisp form
then break forms' lock, stock, and hold
on flesh. All night couples pledge
to stay flux, the hit-run stuff
of cracked homes. Men trim their quick
lawns each weekend, trailing power
mowers. Heartslaves, you've seen them: wives
with flexed hair, hitched to bored kids,
twiddling in good living rooms,
their twin beds slept in, changed, made.

1989

ALLEN GINSBERG

Salutations to Fernando Pessoa

◊   ◊   ◊

Everytime I read Pessoa I think
I'm better than he is I do the same thing
more extravagantly—he's only from Portugal,
I'm American greatest Country in the world
right now End of XX Century tho Portugal
had a big empire in the 15th century never mind
now shrunk to a Corner of Iberian peninsula
whereas New York take New York for instance
tho Mexico City's bigger N.Y.'s richer think of Empire State
Building not long ago world empire's biggest skyscraper—
be that as't may I've experienced 61 years' XX Century
Pessoa walked down Rua do Ouro only till 1936
He entered Whitman so I enter Pessoa no
matter what they say besides dead he wouldn't object.

What way'm I better than Pessoa?
Known on 4 Continents I have 25 English books he only 3
his mostly Portuguese, but that's not his fault—
U.S.A.'s a bigger Country
merely 2 Trillion in debt a passing freakout,
Reagan's dirty work an American Century aberration
unrepresenting our Nation Whitman sang in Epic manner
tho worried about in Democratic Vistas
As a Buddhist not proud my superiority to Pessoa
I'm humble Pessoa was nuts big difference,
tho apparently gay—same as Socrates,
consider Michelangelo DaVinci Shakespeare
inestimable comrado Walt
True I was tainted Pinko at an early age a mere trifle

Science itself destroys ozone layers this era antiStalinists
poison entire earth with radioactive anticommunism
Maybe I lied somewhat
rarely in verse, only protecting others' reputations
Frankly too Candid about my mother tho meant well
Did Pessoa mention his mother? she's interesting,
powerful to birth sextuplets
Alberto Cairo Alvaro de Campos Ricardo Reis Bernardo Soares
       & Alexander Search simultaneously
with Fernando Pessoa himself a classic sexophrenic
Confusing personae not so popular
outside Portugal's tiny kingdom (till recently a secondrate police state)
Let me get to the point er I forget what it was
but certainly enjoy making comparisons between this Ginsberg
       & Pessoa
people talk about in Iberia hardly any books in English
presently the world's major diplomatic language extended throughout
       China.
Besides he was a shrimp, himself admits in interminable "Salutations
       to Walt Whitman"
Whereas 5' 7½" height
somewhat above world average, no immodesty,
I'm speaking seriously about me & Pessoa.
Anyway he never influenced me, never read Pessoa
before I wrote my celebrated "Howl" already translated into 24 languages,
not to this day's Pessoa influence an anxiety
Midnight April 12 88 merely glancing his book
certainly influences me in passing, only reasonable
but reading a page in translation hardly proves "Influence."
Turning to Pessoa, what'd he write about? Whitman,
(Lisbon, the sea etc.) method peculiarly longwinded,
diarrhea mouth some people say—Pessoa Schmessoa.

1995

Landscape

◇   ◇   ◇

Time passed, turning everything to ice.
Under the ice, the future stirred.
If you fell into it, you died.

It was a time
of waiting, of suspended action.

I lived in the present, which was
that part of the future you could see.
The past floated above my head,
like the sun and moon, visible but never reachable.

It was a time
governed by contradictions, as in
I felt nothing and
I was afraid.

Winter emptied the trees, filled them again with snow.
Because I couldn't feel, snow fell, the lake froze over.
Because I was afraid, I didn't move;
my breath was white, a description of silence.

Time passed, and some of it became this.
And some of it simply evaporated;
you could see it float above the white trees
forming particles of ice.

All your life, you wait for the propitious time.
Then the propitious time
reveals itself as action taken.

I watched the past move, a line of clouds moving
from left to right or right to left,
depending on the wind. Some days

there was no wind. The clouds seemed
to stay where they were,
like a painting of the sea, more still than real.

Some days the lake was a sheet of glass.
Under the glass, the future made
demure, inviting sounds;
you had to tense yourself so as not to listen.

Time passed; you got to see a piece of it.
The years it took with it were years of winter;
they would not be missed. Some days

there were no clouds, as though
the sources of the past had vanished. The world

was bleached, like a negative; the light passed
directly through it. Then
the image faded.

Above the world
there was only blue, blue everywhere.

2003

JORIE GRAHAM

Manifest Destiny

◊   ◊   ◊

(Note: Rebbibia is the name of the women's jail in Rome.)
(F.H. 1947–1990)

Northbound, on the way to the station, through the narrow
                                                    rutted
place in the patch of woods,
        the dust from the car ahead rose up
into the wide still shafts of morning-light the trees let
        through,
its revolutionary swirls uplifted in some kind of
        cosmic merriment, up

        all round the sleek whiskey-colored slice
of time
        passing—though perfectly still to our eyes, passengers—
a blade of stillness, the intravenous access
        of the unearthly
into this soil.
        The dust rose into it. No, the dust

        slapped round, falling, a thick curiosity, shabby but
extravagant, crazy pulverized soliloquy, furled up, feathery,
        around the
metronome, raking, as if to transfuse itself onto what won't be
        touched,
a thick precipitate, feudal, a glossary of possible entrances
                                        replete
        with every conceivable version of
change.

Change! It seemed to almost screech as it rose again and
                                                        again
out of our drought into the stiff and
        prosperous stillness—*change, change*—into, onto
that shaft driven in firm,

        steely backbone of the imperial
invisible.
        I watched the stationary golden avenue. At every curve
watched the dust
        thrown up like some mad prophet taking on
all the shapes, all the contortions of the
        human form—bent over, flayed, curled back

onto itself.
        It was hard not to see the grief in it, the
cowardice—
        this carnage of fictive
possibilities, this prolonged
        carnage.
The gold bars gleam.
        The money is put down on the gleaming platter.
Like an eyelid forced back down.
        And another bill, and another bill, down,—
onto the open hand, onto the open,—

        —how long till the blazing gaze is dulled, the wide
need, bristling with light,
        unwavering, shimmering with rightfulness, god,
so still!—
        and the dusty money coming down onto it.

We rose from the table having paid our bill.

        Rome stepped back all round us as we rose up

—colonnades, promenades, porticoes,
        shadows of warriors, lovers and the various queens of
heaven—

arms raised holding the stone fruit, lips parted uttering the
stone word—stone child in the stone arms—stone

    sword held up into the stone
cry—.
     I look into the air
for your face—
     a fold in the invisible out of which features
slip—
     until you put it on again, there, in the dusty air, the
expression you wore, click,
     among the shadows of the sculptures in the

Vatican arcade—3 miles of corridor we hurry through
    to reach the reliquary before it shuts,
to see the Veronica,
    your hands pressed to the glass till the guard
speaks—
    and the eyes in brine,
and the index finger of Aquinas,
    and the burned head of Lawrence so black it seems
to face on all four

sides—then back out into the noon
    sun. *Rome.* And the word pulverizes. In the restaurant
you were gone so long I
    came to look for you.
Your face started up from the two arms below you—
    one holding the needle into the other—

white kiss on the brow of the forever waiting white maiden,
    forever and forever, forever and forever.
We paid up and left there too.
    The city even whiter now. White noise. White light.
    Walking the back way we passed the length of Rebibbia.
Cooler down there. Riverside traffic above to the left.
    We were used to them, the women's shrieks—hanging their arms,
hundreds of them, out through the bars into the steamy
heat—pointing, cursing, all the fingers in the dark noonlight
    screaming down the stories—who was killed, why, where
the children are, will you take a message, I'd do it again,

I'd do it to you, come on, let me give it to you—thousands
of white fingers all over the dark facade, no faces
visible—just

listen, listen and I'll make you
come they'd shriek, trellis of iron and white fleshgrowth,
3 blocks long this queen of the skies—huntress—no face—

all stone and fingerclutch, white, raking the air.
You stood below looking up,
the thing which is your laugh sucked up like a small down-
payment—so small—
then taking my arm, hard, forced me to stand there
before them, below them—*here, do you want her, will she do* you
screamed—
thousands of fingers moving—*tell me, will she do*—

screech of muscle,
throbbing facade,
how should we make her you screamed
do her time, drunk too I thought, the clamp of your hand
hard on my upper arm,
the light down harder on my face, something rising in me
as they

screamed down give her to us, let us have her,
their one scream going in through
the hold where your hand gripped, the narrow opening
through which I knew
that you would not believe in life,
that you would hand the piece you were holding back up,
the debt too heavy to carry,
up to the balcony there, in full sun,

like a caress on the infinite
this handing up of the full amount,
a handful of cloth, cash, skin—
2:53 pm—Rome time—
in the marketplace now, in the arcade,
arms waving the flies off
over the cut meats, beside the statue of Caesar—

two dancers with a hat out for change—
the swallower of flames, the fabric merchant

holding the star-spangled yardage out on her arms,
and singing the price out—loud, clear,
    —what is love what is creation what is longing what
is a star—
    behold I show you the last man—
the price rising up on the gold track of its note,
    the cloth on her arms lifting,

catching the light, dustmotes in the light,
    and the voice thrusting round it,
and the unalterable amount—
    high, hard, doth she and did she and shall she ever more—
sleeps she a thousand years and then and then—
    a motorcycle through it now then a dog—
the last man grows, lives longest,
    is ineradicable—blink—
"we have invented happiness" he says—
    meats sizzling on the silver spit,
price aloft,

    perfect price in the dusty air,
us swirling round its upwardmoving note,
    milling, taking this shape then that, hot wind,
until I have to turn to let her voice in,
    to feel the blue velveteen spangly brocade,
the invisible sum with its blazing zero ajar, there, midair—

and something so quick darting through it—
what will my coin repair? what does my meaning mend?

    I pay her now. I pay her again. Again.
Gold open mouth hovering—no face.

    Until you're pulling me away. Saying *love.*
As if to find me with that.
    But I want to pay her again.
To keep the hole open.
    The zero. The gold lidless pupil.

She will not look away.
   Change change it shrieks   the last man blinks   we have invented,
                                            invented—

Oh why are you here on this earth, you—*you*—swarming, swirling,
      carrying valises, standing on line,
ready to change your name if need be—?

1992

LINDA GREGERSON

Safe

◊   ◊   ◊

K.M.S. 1948–1986

The tendons sewn together and the small bones
        healed, that your hand
    might close on a pencil again

or hold a cup. The delicate muscles made
        whole again,
    to lift your eyelid and govern your smile,

and the nerves new-laid in their tracks.
        The broken
    point of the kitchen knife—and here

let the surgeon be gentle—removed and the skull
        knit closed
    and the blood lifted out of the carpet and washed

from the stairs. And the nineteen-year-old burglar returned
        to the cradle or
    his mother's arms—he must have been harmless

once, even he, who is not sorry, had
        nothing
    to lose, and will never be harmless again.

*   *   *

Emma is learning to wield her own spoon—
        silver for abundance,
    though it seldom finds her mouth as yet.

She hates to be fed, would rather starve,
        but loves
    to steer the precarious course herself.

Silver for pride, then, or luck of the sort
        some children
    are born with, omitting

the manifold slippage
        that separates
    privilege and weal. Luck in this popular figure

is three parts silver anyway,
        that the child
    not succumb to crack in the schoolyard,

rats in the hall, the clever fence with a
        shopping list,
    bad plumbing, bad food, and hatred-on-a-staircase

with a knife in hand and dim designs
        on jewelry
    or a VCR. The spoon was superfluity—

the best part of your paycheck for a child
        you haven't lived
    to see. Friend, her cheek is fresh as hope

of paradise. And every passing minute in the hours
        of light
    and the hours of darkness, in the fever

of pneumonia or the ignorant sweet wash
        of health,
    the miraculous breath

moves into her lungs and, stitch
             by mortal
      stitch, moves out.

                    *   *   *

When the paramedics came at last, my friend
             apologized:
      she must have hit her head, she thought,

she'd just take a minute to mop up the mess
             by the phone.
      Her broken hands, for which

the flaw in memory had provided no such
             alibi,
      her broken hands had kept him two or

three times from her face.
             And later
      when the anesthesiologist had

launched her on his good green gas
             and launched her,
      as they do sometimes, a shade too fast,

she slipped the bonds of recall altogether.
             Safe
      as houses. You know what a house is for the likes

of us: down payment on the nursing home,
             our four-square
      pledge to be debtors of conscience, if debtors

in conscience may not look too closely
             where credit's
      refused. Our piece of the here for here-

after, which shows us diminished regard
             and just
      such a face as fear has made:

one night a woman came home to her house
and locked its useless
locks, and buttoned her nightdress and read

for a while, and slept till she was wakened.

1991

LINDA GREGG

The War

◊　◊　◊

We were at the border and they were checking
the luggage. We had been talking about Lermontov's
novel, *A Hero of Our Time.* John liked Petorin
because he was so modern during that transition
from one history to another. I talked about Vera
and Princess Mary, the old man and the others
Petorin hurt. I said there was no reckoning,
that he was not made accountable as in Tolstoy
or Dostoevsky. Maybe morality does change,
I was thinking, but suffering does not. Then
a scorpion crawled from a satchel on the table.
He fell to the floor and scurried across the room.
The men were delighted. One crouched down and held
the scorpion with a ballpoint pen while he cut off
the poisoned stinger at the end of the tail.
The scorpion stretched out was as long as a hand.
The men gathered around, their open pocket knives
held shoulder high. The man picked up the scorpion
by the tail and put it on his friend who yelped,
jumping. The men laughed. The scorpion fell.
Another man picked it up and threw it lightly
against the wall. The scorpion fell and kept trying,
scuttling across the tiles toward the open door.
He kept his tail high, threatening, but looked tired.
There was excitement in the men, and happiness.
Somebody else picked up the scorpion and I told John
I was going. We went outside where there was nothing.

1990

THOM GUNN

Cafeteria in Boston

◇ ◇ ◇

I could digest the white slick watery mash,
The two green peppers stuffed with rice and grease
In Harry's Cafeteria, could digest
Angelfood cake too like a sweetened sawdust.
I sought to extend the body's education,
Forced it to swallow down the blunted dazzle
Sucked from the red formica where I leaned.
Took myself farther, digesting as I went,
Course after course: even the bloated man
In cast-off janitor's overalls, who may
Indeed have strayed through only for the toilets;
But as he left I caught his hang-dog stare
At the abandoned platefuls crusted stiff
Like poisoned slugs that froth into their trails.
I stomached him, him of the flabby stomach,
Though it was getting harder to keep down.
But how about the creature scurrying in
From the crowds wet on the November sidewalk,
His face a black skull with a slaty shine,
Who slipped his body with one fluid motion
Into a seat before a dish on which
Scrapings had built a heterogeneous mound,
And set about transferring them to his mouth,
Stacking them faster there than he could swallow,
To get a start on the bus-boys. My mouth too
Was packed, its tastes confused: what bitter juices
I generated in my stomach as
Revulsion met revulsion. Yet at last
I lighted upon meat more to my taste
When, glancing off into the wide fluorescence,

I saw the register, where the owner sat,
And suddenly realized that he, the cooks,
The servers of the line, the bus-boys, all
Kept their eyes studiously turned away
From the black scavenger. Digestively,
That was the course that kept the others down.

1989

Prophecy

◇ ◇ ◇

I will strike down wooden houses; I will burn aluminum
clapboard skin; I will strike down garages
where crimson Toyotas sleep side by side; I will explode
palaces of gold, silver, and alabaster:—the summer
great house and its folly together. Where shopping malls
spread plywood and plaster out, and roadhouses
serve steak and potatoskins beside Alaska King Crab;
where triangular flags proclaim tribes of identical campers;
where airplanes nose to tail exhale kerosene,
weeds and ashes will drowse in continual twilight.

I reject the old house and the new car; I reject
Tory and Whig together; I reject the argument
that modesty of ambition is sensible because the bigger
they are the harder they fall; I reject Waterford;
I reject the five-and-dime; I reject Romulus and Remus;
I reject Martha's Vineyard and the slamdunk contest;
I reject leaded panes; I reject the appointment made
at the tennis net or on the seventeenth green; I reject
the Professional Bowling Tour; I reject matchboxes;
I reject purple bathrooms with purple soap in them.

Men who lie awake worrying about taxes, vomiting
at dawn, whose hands shake as they administer Valium,—
skin will peel from the meat of their thighs.
Armies that march all day with elephants past pyramids
and roll pulling missiles past Generals weary of saluting
and past President-Emperors splendid in cloth-of-gold,—
soft rumps of armies will dissipate in rain. Where square
miles of corn waver in Minnesota, where tobacco ripens

in Carolina and apples in New Hampshire, where wheat
turns Kansas green, where pulpmills stink in Oregon,

dust will blow in the darkness and cactus die
before it flowers. Where skiers wait for chairlifts,
wearing money, low raspberries will part rib-bones.
Where the drive-in church raises a chromium cross,
dandelions and milkweed will straggle through blacktop.
I will strike from the ocean with waves afire;
I will strike from the hill with rainclouds of lava;
I will strike from darkened air
with melanoma in the shape of decorative hexagonals.
I will strike down embezzlers and eaters of snails.

I reject Japanese smoked oysters, potted chrysanthemums
allowed to die, Tupperware parties, Ronald McDonald,
Karposi's sarcoma, the Taj Mahal, holsteins wearing
electronic necklaces, the Algonquin, Tunisian aqueducts,
Phi Beta Kappa keys, the Hyatt Embarcadero, carpenters
jogging on the median, and betrayal that engorges
the corrupt heart longing for criminal surrender:
I reject shadows in the corner of the atrium
where Phyllis or Phoebe speaks with Billy or Marc
who says that afternoons are best although not reliable.

Your children will wander looting the shopping malls
for forty years, suffering for your idleness,
until the last dwarf body rots in a parking lot.
I will strike down lobbies and restaurants in motels
carpeted with shaggy petrochemicals
from Maine to Hilton Head, from the Skagit to Tucson.
I will strike down hanggliders, wiry adventurous boys;
their thighbones will snap, their brains
slide from their skulls. I will strike down
families cooking wildboar in New Mexico backyards.

Then landscape will clutter with incapable machinery,
acres of vacant airplanes and schoolbuses, ploughs
with seedlings sprouting and turning brown through colters.
Unlettered dwarves will burrow for warmth and shelter
in the caves of dynamos and Plymouths, dying

of old age at seventeen. Tribes wandering
in the wilderness of their ignorant desolation,
who suffer from your idleness, will burn your illuminated
missals to warm their rickety bodies.
Terrorists assemble plutonium because you are idle

and industrious. The whip-poor-will shrivels and the pickerel
chokes under the government of self-love. Vacancy burns
air so that you strangle without oxygen like rats
in a biologist's bell jar. The living god sharpens
the scythe of my prophecy to strike down red poppies
and blue cornflowers. When priests and policemen
strike my body's match, Jehovah will flame out;
Jehovah will suck air from the vents of bombshelters.
Therefore let the Buick swell until it explodes;
therefore let anorexia starve and bulimia engorge.

When Elzira leaves the house wearing her tennis dress
and drives her black Porsche to meet Abraham,
quarrels, returns to husband and children, and sobs
alseep, drunk, unable to choose among them,—
lawns and carpets will turn into tar together
with lovers, husbands, and children.
Fat will boil in the sacs of children's clear skin.
I will strike down the nations, astronauts and judges;
I will strike down Babylon, I will strike acrobats,
I will strike algae and the white birches.

Because Professors of Law teach ethics in dumbshow,
let the Colonel become President; because Chief Executive
Officers and Commissars collect down for pillows,
let the injustice of cities burn city and suburb;
let the countryside burn; let the pineforests of Maine
explode like a kitchenmatch and the Book of Kells turn
ash in a microsecond; let oxen and athletes
flash into grease:—I return to Appalachian rocks;
I shall eat bread; I shall prophesy through millennia
of Jehovah's day until the sky reddens over cities:

Then houses will burn, even houses of alabaster;
the sky will disappear like a scroll rolled up

and hidden in a cave from the industries of idleness.
Mountains will erupt and vanish, becoming deserts,
and the sea wash over the sea's lost islands
and the earth split open like a corpse's gassy
stomach and the sun turn as black as a widow's skirt
and the full moon grow red with blood swollen inside it
and stars fall from the sky like wind-blown apples,—
while Babylon's managers burn in the rage of the Lamb.

1988

The Opaque

◇　　◇　　◇

We crave it because we feel it is secretly us
after the ideas wearing name-tags have had their
   big convention.
But that's an idea; that's not it.

Bumpy muddy fields with stands of scruffy trees.

Blueprints for the wiring of public buildings in Singapore.

The life lived in a purple Volkswagen
parked next to the Almstead Tree Company in New Rochelle.

A quick-stepping woman in a corridor, moving away;
her calves.

In the opaque, there are only examples.

Venezuela.

Any one word said over and over. Opaque.

Ed Skoog. Opaque. Mitch Green. Opaque.
Serina Mammon. Out of reach.

Gusto of deer hunters. Venison draining.

Speckly smudged static of when we are too tired, when are we
too tired for one more example?

Seventy-year-old twins who sing together of baby Jesus.

Juliette Gréco singing at Le Boeuf Sur Le Toit
and how some guy named Bernard interpreted her phrasing.
Years back, years back years back.

Hundreds of people standing in rain to watch golf.

The next thing, the next thing you get stuck on
before it becomes a handy metaphor . . .

A news item in Arabic about stolen bicycles.

If there were a tribe of Indians called the Opakis,
their way of stitching beaver pelts would be opaque.

Those gray people politely serving around the edges
of your life and how they can stand it.

Bumpy muddy fields with stands of scruffy trees
and why the trees bother to stand up.

Silence of a stuffed bag of laundry.
Laundry, laundry.

That blonde woman on the subway, she wasn't Sophie
she couldn't have been Sophie

Cheddar cheese soup

The waitress who served me my cheddar cheese soup today
without a word and walked out of the restaurant
ten minutes later in her gray-blue winter jacket

The pain of that person you said you loved six years ago.

We get tired, but what would it mean to be tired enough?
Congested heart of a man committing murder
this very hour in Tennessee
(not yet a character in a novel).

What peels away from or pokes out through yesterday's
poem, poamb, poeem, pom-pom
in that black behind black ink . . .

Tintex—Japalac—
Kish & Sons Electric. Zelda's Diner.
Combo Basket at the Big Top.

Mister Thasildar of Bombay ignoring three young
dying prostitutes in a parlor of his Naazma bordello.

Beans in the middle of the night.

Who built this tunnel? How long is this tunnel?
Does it go somewhere? Oh never mind,
here comes the light of day.

2003

Bush's War

◇ ◇ ◇

I typed the brief phrase, "Bush's War,"
At the top of a sheet of white paper,
Having some dim intuition of a poem
Made luminous by reason that would,
Though I did not have them at hand,
Set the facts out in an orderly way.
Berlin is a northerly city. In May
At the end of the twentieth century
In the leafy precincts of Dahlem Dorf,
South of the Grunewald, near Krumme Lanke,
Spring is northerly; it begins before dawn
In a racket of bird song. The *amsels*
Shiver the sun up as if they were shaking
A liquid tangle of golden wire. There are two kinds
Of flowering chestnuts, red and white,
And the wet pavements are speckled
With petals from the incandescent spikes
Of their flowers and shoes at U-bahn stops
Are flecked with them. Green of holm oaks,
Birch tassels, the soft green of maples,
And the odor of lilacs is everywhere.
At Oskar Helene Heim station a farmer
Sells white asparagus from a heaped table.
In a month he'll be selling chanterelles;
In the month after that, strawberries
And small, rosy crawfish from the Spree.
The piles of stalks of the asparagus
Are startlingly phallic, phallic and tender
And deathly pale. Their seasonal appearance
Must be the remnant of some fertility ritual

Of the German tribes. Steamed, they are the color
Of old ivory. In May, in restaurants
They are served on heaped white platters
With boiled potatoes and parsley butter,
Or shavings of Parma ham and lemon juice
Or sorrel and smoked salmon. And,
Walking home in the slant, widening,
Brilliant northern light that falls
On the new-leaved birches and the elms,
Nightingales singing at the first, subtlest,
Darkening of dusk, it is a trick of the mind
That the past seems just ahead of us,
As if we were being shunted there
In the surge of a rattling funicular.
Flash forward: the firebombing of Hamburg,
Fifty thousand dead in a single night,
"The children's bodies the next day
Set in the street in rows like a market
In charred chicken." Flash forward:
Firebombing of Tokyo, a hundred thousand
In a night. Flash forward: forty-five
Thousand Polish officers slaughtered
By the Russian army in the Katyn Woods,
The work of half a day. Flash forward:
Two million Russian prisoners of war
Murdered by the German army all across
The eastern front, supplies low,
Winter of 1943. Flash: Hiroshima.
And then Nagasaki, as if the sentence
Life is fire and flesh is ash needed
To be spoken twice. Flash: Auschwitz,
Dachau, Theresienstadt, the train lurching,
The stomach woozy, past displays of falls
Of hair, piles of valises, spectacles
With frames designed to curl delicately
Around a human ear. Flash:
The gulags, seven million in Byelorussia
And Ukraine. In innocent Europe on a night
In spring, among the light-struck birches,
Students holding hands. One of them
Is carrying a novel, the German translation

Of a slim book by Marguerite Duras
About a love affair in old Saigon. (Flash:
Two million Vietnamese, fifty-five thousand
Of the American young, whole races
Of tropical birds extinct from saturation bombing)
The kind of book the young love
To love, about love in time of war.
Forty-five million, all told, in World War II.
In Berlin, pretty Berlin, in the spring time,
You are never not wondering how
It happened, and the people around you
In the station with chestnut petals on their shoes,
Children then, or unborn, never not
Wondering. Is it that we like the kissing
And bombing together, in prospect
At least, girls in their flowery dresses?
Someone will always want to mobilize
Death on a massive scale for economic
Domination or revenge. And the task, taken
As a task, appeals to the imagination.
The military is an engineering profession.
Look at boys playing: they love
To figure out the ways to blow things up.
But the rest of us have to go along.
Why do we do it? Certainly there's a rage
To injure what's injured us. Wars
Are always pitched to us that way.
The well-paid news readers read the reasons
On the air. And we who are injured,
Or have been convinced that we are injured,
Are always identified with virtue. It's that—
The rage to hurt mixed with self-righteousness
And fear—that's murderous.
The young Arab depilated himself
As an act of purification before he drove
The plane into the office building. It's not
Just violence, it's a taste for power
That amounts to loathing for the body.
Perhaps it's this that permits people to believe
That the dead women in the rubble of Baghdad
Who did not cast a vote for their deaths

Or the glimpse afforded them before they died
Of the raw white of the splintered bones
In the bodies of their men or their children
Are being given the gift of freedom
Which is the virtue of their injured killers.
It's hard to say which is worse about this,
The moral sloth of it or the intellectual disgrace.
And what good are our judgments to the dead?
And death the cleanser, Walt Whitman's
Sweet death, the scourer, the tender
Lover, shutter of eyelids, turns
The heaped bodies into summer fruit,
Magpies eating dark berries in the dusk
And birch pollen staining sidewalks
To the faintest gold. *Balde nur*—Goethe—no,
Warte nur, balde ruhest du auch. Just wait.
You will be quiet soon enough. In Dahlem,
Under the chestnuts, in the leafy spring.

2007

A House Is Not a Home

◊   ◊   ◊

It was the night I embraced Ron's wife a bit too long
because he'd refused to kiss me goodbye
that I realized the essential nature of sound.
When she slapped me across one ear,
and he punched me in the other, I recalled,
almost instantly, the purr of liquor sliding
along the neck of the bottle a few hours earlier
as the three of us took turns imitating the croon
of the recently-deceased Luther Vandross.
I decided then, even as my ears fattened,
to seek employment at the African-American
Acoustic and Audiological Accident Insurance Institute,
where probably there is a whole file devoted
to Luther Vandross. And probably it contains
the phone call he made once to ask a niece
the whereabouts of his very first piano.
I already know there is a difference
between hearing and listening,
but to get the job, I bet I will have to learn
how to transcribe church fires or how to categorize
the dozen or so variations of gasping, one of which
likely includes Ron and me in the eighth grade
the time a neighbor flashed her breasts at us.
That night at Ron's house I believed he, his wife,
and Luther loved me more than anything
I could grasp. "I can't believe you won't kiss me,
you're the gayest man I know!" I told him
just before shackling my arms around his wife.
"My job is all about context," I will tell friends
when they ask. "I love it, though most days

all I do is root through noise like a termite
with a number on his back." What will I steal?
Rain falling on a picket sign, breathy epithets—
you think I'm bullshitting. When you have no music,
everything becomes a form of music. I bet
somewhere in Mississippi there is a skull
that only a sharecropper's daughter can make sing.
I'll steal that sound. More than anything,
I want to work at the African-American
Acoustic and Audiological Accident Insurance Institute
so that I can record the rumors and raucous rhythms
of my people, our jangled history, the slander
in our sugar, the ardor in our anger, a subcategory
of which probably includes the sound particular to one
returning to his feet after a friend has knocked him down.

2009

The Polar Circle

◊   ◊   ◊

for Lauri Nykopp

The world is between tips
We say so to know
We go to look over or out to its pivot, to its
    wobble and drift
Terrible
We are leaving
There's nothing to come to there but
    transformation and tint
Seductions
So we can't be repeating
What one knows in this state can't be known in
    another
Time matches nothing

People don't circle, certainly not unless they are
    responsible
But sleeps pine or eagle or tide to gratify
And thousands depend on one
Repeated
And all that's repeated is mediated
Thought
The order is such that it situates
At the farthest extent of a scene are its
    reachings
Night life is search of its kind
Hands open and fingers shuffle

I could gesture not of persons but of crevice,
    preface, and prelude
I imagine without standpoint poised at loss point
At pole
I easily sleep in its entered light but don't
    write
It doesn't behoove me to make myself smaller than
    I am
And the horizon doesn't hold there
It isn't grained
Its gaping point of contact spreads the latitudes
The pole is interminable, coming and going as if
    solely on rock
But it isn't singular
It shares the mobility of an oblivion I want to
    witness

The world looks like
The pole draws the whirlpools
And to express scope one turns the top of one's
    head
In time the berries unfold of nothing but gold
    cloud
Every color is gathered and then flown
We were even in the red bogs—everything is always
    even
The rivers were amber as tea
And I didn't want to tell, though I seemed to
I always wanted what has no beginning but not what
    has no end
There must be point and it might be tide
Time—North
I think of reason everywhere and it overlaps
Reasonable eventuality and long partition—
    grammar, supper, and sleep ideas are chasing
To pole
It says the dog joined in and tore off the whole
    of a man's face while the man, his arms
    clasped round its back, broke every bone in

the dog's body, and there the pair of them
lay, dead, seizing what seemed to be the only
chance

We dream with our limbs on our heads
As Poe says, It is a happiness to wonder
Our ankles are the hottest
It is happiness to dream
The men ask me where is the charred pot and I say
    it is in the car trunk
The men deny that the slopes have walked into the
    creek
They are probably right and keep consuming
Fire they need—they who come in and fall to their
    knees
To ground

Human curiosity contradicts the human will to
    believe
Before going north I almost had been stopping
But what's the denial of solving
Night visions rhyme—peaks, language, sleep,
    light, tundra, lichen
Because of the obscurity of such phenomena Nature
    seems uncanny
It lets us mock and destroy the utterly complete
Sleep is what remains of Nature
That merely mathematical recognition of equality,
    Poe says, which seems to be the root of all
    beauty
With night thoughts like these, are we not
    logicians
The lower teeth fall out and point saying,
    "Ourselves!"
We are barbarian, recalcitrant, in sleep
Probably we sleep beyond our strength
But what has happened?
As herself at the Arctic limit I would leave
    myself

Still I ask, "Am I contributing something?"
A sleeper leaning over more than ever to make
     contact with reality
Everything is scattered beyond the face
Detached
But persons have their immortality to sacrifice—
     and why stop?

1994

Having Intended to Merely Pick on an Oil Company, the Poem Goes Awry

◊   ◊   ◊

Never before have I so resembled British Petroleum.
They—it?—are concerned about the environment.
I—it?—am concerned about the environment.
They—him?—convey their concern through commercials,
in which a man talks softly about the importance
of the Earth. I—doodad?—convey my concern
through poems, in which my fingers type softly
about the importance of the Earth. They—oligarchs?—
have painted their slogans green. I—ineffectual
left-leaning emotional black hole of a self-semaphore?—
recycle. Isn't a corporation technically a person
and responsible? Aren't I technically a person
and responsible? In a legal sense, in a regal sense,
if romanticism holds sway? To give you a feel
for how soft his voice is, imagine a kitty
that eats only felt wearing a sable coat on a bed
of dandelion fluff under sheets of the foreskins
of seraphim, that's how soothingly they want to drill
in Alaska, in your head, just in case. And let's be honest,
we mostly want them to, we mostly want to get to the bank
by two so we can get out of town by three and beat
the traffic, traffic is murder, this time of year.
How far would you walk for bread? For the flour
to make bread? A yard, a mile, a year, a life?
Now you ask me, when are you going to fix your bike

and ride it to work? Past the plain horses
and spotted cows and the spotted horses and plain cows,
along the river, to the left of the fallen-down barn
and the right of the falling-down barn, up the hill,
through the Pentecostal bend and past the Methodist
edifice, through the speed trap, beside the art gallery
and cigar shop, past the tattoo parlor and the bar
and the other bar and the other other bar and the other
other other bar and the bar that closed, where I swear,
Al-Anon meets, since I'm wondering, what is the value
of the wick or wire of soul, be it emotional
or notional, now that oceans are wheezing to a stop?

2011

Phone Booth

◇   ◇   ◇

There should be more nouns
For objects put to sleep
Against their will
The "booth" for instance
With coiled hidden wires
Lidded chrome drawers
Tipping up like lizards' eyes
We looked out into rhymed rain
We heard varying vowels
Rimbaud's vowels with colors
Orange or blue beeps
Types of ancient punctuation
The interpunct between words
A call became twenty-five cents
Times in a marriage we went there
To complain or flirt
A few decades and we wised up
Got used to the shadow
The phone booth as reliquary
An arm could rest
On the triangular shelf
A briefcase between the feet
A pen poked into acoustic holes
While we gathered our actions/wits
For magic and pain
The destiny twins
Some of us scratched pale glyphs
Onto the glass door while talking

One day we started to race past
And others started racing
Holding phones to their ears
Holding a personal string
To their lips
If there are overages
There might be nouns for
The clotting of numbers in the sky
So thick the stars can't shine through
A word for backing away
From those who shout to their strings
In the airport while eating
We loved the half-booths
Could cup one hand on the mouthpiece
Lean two-thirds out to talk to a friend
Sitting in the lobby
The universe grows
We are dizzy as mercury
We are solitudes aided by awe
Let us mourn secrets told to
Fake wood and the trapezoidal seat
Perfume in the mouthpiece
Like a little Grecian sash
Why did we live so fast
The booth hid our ankles
We twisted the rigid cord
As we spoke
It made a kind of whorl

2008

Man on a Fire Escape

◇　◇　◇

He couldn't remember what propelled him
out of the bedroom window onto the fire escape
of his fifth-floor walkup on the river,

so that he could see, as if for the first time,
sunset settling down on the dazed cityscape
and tugboats pulling barges up the river.

There were barred windows glaring at him
from the other side of the street
while the sun deepened into a smoky flare

that scalded the clouds gold-vermillion.
It was just an ordinary autumn twilight—
the kind he had witnessed often before—

but then the day brightened almost unnaturally
into a rusting, burnished, purplish-red haze
and everything burst into flame;

the factories pouring smoke into the sky,
the trees and shrubs, the shadows,
of pedestrians scorched and rushing home. . . .

There were storefronts going blind and cars
burning on the parkway and steel girders
collapsing into the polluted waves.

Even the latticed fretwork of stairs
where he was standing, even the first stars
climbing out of their sunlit graves

were branded and lifted up, consumed by fire.
It was like watching the start of Armageddon,
like seeing his mother dipped in flame. . . .

And then he closed his eyes and it was over.
Just like that. When he opened them again
the world had reassembled beyond harm.

So where had he crossed to? Nowhere.
And what had he seen? Nothing. No foghorns
called out to each other, as if in a dream,

and no moon rose over the dark river
like a warning—icy, long forgotten—
while he turned back to an empty room.

1992

In Praise of Coldness

◇ ◇ ◇

"If you wish to move your reader,"
Chekhov wrote, "you must write more coldly."

Herakleitos recommended, "A dry soul is best."

And so at the center of many great works
is found a preserving dispassion,
like the vanishing point of quattrocento perspective,
or the tiny packets of desiccant enclosed
in a box of new shoes or seeds.

But still the vanishing point
is not the painting,
the silica is not the blossoming plant.

Chekhov, dying, read the timetables of trains.
To what more earthly thing could he have been faithful?—
Scent of rocking distances,
smoke of blue trees out the window,
hampers of bread, pickled cabbage, boiled meat.

Scent of the knowable journey.

Neither a person entirely broken
nor one entirely whole can speak.

In sorrow, pretend to be fearless. In happiness, tremble.

2001

In a Quiet Town by the Sea

◇   ◇   ◇

Once I listened to two guys talk about fucking around.
One of them said he liked to meet someone
in a city far away from where he lives
and to get her into the strange clean sheets of a hotel bed.

He said skin was the holiest testament of all
and that to remove the clothes of a sexualized stranger

was like filling your lungs with oxygen
before diving into the swimming pool of god.

He said, Pleasure doesn't care
whose cup you drink it from—
and you could tell it was something he had read once in a book,
written down and practiced in his head.

The other guy said that the stink from secrets in a marriage
was like the smell of decomposing flesh
rising from under the foundation of your house.

He said love is writing your name in cement,

and anyway his wife would know in a NASCAR minute
if he came home with the smell of pussy on his clothes.

There were drinks on the table of course
and a blonde waitress buzzing around
like the goddess of temptation in a budget film
—whose breasts, silhouetted in her blouse,
were like exhibits A and B in the impending criminal case

—as she herself was clearly
destined to be evidence
for both the defense and prosecution.

And there was something so typical about these guys
with their alcohol and self-glorifying memories,

their longing to conquer the world
and yet to still be coddled by their mommy-wives,

you wanted to have them dipped in plastic for a keychain,
or to turn to the salesman and say,
Can we see something a little, no, please, something *completely* different?

Outside the moon gazed upon the earth with wary ardor;
the church cast its shadow upon the plaza
like a triangle and square
in a troubling geometry problem. . . .

And in the houses and the neighborhoods, it's distressing to report,
there was no one sleeping. There was no one sleeping
who did not dream of being touched.

2005

JOHN HOLLANDER

The See-Saw

◇　◇　◇

Of the remedies acting primarily on the body, the see-saw especially has proved efficacious, especially with raving lunatics. The see-saw movement induces giddiness in the patient and loosens his fixed idea.
　　　　　　　—G. W. F. Hegel, Zusatz to section 408 of the
　　　　　　　　Encyclopedia of the Philosophical Sciences
　　　　　　　　(trans. A. V. Miller)

Margery daw.
And up she went as I went down
And up she went and then I saw
The hair between her legs was brown.

Hold the handle with just your thumbs
And flap your fingers. Smile and frown
And giggle and sigh . . . we know what comes
Up must come down.

Up! and the end of the tip of me thrills:
Now I see over
The playground fence to the lovely hills,
The shadowy dales, the meadows of clover.

Down! and I bump . . . a hardened cough . . .
Against the place where I have a tail
(Do I have a tail? If I do, then they'll
Cut it all off.)

Mechanical Operations of
The Spirit oscillate between

The high of hate, the low of love,
As we have seen;

As we have sawn
So shall we rip, this way and that
Way, up and down, and my peace has gone
Off to war in a funny hat.

Two bolts on the handle dream of me
Like eyes (those very eyes I see
Saw something dirty they did to you,
Margery Doo)

A fulcrum with an idée fixe
(Hear how it creaks!)
Won't be shaken, *Balance is all.*
I'm unbalanced, a head-shaped ball.

Margery Dall:
I'd fill her up but my thing's too small,
She'd fill me down with her legs apart.
Every stopper gives me a start.

Here I come and she goes there,
Each of us President of the Air,
Slave of the Ground.
It's square that makes the world go round.

Toes just touch the ground, she and I,
Gravel and sky,
Balanced now in the midst of flight
Listen for yesterday, wait for night.

Something bad back-and-forth was there
Under Grandmother's rocking chair,
With his hanging weights and his swinging cock,
Grandfather Clock

Punishes Pa,
Ravishes Ma, and ticks the tock

Of now and then and the Time they mock.
Und ich bin hier und Margery da.

And she goes low and I go high
By an inexorable law:
See me be born? I saw Margery die,
Margery Daw.

See saw.

My wooden slope can't get to sleep,
The peaks are sunken, the moon down deep,
The desert damp and the sea sere
Margery Dear
I'm here there, and you're there here.
Margery Day,
Sold her old bed to lie on straw
To die on straw on the Days of Awe;
Margery Daw on the Days of Play
Goes up and down in the same old way

Und ich bin hier und Margery da
Tra la la la.

Out and down and up and back,
All comes on now faster and faster
When will I rest? and when will Jack
"Have a new master"?

I watch the light by which I see
Saw away at my wooden head,
Living or dead?
I haven't been told and I'll never be.

Who is it calls us home from play?
That nurse of darkness with Nothing to say.
One last up and down. And then
Never again.

1991

Like Most Revelations

◇　◇　◇

after Morris Louis

It is the movement that incites the form,
discovered as a downward rapture—yes,
it is the movement that delights the form,
sustained by its own velocity. And yet

it is the movement that delays the form
while darkness slows and encumbers; in fact
it is the movement that betrays the form,
baffled in such toils of ease, until

it is the movement that deceives the form,
beguiling our attention—we supposed
it is the movement that achieves the form.
Were we mistaken? What does it matter if

it is the movement that negates the form?
Even though we give (give up) ourselves
to this mortal process of continuing,
it is the movement that creates the form.

1992

9-11-01

◇   ◇   ◇

The first person is an existentialist

Like trash in the groin of the sand dunes
Like a brown cardboard home beside a dam

Like seeing like things the same
Between Death Valley and the desert of Pavan

An earthquake a turret with arms and legs
The second person is the beloved

Like winners taking the hit
Like looking down on Utah as if

It was Saudi Arabia or Pakistan
Like war-planes out of Miramar

Like a split cult a jolt of coke New York
Like Mexico in its deep beige couplets

Like this, like that . . . like call us all It,
Thou It. "Sky to Spirit! Call us all It!"

The third person is a materialist.

2002

Magdalene—
The Seven Devils

◊   ◊   ◊

Mary, called Magdalene, from whom seven devils had been cast out

—Luke 8:2

The first was that I was very busy.
The second—I was different from you: whatever happened to you could
    not happen to me, not like that.

The third—I worried.
The fourth—envy, disguised as compassion.
The fifth was that I refused to consider the quality of life of the aphid,
the aphid disgusted me. But I couldn't stop thinking about it.
The mosquito too—its face. And the ant—its bifurcated body.

Ok the first was that I was so busy.

The second that I might make the wrong choice,
because I had decided to take that plane that day,
that flight, before noon, so as to arrive early
    and, I shouldn't have wanted that.

The third was that if I walked past the certain place on the street
    the house would blow up.

The fourth was that I was made of guts and blood with a thin layer
    of skin lightly thrown over the whole thing.

The fifth was that the dead seemed more alive to me than the living

The sixth—if I touched my right arm I had to touch my left arm, and if I touched the left arm a little harder than I'd first touched the right then I had to retouch the left and then touch the right again so it would be even.

The seventh—I knew I was breathing the expelled breath of everything that was alive and I couldn't stand it,

I wanted a sieve, a mask, a, I hate this word—cheesecloth— to breathe through that would trap it—whatever was inside everyone else that entered me when I breathed in

No. That was the first one.

The second was that I was so busy. I had no time. How had this happened? How had our lives gotten like this?

The third was that I couldn't eat food if I really saw it—distinct, separate from me in a bowl or on a plate.

Ok. The first was that I could never get to the end of the list.

The second was that the laundry was never finally done.

The third was that no one knew me, although they thought they did. And that if people thought of me as little as I thought of them then what was love?

The fourth was I didn't belong to anyone. I wouldn't allow myself to belong to anyone.

Historians would assume my sin was sexual.

The fifth was that I knew none of us could ever know what we didn't know.

The sixth was that I projected onto others what I myself was feeling.

The seventh was the way my mother looked when she was dying. The sound she made—the gurgling sound—so loud we had to speak louder to hear each other over it.

And that I couldn't stop hearing it—years later—
grocery shopping, crossing the street—

No, not the sound—it was her body's hunger
finally evident—what our mother had hidden all her life.

For months I dreamt of knucklebones and roots,
the slabs of sidewalk pushed up like crooked teeth by what grew underneath.

The underneath—that was the first devil. It was always with me.
And that I didn't think you—if I told you—would understand any of this—

2012

From "Urban Renewal"

◊   ◊   ◊

XVI.

What of my fourth grade teacher at Reynolds Elementary,
who weary after failed attempts to set to memory
names strange and meaningless as grains of dirt around
the mouthless, mountain caves at Bahrain Karai—
Tarik, Shanequa, Imani, Aisha—nicknamed the entire class
after French painters whether boy or girl. Behold,
the beginning of sentient formless life. And so,
my best friend Darnell became Marcel, and Tee-tee
was Braque, and Stacy James was Fragonard,
and I, Eduard Charlemont. Time has come to look
at these signs from other points of view. Days passed
in inactivity before I corrected her, for Eduard was
Austrian and painted the black chief in a palace in 1878
to the question whether intelligence exists. All of Europe
swooned to Venus of Willendorf. Outside her tongue,
yet of it, in textbooks Herodotus declares the legend
of Sewosret of black Egypt, colonizer of Greece,
founder of Athens. What's in a name? Sagas rise and
fall in the orbs of jumpropes, Hannibal grasps a Roman
monkeybar on history's rung, and the mighty heroes at recess
lay dead in woe on the imagined battlefields of Halo.

2004

Plea for Forgiveness

◇　◇　◇

The old man William Carlos Williams, who had been famous for kindness
And for bringing to our poetry a mannerless speaking,

In the aftermath of a stroke was possessed by guilt
And began to construct for his wife the chronicle

Of his peccadilloes, an unforgivable thing, a mistake
Like all pleas for forgiveness, but he persisted

Blindly, obstinately, each day, as though in the end
It would relieve her to know the particulars

Of affairs she must have guessed and tacitly permitted,
For she encouraged his Sunday drives across the river.

His poems suggest as much; anyone can see it.
The thread, the binding of the voice, is a single hair

Spliced from the different hairs of different lovers,
And it clings to his poems, blond and dark,

Tangled and straight, and runs on beyond the page.
I carry it with me, saying, "I have found it so."

It is a world of human blossoming, after all.
But the old woman, sitting there like rust—

For her, there would be no more poems of stolen
Plums, of round and firm trunks of young trees,

Only the candor of the bedpan and fouled sheets,
When there could no longer have been any hope

That he would recover, when the thing she desired
Was not his health so much as his speechlessness.

2000

So Where Are We?

◇　◇　◇

So where were we? The fiery
avalanche headed right at us—falling,

flailing bodies in mid-air—
the neighborhood under thick gray powder—

on every screen. I don't know
where you are, I don't know what

I'm going to do, I heard a man say;
the man who had spoken was myself.

What year? Which Southwest Asian war?
Smoke from infants' brains

on fire from the phosphorus hours
after they're killed, killers

reveling in the horror. The more obscene
the better it works. The point

at which a hundred thousand massacred
is only a detail. Asset and credit bubbles

about to burst. Too much consciousness
of too much at once, a tangle of tenses

and parallel thoughts, a series of feelings
overlapping a sudden sensation

felt and known, those chains of small facts
repeated endlessly, in the depths

of silent time. So where are we?
My ear turns, like an animal's. I listen.

Like it or not, a digital you is out there.
Half of that city's buildings aren't there.

Who was there when something was, and a witness
to it? The rich boy general conducts the Pakistani

heroin trade on a satellite phone from his cave.
On the top floor of the Federal Reserve

in an office looking out onto Liberty
at the South Tower's onetime space,

the Secretary of the Treasury concedes
they got killed in terms of perceptions.

Ten blocks away is the Church of the Transfiguration,
in the back is a Byzantine Madonna—

there is a God, a God who fits the drama
in a very particular sense. What you said—

the memory of a memory of a remembered
memory, the color of a memory, violet and black.

The lunar eclipse on the winter solstice,
the moon a red and black and copper hue.

The streets, the harbor, the light, the sky.
The blue and cloudless intense and blue morning sky.

2012

Reading Aloud to My Father

◇   ◇   ◇

I chose the book haphazard
from the shelf, but with Nabokov's first
sentence I knew it wasn't the thing
to read to a dying man:
The cradle rocks above an abyss, it began,
and common sense tells us that our existence
is but a brief crack of light
between two eternities of darkness.

The words disturbed both of us immediately,
and I stopped. With music it was the same—
Chopin's piano concerto—he asked me
to turn it off. He ceased eating, and drank
little, while the tumors briskly appropriated
what was left of him.

But to return to the cradle rocking. I think
Nabokov had it wrong. This is the abyss.
That's why babies howl at birth,
and why the dying so often reach
for something only they can apprehend.

At the end they don't want their hands
to be under the covers, and if you should put
your hand on theirs in a tentative gesture
of solidarity, they'll pull the hand free;
and you must honor that desire,
and let them pull it free.

1996

Proverb

◇   ◇   ◇

Les morts vont vite, the dead go fast, the next day absent!
Et les vivants sont dingues, the living are haywire.
Except for a few who grieve, life rapidly readjusts itself
The milliner trims the hat not thinking of the departed
The horse sweats and throws his stubborn rider to the earth
Uncaring if he has killed him or not
The thrown man rises. But now he knows that he is not going,
Not going fast, though he was close to having been gone.
The day after Caesar's death, there was a new, bustling Rome
The moment after the racehorse's death, a new one is sought for
    the stable
The second after a moth's death there are one or two hundred other
    moths
The month after Einstein's death the earth is inundated with new
    theories
Biographies are written to cover up the speed with which we go:
No more presence in the bedroom or waiting in the hall
Greeting to say hello with mixed emotions. The dead go quickly
Not knowing why they go or where they go. To die is human,
To come back divine. Roosevelt gives way to Truman
Suddenly in the empty White House a brave new voice resounds
And the wheelchaired captain has crossed the great divide.
Faster than memories, faster than old mythologies, faster than the
    speediest train.
Alexander of Macedon, on time!
Prudhomme on time, Gorbachev on time, the beloved and the lover
    on time!
Les morts vont vite. We living stand at the gate
And life goes on.

2003

Sally's Hair

◇   ◇   ◇

It's like living in a lightbulb, with the leaves
Like filaments and the sky a shell of thin, transparent glass
Enclosing the late heaven of a summer day, a canopy
Of incandescent blue above the dappled sunlight golden on the grass.

I took the train back from Poughkeepsie to New York
And in the Port Authority, there at the Suburban Transit window,
She asked, "Is this the bus to Princeton?"—which it was.
"Do you know Geoffrey Love?" I said I did. She had the blondest hair,

Which fell across her shoulders, and a dress of almost phosphorescent blue.
She liked Ayn Rand. We went down to the Village for a drink,
Where I contrived to miss the last bus to New Jersey, and at 3 a.m. we
Walked around and found a cheap hotel I hadn't enough money for

And fooled around on its dilapidated couch. An early morning bus
(She'd come to see her brother), dinner plans and missed connections
And a message on his door about the Jersey Shore. Next day
A summer dormitory room, my roommates gone: "Are you," she asked,

"A hedonist?" I guessed so. Then she had to catch her plane.
Sally—Sally Roche. She called that night from Florida,
And then I never heard from her again. I wonder where she is now,
Who she is now. That was thirty-seven years ago

And I'm too old to be surprised again. The days are open,
Life conceals no depths, no mysteries, the sky is everywhere,
The leaves are all ablaze with light, the blond light
Of a summer afternoon that made me think again of Sally's hair.

2006

Facing It

◇　◇　◇

My black face fades,
hiding inside the black granite.
I said I wouldn't,
dammit: No tears.
I'm stone. I'm flesh.
My clouded reflection eyes me
like a bird of prey, the profile of night
slanted against morning. I turn
this way—the stone lets me go.
I turn that way—I'm inside
the Vietnam Veterans Memorial
again, depending on the light
to make a difference.
I go down the 58,022 names,
half-expecting to find
my own in letters like smoke.
I touch the name Andrew Johnson;
I see the booby trap's white flash.
Names shimmer on a woman's blouse
but when she walks away
the names stay on the wall.
Brushstrokes flash, a red bird's
wings cutting across my stare.
The sky. A plane in the sky.
A white vet's image floats
closer to me, then his pale eyes
look through mine. I'm a window.
He's lost his right arm

inside the stone. In the black mirror
a woman's trying to erase names:
No, she's brushing a boy's hair.

1990

Touch Me

◇　◇　◇

Summer is late, my heart.
Words plucked out of the air
some forty years ago
when I was wild with love
and torn almost in two
scatter like leaves this night
of whistling wind and rain.
It is my heart that's late,
it is my song that's flown.
Outdoors all afternoon
under a gunmetal sky
staking my garden down,
I kneeled to the crickets trilling
underfoot as if about
to burst from their crusty shells;
and like a child again
marvelled to hear so clear
and brave a music pour
from such a small machine.
What makes the engine go?
Desire, desire, desire.
The longing for the dance
stirs in the buried life.
One season only
　　　　　　　and it's done.
So let the battered old willow
thrash against the windowpanes
and the house timbers creak.

Darling, do you remember
the man you married? Touch me,
remind me who I am.

1996

Operation Memory

◊   ◊   ◊

We were smoking some of this knockout weed when
Operation Memory was announced. To his separate bed
Each soldier went, counting backwards from a hundred
With a needle in his arm. And there I was, in the middle
Of a recession, in the middle of a strange city, between jobs
And apartments and wives. Nobody told me the gun was loaded.

We'd been drinking since early afternoon. I was loaded.
The doctor made me recite my name, rank, and serial number
    when
I woke up, sweating, in my civvies. All my friends had jobs
As professional liars, and most had partners who were good in bed.
What did I have? Just this feeling of always being in the middle
Of things, and the luck of looking younger than fifty.

At dawn I returned to draft headquarters. I was eighteen
And counting backwards. The interviewer asked one loaded
Question after another, such as why I often read the middle
Of novels, ignoring their beginnings and their ends. When
Had I decided to volunteer for intelligence work? "In bed
With a broad," I answered with locker-room bravado.
    The truth was, jobs

Were scarce, and working on Operation Memory was better than
    no job
At all. Unamused, the judge looked at his watch. It was 1970
By the time he spoke. Recommending clemency, he ordered
    me to go to bed
At noon and practice my disappearing act. Someone must have
    loaded

The harmless gun on the wall in Act I when
I was asleep. And there I was, without an alibi, in the middle

Of a journey down nameless, snow-covered streets, in the middle
Of a mystery—or a muddle. These were the jobs
That saved men's souls, or so I was told, but when
The orphans assembled for their annual reunion, ten
Years later, on the playing fields of Eton, each unloaded
A kit bag full of troubles, and smiled bravely, and went to bed.

Thanks to Operation Memory, each of us woke up in a
    different bed
Or coffin, with a different partner beside him, in the middle
Of a war that had never been declared. No one had time to load
His weapon or see to any of the dozen essential jobs
Preceding combat duty. And there I was, dodging bullets,
    merely one
In a million whose lucky number had come up. When

It happened, I was asleep in bed, and when I woke up,
It was over: I was 38, on the brink of middle age,
A succession of stupid jobs behind me, a loaded gun on my lap.

1988

The Return

◊   ◊   ◊

All afternoon my father drove the country roads
between Detroit and Lansing. What he was looking for
I never learned, no doubt because he never knew himself,
though he would grab any unfamiliar side road
and follow where it led past fields of tall sweet corn
in August or in winter those of frozen sheaves.
Often he'd leave the Terraplane beside the highway
to enter the stunned silence of mid-September,
his eyes cast down for a sign, the only music
his own breath or the wind tracking slowly through
the stalks or riding above the barren ground. Later
he'd come home, his dress shoes coated with dust or mud,
his long black overcoat stained or tattered
at the hem, sit wordless in his favorite chair,
his necktie loosened, and stare at nothing. At first
my brothers and I tried conversation, questions
only he could answer: Why had he gone to war?
Where did he learn Arabic? Where was his father?
I remember none of this. I read it all later,
years later as an old man, a grandfather myself,
in a journal he left my mother with little drawings
of ruined barns and telephone poles, receding
toward a future he never lived, aphorisms
from Montaigne, Juvenal, Voltaire, and perhaps a few
of his own: "He who looks for answers finds questions."
Three times he wrote, "I was meant to be someone else,"
and went on to describe the perfumes of the damp fields.
"It all starts with seeds," and a pencil drawing
of young apple trees he saw somewhere or else dreamed.
I inherited the book when I was almost seventy,

and with it the need to return to who we were.
In the Detroit airport I rented a Taurus;
the woman at the counter was bored or crazy:
Did I want company? she asked; she knew every road
from here to Chicago. She had a slight accent,
Dutch or German, long black hair, and one frozen eye.
I considered but decided to go alone,
determined to find what he had never found.
Slowly the autumn morning warmed; flocks of starlings
rose above the vacant fields and blotted out the sun.
I drove on until I found the grove of apple trees
heavy with fruit, and left the car, the motor running,
beside a sagging fence, and entered his life
on my own for maybe the first time. A crow welcomed
me home, the sun rode above, austere and silent,
the early afternoon was cloudless, perfect.
When the crow dragged itself off to another world,
the shade deepened slowly in pools that darkened around
the trees; for a moment everything in sight stopped.
The wind hummed in my good ear, not words exactly,
not nonsense either, nor what I spoke to myself,
just the language creation once wakened to.
I took off my hat, a mistake in the presence
of my father's God, wiped my brow with what I had,
the back of my hand, and marveled at what was here:
nothing at all except the stubbornness of things.

1999

AMIT MAJMUDAR

The Autobiography
of Khwaja Mustasim

◊ ◊ ◊

I stood for twenty years a chess piece in Córdoba, the black rook.
I was a parrot fed melon seeds by the eleventh caliph.
I sparked to life in a Damascus forge, no bigger than my own pupil.
I was the mosquito whose malarial kiss conquered Alexander.
I bound books in Bukhara, burned them in Balkh.
In my four hundred and sixteenth year I came to Qom.
I tasted Paradise early as an ant in the sugar bin of Mehmet Pasha's chief chef.
I was a Hindu slave stonemason who built the Blue Mosque without believing.
I rode as a louse under Burton's turban when he sneaked into Mecca.
I butchered halal in Jalalabad.
I had been a vulture just ten years when I looked down and saw Karbala set for
    me like a table.
I walked that lush Hafiz home and held his head while he puked.
I was one of those four palm trees smart-bomb-shaken behind the reporter's
    khaki vest.
I threw out the English-language newspaper that went on to hide the roadside
    bomb.
The nails in which were taken from my brother's coffin.
My sister's widowing sighed sand in a thousand Kalashnikovs.
I buzzed by a tube light, and three intelligence officers, magazines rolled,
    hunted me in vain.
Here I am at last, born in a city whose name, on General Elphinstone's 1842
    map, was misspelt "Heart."
A mullah for a mauled age, a Muslim whose memory goes back farther than
    the Balfour Declaration.
You may remember me as the grandfather who guided the gaze of a six-year-
    old Omar Khayyám to the constellations.

Also maybe as the inmate of a Cairo jail who took the top bunk and shouted down at Sayyid Qutb to please please please shut up.

2012

Hell

◇   ◇   ◇

The second-hardest thing I have to do is not be longing's slave.

Hell is that. Hell is that, others, having a job, and not having a
job. Hell is thinking continually of those who were truly great.

Hell is the moment you realize that you were ignorant of the fact,
when it was true, that you were not yet ruined by desire.

The kind of music I want to continue hearing after I am dead is
the kind that makes me think I will be capable of hearing it then.

There is music in Hell. Wind of desolation! It blows past the egg-
eyed statues. The canopic jars are full of secrets.

The wind blows through me. I open my mouth to speak.

I recite the list of people I have copulated with. It does not take long.
I say the names of my imaginary children. I call out four-syllable
words beginning with B. This is how I stay alive.

Beelzebub. Brachiosaur. Bubble-headed. I don't know how I stay alive.
What I do know is that there is a light, far above us, that goes out
when we die,

and that in Hell there is a gray tulip that grows without any sun.
It reminds me of everything I failed at,

and I water it carefully. It is all I have to remind me of you.

2005

My Mammogram

◇　◇　◇

I.

In the shower, at the shaving mirror or beach,
For years I'd led . . . the unexamined life?
When all along and so easily within reach
(Closer even than the nonexistent wife)

Lay the trouble—naturally enough
Lurking in a useless, overlooked
Mass of fat and old newspaper stuff
About matters I regularly mistook

As a horror story for the opposite sex,
Nothing to do with what at my downtown gym
Are furtively ogled as The Guy's Pecs.

But one side is swollen, the too tender skin
Discolored. So the doctor orders an X-
Ray, and nervously frowns at my nervous grin.

II.

Mammography's on the basement floor.
The nurse has an executioner's gentle eyes.
I start to unbutton my shirt. She shuts the door.
Fifty, male, already embarrassed by the size

Of my "breasts," I'm told to put the left one
Up on a smudged, cold, Plexiglas shelf,
Part of a robot half menacing, half glum,
Like a three-dimensional model of the Freudian self.

Angles are calculated. The computer beeps.
Saucers close on a flatness further compressed.
There's an ache near the heart neither dull nor sharp.

The room gets lethal. Casually the nurse retreats
Behind her shield. Anxiety as blithely suggests
I joke about a snapshot for my Christmas card.

III.

"No sign of cancer," the radiologist swans
In to say—with just a hint in his tone
That he's done me a personal favor—whereupon
His look darkens. "But what these pictures show . . .

Here, look, you'll notice the gland on the left's
Enlarged. See?" I see an aerial shot
Of Iraq, and nod. "We'll need further tests,
Of course, but I'd bet that what *you've* got

Is a liver problem. Trouble with your estrogen
Levels. It's time, my friend, to take stock.
It happens more often than you'd think to men."

Reeling from its millionth Scotch on the rocks,
In other words, my liver's sensed the end.
Why does it come as something less than a shock?

IV.

The end of life as I've known it, that is to say—
Testosterone sported like a power tie,
The matching set of drives and dreads that may
Now soon be plumped to whatever new designs

My apparently resentful, androgynous
Inner life has on me. Blind seer?
The Bearded Lady in some provincial circus?
Something that others both desire and fear.

Still, doesn't everyone *long* to be changed,
Transformed to, no matter, a higher or lower state,
To know the leathery D-Day hero's strange

Detachment, the queen bee's dreamy loll?
Oh, but the future each of us blankly awaits
Was long ago written on the genetic wall.

V.

So suppose the breasts fill out until I look
Like my own mother . . . ready to nurse a son,
A version of myself, the infant understood
In the end as the way my own death had come.

Or will I in a decade be back here again,
The diagnosis this time not freakish but fatal?
The changes in one's later years all tend,
Until the last one, toward the farcical,

Each of us slowly turned into something that hurts,
Someone we no longer recognize.
If soul is the final shape I shall assume,

The shadow brightening against the fluorescent gloom,
An absence as clumsily slipped into as this shirt,
Then which of my bodies will have been the best disguise?

1995

HEATHER McHUGH

Past All Understanding

◇   ◇   ◇

Gasworks Park, 1996

A woman there was balancing her baby
back-to-back. They held each other's hands,
did tilts and bends and teeter-totters on
each other's inclinations, making
casual covalency into
a human ideogram,
spontaneous Pilobolus—
a spectacle at which
the estimable Kooch
(half Border and half Lab)

began to bark. He wouldn't stop. The child slid off
the woman's back; now they were two
who scowled and stared. You looked,
I started to explain, like one
big oddity to him. (They weren't appeased.) He barks at
crippled people too. (Now they were horrified.) Meanwhile a wind

rose at the kiosk, stapled with yard jobs, sub-clubs, bands somebody-
      named
for animals. The whole park fluttered up and flailed, and Kooch,
      unquenchable,
perceived the higher truth. By now the uproar was enough
to make the bicyclists bypassing (bent beneath their packs),
an assortment of teaching assistants (harried, earnest, hardly earning)—
and even some white-haired full professorships all come to a halt,
in the wake of the wave of their tracks.
What brouhahas! What flaps!

146

To Kooch's mind, if you
could call it that,
the worst was
yet to come—

for looming overhead, a host of red and yellow kites appeared
intent on swooping even to the cowlicks of the humans—Were
these people blind—the woman in pink, the man in blue, who paused
     there
in his purview, stupidly, to shake their heads? He thinks
we're in danger, I tried again
to reason with my fellow-man.
But now the dog

was past all understanding; he was uncontainable. He burst
into a pure fur paroxysm, blaming the sky for all that we
were worth, holding his ground with four feet braced
against an over-turning earth. . . .

1998

JAMES McMICHAEL

From "The Person She Is"

◇　◇　◇

I know I'll lose her.
One of us will decide. Linda will say she can't
do this anymore or I'll say I can't. Confused
only about how long to stay, we'll meet and close it up.
She won't let me hold her. I won't care that my
eyes still work, that I can lift myself past staring.
Nothing from her will reach me after that.
I'll drive back to them, their low white T-shaped house
mine too if I can make them take her place.
I'll have to. I mustn't think her room and whether if by
nine one morning in a year she will have left it,
sleepy, late, remembering tomorrow is New York,
her interview with UN General Services a
cinch to go well. What I must think instead is Bobby's
follow-through from the left side. He pulls my lob past Geoff,
who's bored. Shagging five soaked balls isn't
Geoff's idea. I tell him he can hit soon. He takes his time,
then underhands the first off line and half way back.
Groundfog, right field, the freeway, LAX. She has
both official languages. For the International Court,
"The Registrar shall arrange to have interpreted
from French to English and from English into French
each statement, question and response." Or maybe it will be
Washington she'll work for. On mission to a new
West African republic, she might sign on with
Reynolds, Kaiser, Bethlehem Steel. They needed Guinea's
bauxite for aluminum, manganese from Gabon,
their dealings for more plants and harbors slowed by lengthy
phonecalls through Paris. When there were snags, she'd
fly there that same afternoon, her calendar a mix of

eighty hours on and whole weeks off. There'd be
sidetrips to England by Calais and one aisle
over from her on the crossing, by himself,
the man I saw this week I fear she'd like.
He'd have noticed her before they cleared the dock, she'd been
writing something, left wrist bent toward him, the card almost
filled, now, with whatever she'd been telling someone else.
She'd start another, the address first. Eased that he'd
sense it in his shoulders when she stood to leave,
he'd keep himself from looking, it was much better
not to look, he might not interest her, better
not to be left remembering how she looked.
Dover. He'd follow her to the train and sit
across from her, apply himself convincingly to his four
appointments and their dossiers. After she'd make
notes to herself from a bed and breakfast guide,
from *The Guide to the National Trust,* she'd put the books
back in her hemp bag. He didn't mean to be
nosy, he'd say, but was she going to
see some country houses while she's here? Comfortably,
she'd tell him which ones. Though he knew them all, he'd be so
taken with her that he'd lose what she was saying,
he'd undergo the list and ask if she'd be
hiring a car. She'd pick one up tomorrow in
Hammersmith and then drive west. Would she have
dinner with him tonight? She'd say she'd like that:
she was booked at the St. Margaret's, off Russell Square,
could he meet her there at seven? When she'd close her eyes,
her head against the cushioned wing of the seat,
he'd think her managing to rest was not so much a
carelessness to his attentions as that she wasn't vain.
She wouldn't catch him watching if he angled his look
away from her toward the window, in the tunnels
especially he'd see reflected in its glass her gradual
full outline as she breathed. There would be time all
evening to talk. He'd tell her then about his
uncle's place in Surrey where they'd both be welcome,
its rubble-stone and leaded casements, tile, an east
loggia to the lawns and wooded slope. He'd loved the
kitchen garden as a boy, the path there, silver
lavender and catmint borders, an oak-doored archway

framing for him on chains above a well the twin
coronas of roses in the cool damp light.

My wife is taking it well enough.
If there's another woman she doesn't want to know.
In LA, where no one knows us and would tell,
I rent a studio above a garage. Linda moves
out of the Y to the front unit of a duplex.
She's at the Ambassador for Bobby Kennedy's
victory party the night I leave. Dumbfoundedness,
one more impossible cortege, but she can come
over now, I can go see her, summer, our walks up the
fireroad in the last light, rabbits and even
deer sometimes across the reservoir on the grassy fans.
We go to the store together. There's time for
movies, now, and double solitaire. We wrestle.
She cuts my hair one Saturday outside her kitchen.

I have to teach again that fall and move back
down to Laguna. The days alone are less baleful,
they're just for a year. No one ever stops by,
but when she drives down on Thursdays after class
I meet her at the Tic-Toc Market. My apartment's
little more than the bed, and we can't wait.
Safe-harbored, whispering, with always more to tell,
we stay put, the dark catching up with us each week
until it's there in our first hour. From upstairs,
the muffled after-dinner clatter. Somebody's phone.
We start over at her knee, we're slower, the prolonged
fine sadnesses we'd hoarded from the years before
slow to give way and slowing so that only after
nothing for awhile does what we're doing take us
not toward her finishing again (or not right now) but
anywhere we've missed, her ribs, only the lightest
grazing of them, down and forward, not too far
nor too far back again across, each furrow
closer by its width to that last ridge below the pliant
dominating compass of her breast. We're being
pulled, of course. She hasn't stopped me. She won't.
At its outermost, her body's what she touches with.
It isn't long before she's moving too. Our skins

poised for the next just barely altered place, we're
thread-like stalks, light-running, sheer, our tiny leaves
flush with the basin's wide paved curb. It's still
gate-piered courtyard, ashlar dressed, a balustrade.
From jets above the circular pool alcoves,
water, its affection for an always lower point
tight-channeled in the iris rills, then underground,
the land dropping away through poplars to the dell.
Damp peaty banks easing to the full pond-hollow,
I'd never married, she'd been born to someone else.

1993

The "Ring" Cycle

◇　◇　◇

1

They're doing a "Ring" cycle at the Met,
Four operas in one week, for the first time
Since 1939. I went to that one.
Then war broke out, Flagstad flew home, tastes veered
To tuneful deaths and dudgeons. Next to Verdi,
Whose riddles I could whistle but not solve,
Wagner had been significance itself,
Great golden lengths of it, stitched with motifs,
A music in whose folds the mind, at twelve,
Came to its senses: Twin, Sword, Forest Bird,
Envy, Redemption Through Love . . . But left unheard
These fifty years? A fire of answered prayers
Burned round that little pitcher with big ears
Who now wakes. Night. E-flat denotes the Rhine,
Where everything began. The world's life. Mine.

2

Young love, moon-flooded hut, and the act ends.
Houselights. The matron on my left exclaims.
We gasp and kiss. Our mothers were best friends.
Now, old as mothers, here we sit. Too weird.
That man across the aisle, with lamb's-wool beard,
Was once my classmate, or a year behind me.
Alone, in black, in front of him, Maxine. . . .
It's like the "Our Town" cemetery scene!

We have long evenings to absorb together
Before the world ends: once familiar faces
Transfigured by hi-tech rainbow and mist,
Fireball and thunderhead. Make-believe weather
Calling no less for prudence. At our stage,
When recognition strikes, who can afford
The strain it places on the old switchboard?

3

Fricka looks pleased with her new hairdresser.
Brünnhilde (Behrens) has abandoned hers.
Russet-maned, eager for battle, she butts her father
Like a playful pony. They've all grown, these powers,
So young, so human. So exploitable.
The very industries whose "major funding"
Underwrote the production continue to plunder
The planet's wealth. Erda, her cobwebs beaded
With years of seeping waste, subsides unheeded
—Right, Mr. President? Right, Texaco?—
Into a gas-blue cleft. Singers retire,
Yes, but take pupils. Not these powers, no, no.
What corporation Wotan, trained by them,
Returns gold to the disaffected river,
Or preatomic sanctity to fire?

4

Brünnhilde confronts Siegfried. That is to say,
Two singers have been patiently rehearsed
So that their tones and attitudes convey
Outrage and injured innocence. But first
Two youngsters became singers, strove to master
Every nuance of innocence and outrage
Even in the bosom of their stolid
Middle-class families who made it possible
To study voice, and languages, take lessons
In how the woman loves, the hero dies. . . .

Tonight again, each note a blade reforged,
The dire oath ready in their blood is sworn.
Two world-class egos, painted, overweight,
Who'll joke at supper side by side, now hate
So plausibly that one old stagehand cries.

5

I've worn my rings—all three of them
At once for the first time—to the "Ring."

Like pearls in seawater they gleam,
A facet sparkles through waves of sound.

Of their three givers one is underground,
One far off, one here listening.

One ring is gold; one silver, set
With two small diamonds; the third, bone
—Conch shell, rather. Ocean cradled it

As Earth did the gems and metals. All unknown,
Then, were the sweatshops of Nibelheim

That worry Nature into jewelry,
Orbits of power, Love's over me,

Or music's, as his own chromatic scales
Beset the dragon, over Time.

6

Back when the old house was being leveled
And this one built, I made a contribution.
Accordingly, a seat that bears my name
Year after year between its thin, squared shoulders
(Where Hagen is about to aim his spear)
Bides its time in instrumental gloom.

These evenings we're safe. Our seats belong
To Walter J. and Ortrud Fogelsong
—Whoever they are, or were. But late one night
(How is it possible? I'm sound asleep!)
I stumble on "my" darkened place. The plaque
Gives off that phosphorescent sheen of Earth's
Address book. Stranger yet, as I sink back,
The youth behind me, daybreak in his eyes—
A son till now undreamed of—makes to rise.

1991

The Stranger

◇   ◇   ◇

After a Guarani legend recorded by Ernesto Morales

One day in the forest there was somebody
who had never been there before
it was somebody like the monkeys but taller
and without a tail and without so much hair
standing up and walking on only two feet
and as he went he heard a voice calling Save me

as the stranger looked he could see a snake
a very big snake with a circle of fire
that was dancing all around it
and the snake was trying to get out
but every way it turned the fire was there

so the stranger bent the trunk of a young tree
and climbed out over the fire until he
could hold a branch down to the snake
and the snake wrapped himself around the branch
and the stranger pulled the snake up out of the fire

and as soon as the snake saw that he was free
he twined himself around the stranger
and started to crush the life out of him
but the stranger shouted No No
I am the one who has just saved your life
and you pay me back by trying to kill me
but the snake said I am keeping the law
it is the law that whoever does good
receives evil in return

and he drew his coils tight around the stranger
but the stranger kept on saying No No
I do not believe that is the law

so the snake said I will show you
I will show you three times and you will see
and he kept his coils tight around the stranger's neck
and all around his arms and body
but he let go of the stranger's legs
Now walk he said to the stranger Keep going

so they started out that way and they came
to a river and the river said to them
I do good to everyone and look what they
do to me I save them from dying of thirst
and all they do is stir up the mud
and fill my water with dead things

the snake said One

the stranger said Let us go on and they did
and they came to a carandá-i palm
there were wounds running with sap on its trunk
and the palm tree was moaning I do good
to everyone and look what they do to me
I give them my fruit and my shade and they cut me
and drink from my body until I die

the snake said Two

the stranger said Let us go on and they did
and came to a place where they heard whimpering
and saw a dog with his paw in a basket
and the dog said I did a good thing
and this is what came of it
I found a jaguar who had been hurt
and I took care of him and he got better

and as soon as he had his strength again
he sprang at me wanting to eat me up
I managed to get away but he tore my paw

I hid in a cave until he was gone
and here in this basket I have
a calabash full of milk for my wound
but now I have pushed it too far down to reach

will you help me he said to the snake
and the snake liked milk better than anything
so he slid off the stranger and into the basket
and when he was inside the dog snapped it shut
and swung it against a tree with all his might
again and again until the snake was dead

and after the snake was dead in there
the dog said to the stranger Friend
I have saved your life
and the stranger took the dog home with him
and treated him the way the stranger would treat a dog

1993

THYLIAS MOSS

There Will Be Animals

◇   ◇   ◇

There will be animals to teach us
what we can't teach ourselves.

There will be a baboon who is neither stupid nor clumsy
as he paints his mandrill face for the war being waged
against his jungle.

There will be egrets in a few thousand years
who will have evolved without plumes so we cannot take them.

There will be ewes giving and giving their wool
compensating for what we lack in humility.

There will be macaws with short arched bills
that stay short because they talk without telling lies.

Mackerel will continue to appear near Cape Hatteras each spring
and swim north into Canadian waters so there can be continuity.

There will be penguins keeping alive Hollywood's golden era.

The chaparral cock will continue to outdistance man
twisting and turning on a path unconcerned with shortcuts.

Coffin fly dun will leave the Shawsheen River
heading for the lights of Lawrence. What they see in 48 hours
makes them adults who will fast for the rest of their short lives,
mating once during the next hour and understanding everything
as they drop into a communal grave three feet thick with family
reaching the same conclusions.

The coast horned lizard still won't be found
without a bag of tricks; it will inflate and the first
of six million Jewfish will emerge from its mouth.
We will all be richer.

John Dory will replace John Doe
so the nameless among us will have Peter's thumbmark on their
  cheek
and the coin the saint pulled from their mouths in their pockets.
Then once and for all we will know it is no illusion:
the lion lying with the lamb, the grandmother and Little Red Riding
  Hood
walking out of a wolf named Dachau.

1990

The Loaf

◊   ◊   ◊

When I put my finger to the hole they've cut for a dimmer switch
in a wall of plaster stiffened with horsehair
it seems I've scratched a two-hundred-year-old itch

with a pink and a pink and a pinkie-pick.

When I put my ear to the hole I'm suddenly aware
of spades and shovels turning up the gain
all the way from Raritan to the Delaware

with a clink and a clink and a clinky-click.

When I put my nose to the hole I smell the flood-plain
of the canal after a hurricane
and the spots of green grass where thousands of Irish have lain

with a stink and a stink and a stinky-stick.

When I put my eye to the hole I see one holding horsedung to the
        rain
in the hope, indeed, indeed,
of washing out a few whole ears of grain

with a wink and a wink and a winkie-wick

And when I do at last succeed
on putting my mouth to the horsehair-fringed niche
I can taste the small loaf of bread he baked from that whole seed

with a link and a link and a linky-lick.

2003

From Muse & Drudge

◇ ◇ ◇

Fatten your animal for sacrifice, poet,
but keep your muse slender.
                              —Callimachus

1.

sapphire's lyre styles
plucked eyebrows
bow lips and legs
whose lives are lonely too

my last nerve's lucid music
sure chewed up the juicy fruit
you must don't like my peaches
there's some left on the tree

you've had my thrills
a reefer a tub of gin
don't mess with me I'm evil
I'm in your sin

clipped bird eclipsed moon
soon no memory of you
no drive or desire survives
you flutter invisible still

another funky Sunday
stone-souled picnic
your heart beats me
as I lie naked on the grass

a name determined by other names
prescribed mediation
unblushingly on display
to one man or all

travelling Jane
no time to settle down
bee in her bonnet
her ants underpants

bittersweet and inescapable
hip signals like later
some handsome man kind on the eyes
a kind man looks good to me

3.

I dream a world
and then what
my soul is resting
but my feet are tired

half the night gone
I'm holding my own
some half forgotten tune
casual funk from a darker back room

handful of gimme
myself when I am real
how would you know
if you've never tasted

a ramble in brambles
the blacker more sweeter juicier
pores sweat into blackberry tangles
going back native natural country wild briers

4.

country clothes hung on her all and sundry
bolt of blue have mercy ink perfume
that snapping turtle pussy
won't let go until thunder comes

call me pessimistic
but I fall for sour pickles
sweets for the sweet
awrr reet peteet patootie

shadows crossed her face
distanced by the medium
riffing through it
too poor to pay attention

sepia bronze mahogany
say froggy jump salty
jelly in a vise
buttered up broke ice

5.

battered like her face
embrazened with ravage
the oxidizing of these
agonizingly worked surfaces

that other scene offstage
where by and for her he descends
a path through tangled sounds
he wants to make a song

blue gum pine barrens
loose booty muddy bosom
my all day contemplation
my midnight dream

something must need fixing
raise your window high
the carpenter's here
with hammer and nail

6.

sun goes on shining
while the debbil beats his wife
blues played lefthanded
topsy-turvy inside out

under the weather
down by the sea
a broke johnny walker
mister meaner

bigger than a big man
cirrus as a heart tack
more power than a loco motive
think your shit don't stink

edge against a wall
wearing your colors
soulfully worn out
stylishly distressed

1994

Hate Mail

◇　◇　◇

You are a whore. You are an old whore.
Everyone hates you. God hates you.
He pretty much has had it with all women

But, let me tell you, especially you. You like
To think that you can think faster than
The rest of us—hah! We drive the car

In which you're a crash dummy! So
Why do you defy our Executive Committee
Which will never cede its floor to you? If a pig

Flew out of a tree & rose to become
A blimp—you would write a poem
About it, ignoring the Greater Good,

The hard facts of gravity. You deserve to be
Flattened by the Greater Good—pigs don't
Fly, yet your arrogance is that of a blimp

Which has long forgotten its place on this earth.
Big arrogance unmoored from its launchpad
Floating free, up with mangy Canadian honkers,

Up with the spy satellites and the ruined
Ozone layer which is, btw, caused by your breath,
Because you were born to ruin everything, hacking

Into the inspiration of the normal human ego.
You are not Queen Tut, honey, you are not
Even a peasant barmaid, you are an aristocrat

Of Trash, land mine of exploding rhinestones,
Crown of thorns, cabal of screech bats!
I am telling you this as an old friend,

Who is offering advice for your own good—
Change now or we will have to Take Measures—
If you know what I mean, which you do—

& now let's hear one of your fucked-up poems:
let's hear you refute this truth any way you can.

2012

Q

◇ ◇ ◇

Q belonged to Q.&A.,
to questions, and to foursomes, and fractions,
it belonged to the Queen, to Quakers, to quintets—
within its compound in the dictionary dwelt
the quill pig, and quince beetle,
and quetzal, and quail. Quailing was part of Q's
quiddity—the Q quaked
and quivered, it quarrelled and quashed. No one was
quite sure where it had come from, but it had
travelled with the K, they were the two voiceless
velar Semitic consonants, they went
back to the desert, to *caph* and *koph*.
And K has done a lot better—
29 pages in Webster's Third
to Q's 13. And though Q has much
to be proud of, from Q.&I. detector
through quinoa, sometimes these days the letter
looks like what medical students called the
Q face—its tongue lolling out.
And sometimes when you pass a folded
newspaper you can hear from within it
a keening, from all the Q's who are being
set in type, warboarded,
made to tell and tell of the quick and the
Iraq dead.

2010

The Window at Arles

◇   ◇   ◇

Even the moon set him going, with its blank stare;
even the walls of the café, which seemed to tilt
and sway as he watched them, green with absinthe.
"It is a wonderful thing to draw a human being."
All night, Van Gogh painted, and then scraped paint from the easel;
the stiff sound of palette knife on canvas,
scratching, made him think of a hungry animal.
Women came and posed.
"It is a wonderful thing to paint a human being, something
that lives," he told Theo; "it is confoundedly difficult,
but after all it is splendid."
When the money for models ran out,
he bought plaster casts of hands and hung them
from the crossbeams of his room,
and woke to the sound of their knocking in the wind.

*

One night Van Gogh sat in a chair, staring.
Brush in one hand, milk saucer in the other.
The tea was weak. Nothing came. In the morning,
one of his models brought bread and cheese
and made him eat. That afternoon,
he broke the plaster casts, banging hand into hand
until he stood in a storm of dust, coughing.

*

When he worked he felt a scratch at his calf,
a scarlet wound, a whoop of blood. He was hungry;
even his eyes were hungry.
All he saw was red: red snow, red legs of women

in the village rues, red pinwheels of hay.
"It is a wonderful thing
to hurt a human being, something
that lives. It is confoundedly difficult, but after all it is splendid."

Beyond the window, a cave opened
in the trees and led into emptiness,
a yellow you couldn't quite see an end to.
Van Gogh walked into it,
and his body began to shake. It was a color-riot.
He could hear, somewhere, a dog
thumping its tail in the dark.
"How splendid yellow is!" he said.

*

Color was electricity, it turned you blind
if you got hold of it.
It turned you blind if something cold
got hold of you and blistered.
Walls falling toward you.
When you turn color into a weapon,
something gets left over:
a charred body.
What you must do is take the plaster
and turn it to praise
as light turns grass in the evening
into fear gone blind into the hunt.

2008

I Do Not

◊   ◊   ◊

"Je ne sais pas l'anglais."
—Georges Hugnet

I do not know English.

I do not know English, and therefore I can have nothing to say
about this latest war, flowering through a nightscope in the
evening sky.

I do not know English and therefore, when hungry, can do no more
than point repeatedly to my mouth.

Yet such a gesture might be taken to mean any number of things.

I do not know English and therefore cannot seek the requisite
permissions, as outlined in the recent protocol.

Such as: May I utter a term of endearment; may I now proceed to
put my arm or arms around you and apply gentle pressure;
may I now kiss you directly on the lips; now on the left tendon
of the neck; now on the nipple of each breast? And so on.

Would not in any case be able to decipher her response.

I do not know English. Therefore I have no way of communicating
that I prefer this painting of nothing to that one of something.

No way to speak of my past or hopes for the future, of my glasses
mysteriously shattered in Rotterdam, the statue of Eros and

Psyche in the Summer Garden, the sudden, shrill cries in the streets of São Paulo, a watch abruptly stopping in Paris.

No way to tell the joke about the rabbi and the parrot, the bartender and the duck, the Pope and the porte-cochère.

You will understand why you have received no letters from me and why yours have gone unread.

Those, that is, where you write so precisely of the confluence of the visible universe with the invisible, and of the lens of dark matter.

No way to differentiate the hall of mirrors from the meadow of mullein, the beetlebung from the pinkletink, the kettlehole from the ventifact.

Nor can I utter the words science, séance, silence, language and languish.

Nor can I tell of the arboreal shadows elongated and shifting along the wall as the sun's angle approaches maximum hibernal declination.

Cannot tell of the almond-eyed face that peered from the well, the ship of stone whose sail was a tongue.

And I cannot report that this rose has twenty-four petals, one slightly chancred.

Cannot tell how I dismantled it myself at this desk.

Cannot ask the name of this rose.

I cannot repeat the words of the Recording Angel or those of the Angel of Erasure.

Can speak neither of things abounding nor of things disappearing.

Still the games continue. A muscular man waves a stick at a ball. A
   woman in white, arms outstretched, carves a true circle in space.
   A village turns to dust in the chalk hills.

Because I do not know English I have been variously called Mr.
   Twisted, The One Undone, The Nonrespondent, The Truly
   Lost Boy, and Laughed-At-By-Horses.

The war is declared ended, almost before it has begun.

They have named it The Ultimate Combat between Nearness and
   Distance.

I do not know English.

2000

Fretwork

◊　◊　◊

Reports are various—
conflicting also:

many fell,
            a few;

like taken cities. . . .
                        *

Whether or not
to any loss there is weight
assignable,

                or a music given

—some play of notes,
slow-trumpeted,

for which to listen
is already to be
too late;

            whether forgetting is
or is not proof of
mercy, henceforth let

others say.

                *

        Is not victory itself
the proof of victory?

                    *

Little hammer, chasing—onto
unmarked metal—pattern,
decoration,

a name,

a scar upon the face
of history, what

has no face

                    *

            Of briar
and thorn, my bed.

                    *

—I stand in clover.

            2002

Samurai Song

◇　◇　◇

When I had no roof I made
Audacity my roof. When I had
No supper my eyes dined.

When I had no eyes I listened.
When I had no ears I thought.
When I had no thought I waited.

When I had no father I made
Care my father. When I had no
Mother I embraced order.

When I had no friend I made
Quiet my friend. When I had no
Enemy I opposed my body.

When I had no temple I made
My voice my temple. I have
No priest, my tongue is my choir.

When I have no means fortune
Is my means. When I have
Nothing, death will be my fortune.

Need is my tactic, detachment
Is my strategy. When I had
No lover I courted my sleep.

2000

A short narrative of breasts and wombs in service of Plot entitled

◇   ◇   ◇

Liv lying on the floor looking at

The Dirty Thought

[The womb similar to fruit that goes uneaten will grow gray fur, the breasts a dying rose, darkening nipples, prickling sickness as it moves toward mold, a spongy moss as metaphor for illness.]

Liv, answer me this: Is the female anatomically in need of a child as a life preserver, a hand, a hand up? And now, and now do you want harder the family you fear in fear of all those answers?

Could you put fear there as having to do with the price of milk, as having to do with prudence? To your health. Cheers. Or against the aging body unused, which way does punishment go?

"Let us not negotiate out of fear . . ." butbutbut . . . Then the wind touched the opened subject until Liv finding herself in light winds, squalls, was without a place to put her ladder.

From the treetop something fell, a bundle, a newspaper, a bug, a bag, still nobody's baby. The sound was desperation dropped down, a falling into place, and not way away—

Statistics show: One in what? One in every what? A child in every pot will help the body grow? No matter, all the minutes will still slip into the first then the ashes will shiver.

Liv, is the graffitied mind sprained? Who sprayed an answer there? Which cancer? What dirtied up intention? No matter. Anyway, which way does your ladder go?

Toward? Or away in keeping with that ant crawling on your ankle? Oh mindless hand, rub hard. Not quite in pain because pain is shorthand for what? One in every what? Cradle all.

Or kiss it up without facing yourself. Knowing the issue, Liv slouches, her chin resting on her folded hands. She thinks: blunt impact, injury. She tosses a but against the wall,

she tosses: boom. boom.

2001

ADRIENNE RICH

Ends of the Earth

◇   ◇   ◇

All that can be unknown is stored in the black screen of a
    broken television set.
Coarse-frosted karst crumbling as foam, eel eyes piercing
    the rivers.
Dark or light, leaving or landfall, male or female demarcations dissolve
into the O of time and solitude. I found here: no inter/
ruption to a version of earth so abandoned and abandoning
I read it my own acedia lashed by the winds
questing shredmeal toward the Great Plains, that ocean. My
    fear.

Call it Galisteo but that's not the name of what happened
    here.

If indoors in an eyeflash (perhaps) I caught the gazer of spaces
lighting the two wax candles in black iron holders
against the white wall after work and after dark
but never saw the hand

how inhale the faint mist of another's gazing, pacing, dozing
words muttered aloud in utter silence, gesture unaware
thought that has suffered and borne itself to the ends of
    the earth
web agitating between my life and another's?
Other whose bed I have shared but never at once together?

2002

The Rev. Larry Love
Is Dead

◇   ◇   ◇

He's dead now,

his balls will
never get itchy
again—
        because he's dead now forever—

his hair having been
hennaed free of charge
for one last time
by the Egyptian cosmetologists
at the Style Connection,
                there's no doubt now that he's dead—

Thanks to a fury
in his bloodhall,

he's good & gone forever.

The sun tho
is bright today,
                a constancy, a slivered glinting in the airstream—

and, musically-speaking,
the bluejay
swinging amid our pines has got himself
a permanent hard-on

it seems—
        on the radio next door
the tunes of another era,
             still very much without error,

the Everlys,
the miscreant pheromone
Sly Stone, Barry White
of the undulant jheri curls,

and every 6th or 7th song
the always early-autumn river foam
of tenor Orbison—

        why is it the world gets in his way like this?

2007

Discounting Lynn

◊   ◊   ◊

I find it in the twenty-five-cent bin,
which I browse biweekly for the book
that will explain why my hand
seems so misty lately, even
with my new glasses on,
why it can't hold on to anything
with the grip of commitment,
not even a fork, which looks
unsettling these days,
like half a set of silver teeth,
so I bend down low and I choose.

This book has been through a lot.
Since it's poetry, I imagine
it had trouble finding a publisher,
so now rub in this further indignity:
abandoned by the bookseller
at a discount of 25%, and then
dumped by the first owner for profit
in a used bookstore ($9.70—
how pathetic, not even $9.99)
relegated then to an even more desperately
used bookstore ($2—handwritten
on a round orange sticker)
and now given up for lost, now
25¢ slashed sloppily in pencil on the flyleaf.
The book looks fairly readable, a Lynn
wrote it. Maybe not, though, maybe just
a pseudonym. Actual name possibly

Lila-Jean, someone trying to abridge
her native floridity, sound more seriously
friendly, solid, actual, northern.

I find the right spot to read this book:
under an oak tree whose acorns are so small
they seem toylike underfoot, scattered by a child's
imagination, not capable of reproduction
or supplying half a squirrel's midnight snack,
here beside the Muffler 'n Brake Shop
and two dumpsters. Stacked railroad ties
form a half-bench beneath the tree.
A place where you can smoke a cigarette
and in effect throw yourself away
to prepare for reading this thrice-junked text.
On the backleaf some notes are scribbled
by one of the owners, presumably the first,
who invested the most to read the book
and needed a return on that investment.

many characters are doing something on the page

I don't mind the lack of punctuation, but I do
like a thought and I think
how fortunate I rescued this book
from such a dodo:

book draws you out of the text

and really it says *texl* because she was so
done with this book she couldn't bother
to cross her *t.* Well, honey, good riddance.
I can't help thinking she. Does some post-
Paleolithic, prefeminist corner of my psyche
suspect that men still tend not to buy
slender poetry paperbacks by Lynns?
But at least there's some substance
to that note and I read some pages to see
if there's anything in it. Could be.
What if this Lynn were to become our era's

Dickinson? What if she already is!
Then I start writing this because my hand
feels misty again, "Lynn" hasn't helped
one jot. Nor has anti-Lynn, or whoever
said the words Lynn's ex-reader wrote,
since it could have been a professor
with a name like a sneeze. Dr. Hatchitt.
I write this on the backleaf, weaving in
and out of his/her scribbles. Then I relent
because an author can't be blamed for her
readers and turn to the last page of texl,
where authors tend to plant their most
magic beans, and just as I'm getting
to the sentence that is about me, I'm
stung on the back of the hand by a sweat bee.
But the sentence turns out to be about Lynn,
Lila-Jean, not me. And I'm not sweating at all,
or I wasn't then, and officially that was no bee.

2006

Middle School

◇　◇　◇

I went to Cesare Pavese Middle School.
The gymnasium was a chapel dedicated to loneliness
and no one played games.
There was a stained glass window over the principal's desk
and innumerable birds flew against it,
reciting Shelley with all their might,
but it was bulletproof, and besides,
our leaders were never immortal.
The classrooms were modeled after motel rooms,
replete with stains, and in remedial cases
saucers of milk on the floor for innumerable cats,
or kittens, depending on the time of year.
In them we were expected to examine ourselves and pass.
The principal himself once jumped off the roof
at noon, to show us school spirit.
Our mascot was Twist-Tie Man.
Our team The Bitter Herbs.
Our club The Reconsiderers.
It was an honor to have gone,
though a tad strict in retrospect.
You have probably heard that we all became janitors,
sitting in basements next to boilers
reading cheap paperback books of Italian poetry,
and never sweep a thing.
Yet the world runs fine.

2012

KAY RYAN

Outsider Art

◇ ◇ ◇

Most of it's too dreary
or too cherry red.
If it's a chair, it's
covered with things
the savior said
or should have said—
dense admonishments
in nail polish
too small to be read.
If it's a picture,
the frame is either
burnt matches glued together
or a regular frame painted over
to extend the picture. There never
seems to be a surface equal
to the needs of these people.
Their purpose wraps
around the backs of things
and under arms;
they gouge and hatch
and glue on charms
till likable materials—
apple crates and canning funnels—
lose their rural ease. We are not
pleased the way we thought
we would be pleased.

1995

Switchblade

◊   ◊   ◊

Most of the past is lost,
and I'm glad mine has vanished
into blackness or space or whatever nowhere
what we feel and do goes,
but there were a few cool Sunday afternoons
when my father wasn't sick with hangover
and the air in the house wasn't foul with anger
and the best china had been cleared after the week's best meal
so he could place on the table his violins
to polish with their special cloth and oil.
Three violins he'd arrange
side by side in their velvet-lined cases
with enough room between for the lids to lie open.
They looked like children in coffins,
three infant sisters whose hearts had stopped for no reason,
but after he rubbed up their scrolls and waists
along the lines of the grain to the highest sheen,
they took on the knowing posture of women in silk gowns
in magazine ads for new cars and ocean voyages,
and, as if a violin were a car in storage
that needed a spin around the block every so often,
for fifteen minutes he would play each one—
though not until each horsehair bow was precisely tightened
and coated with rosin, and we had undergone an eon of tuning.
When he played no one was allowed to speak to him.
He seemed to see something drastic across the room
or feel it through his handkerchief padding the chinboard.
So we'd hop in front of him waving or making pig-noses
the way kids do to guards at Buckingham Palace,

and after he had finished playing and had returned to himself,
he'd softly curse the idiocy of his children
beneath my mother's voice yelling to him from the kitchen
That was beautiful, Paul, play it again.

He never did, and I always hoped he wouldn't,
because the whole time I was waiting for his switchblade
to appear, and the new stories he'd tell me
for the scar thin as a seam
up the white underside of his forearm,
for the chunks of proud flesh on his back and belly,
scarlet souvenirs of East St. Louis dance halls in the twenties,
cornered in men's rooms, ganged in blind alleys,
always slashing out alone with this knife.
First the violins had to be snug again
inside their black cases
for who knew how many more months or years or lifetimes;
then he had to pretend to have forgotten
why I was sitting there wide-eyed across from him
long after my sister and brother had gone off with friends.
Every time, as if only an afterthought,
he'd sneak into his pocket and ease the switchblade
onto the bare table between us,
its thumb-button jutting from the pearl-and-silver plating
like the eye of some sleek prehistoric fish.
I must have known it wouldn't come to life
and slither toward me by itself,
but when he'd finally nod to me to take it
its touch was still warm with his body heat
and I could feel the blade inside aching
to flash open with the terrible click
that sounds now like just a *tsk* of disappointment,
it has become so sweet and quiet.

1990

Let's All Hear It
for Mildred Bailey!

◊　　◊　　◊

The men's can at Café Society Uptown
was need I say it? Upstairs
and as I headed for the stairs I
stumbled slightly
not about to fall
and Mildred Bailey
swept by in a nifty outfit:
off-brown velvet
cut in a simple suit-effect
studded with brass nail heads
(her hair dressed with stark simplicity)
"Take it easy, Sonny," she
advised me and passed on to the supper-club
(surely no supper was
served at Café you-know-which?)
A star spoke to me
in person! No one
less than Mildred Bailey!

Downstairs I nursed one drink
(cheap is cheap)
and Mildred Bailey got it on
and the boys all stood and shouted
"Mama Won't You Scrap Your Fat?"
a lively number
during the brown-out

in war-haunted, death-smeared
NY

   Then things got better, greater:
Mildred Bailey sang immortal hits
indelibly
permanently
marked by that voice
with built-in laughter
perfect attack: always
on the note
not behind or above it
and the extra something nice
that was that voice
a quality, a sound she had
on a disc, a waxing
you know it: Mildred Bailey

   The night progressed:
a second drunk—oops—drink
(over there, boys, in what seemed
like silence box-cars rolled on
loaded with Jews, gypsies, nameless
forever others: The Final Solution
a dream of
Adolf Hitler:
Satan incarnate)
Mildred Bailey winds up the show
with a bouncy
number: when she gets back
to Brooklyn
from cheapo cruise ship
visitation:
Havana, Cuba
(then the door stood wide
to assorted thrills)
the next one in her life
ain't gonna be no loser, a clerk
oh no
"You can bet that he'll be Latin"

And Mildred Bailey, not
quite alone
in her upstate farmhouse
the rain is falling
she listens to another voice
somehow sadly
it is singing a song:
music
in a world gone wrong

1988

Pornography

◇ ◇ ◇

I. FIRST COUPLE

On his knees, his back to us: the pale honeydew melons of his
    bare buttocks, the shapely, muscular hemispheres—

    the voluptuous center.

His knees push into the worn plush of a velvet cushion
    on the floral Oriental beside her cot.

He twists sideways—*contrapposto*—and bends to put his face
    into her crotch, between her limp legs,

    one hoisted by his right shoulder, the other—more
    like an arm—reaching around his back, her ankle
    resting on his naked hip.

    She's wearing shiny slippers with bows; he has on
    bedroom slippers and socks.

He's got a classic profile: straight nose, sharp chin.
    Cowlick. His hair tapers high on his neck,
    outlines his ear, in the current fashion;
                                  her
    curly bob gives away the date (barely '20s).

His mouth grazes her private hair; lips apart, he
    keeps his tongue to himself.

He's serious: if he were wearing clothes, and she were something
        with pipes, he'd be a plumber's assistant—inspecting,
        studious, intent;
                        nothing erotic in his look, hardly
        aroused at all (a little hard to tell, of course,
        from behind).

Flat on her back, on the dark, fringed spread, gravity
        flattening her breasts, she looks

        uncomfortable, but not unhappy. Her eyes
        check out the camera. Her lips are sealed, yet—

        isn't there?—a trace of smile
        playing around the edges . . .

She stretches out an arm to him, places her palm
        flat on his head—guiding him so lightly, she

        might be blessing him.

II. SECOND COUPLE: THE SAILOR AND HIS GIRL

They're hot, half-dressed (upper half only), and they
        can't wait.

        He sports a sailor's midi and a mariner's
        beret (is that a mound of fishing nets
        she's lying back on?)
                        He rests his naked knee
        beside her ample thigh.

Her dress is long—Victorian and striped. If she hadn't
        raised it to her chest, it would be hiding her
        black knee-length stockings and black, mannish shoes.
        (He's also wearing shoes. How did he get his
        pants off?)

No underwear—
                                nothing fallen around her
                                                ankles
        to keep her from spreading her legs.

Not quite supine, she strains forward to eye, and
        hold, his bold erection:
                                bat and hardballs—
        major league (his Fenway Frank; his juicy
        all-day-sucker).

He looks down hungrily at her hungry eyes
        and mouth—one hand pressed flush against
        his own naked thigh.
                                He slouches a little (not all of him is
        standing at attention), to make what she wants
        easier for her to reach.

But the photographer is sharp—he keeps his sharpest focus
        on what he's sure we want it on: all the

        fleshy folds, clefts, crevices—the no-longer-
        secret places—of her welcoming flesh.

He knows the costumes negate the spiritual burden
        (and freedom) of pure nakedness—
                                put us *in*
        medias res (things happening, things about
        to happen); in

        on the guilty secret, complicit—one eye
        furtively glancing over a shoulder . . .

His models rivet their attention on each other (did he
        have to tell them?), so that we can be

        riveted too.

Of course, they're only posing—
        but despite the props and costumes, certain

undeniable details
suggest that it isn't—it

can't be—all an act.

III. Ménage à Trois

It's the heavy one—the one with the little pot belly, sagging
breasts, and double chin (practically all we can
see of her face)—that he's kissing so passionately.

Yet his arms are around them both, he loves them both
(and of course he couldn't kiss them
both at the same time).

Naked except for (like them) shoes and stockings, and garters,
he sits at the edge of an overstuffed easy chair,
his knees spread wide,
his massive cock
rising like the Leaning Tower from his gut.

His chest and neck, calves and thighs, have an athlete's
sculptured musculature:

exercise keeps all his parts in shape.

Both women are on their knees. She—the heavy one on his
left (*our* right)—pushes into him, her round belly
against his knee, her plush, round bottom
a luxurious counterweight.

Her fingers clutch his engorged organ, hang
on to it, almost to steady herself.

The other one is slimmer, prettier, she has a pretty
mouth—a delicate movie-star face.

She's almost crouching, practically sitting on her
own high heels; her right hand tenderly envelops

his testicles.
　　　　　　Hard to tell if she's smiling
up at his face or down at his genitals—probably
both, in equal admiration, adoration, desire.

His own benign, blissed-out look is
　　　　harder to read, his shadowy profile
　　　　half-buried in the intense kiss.

There's something sweet, *humane,* about them all: not
　　　　innocent—
　　　　　　　　but nothing (well, almost nothing) hard,
　　　　or hardened yet.

Only the little they have on reminds us how
openly this was intended to be obscene.

The composition itself is elegant—balanced, symmetrical:
　　　　the sweeping curve of the pretty one's behind
and back, flowing up and across the curve of the
man's shoulders and neck,
　　　　　　　　then down again through the
fuller arcs of the plump one's back and rump—

a harmonious circle of arms: theirs behind his back
supporting him; his around them—his hands resting
on their shoulders; their hands meeting in his lap . . .

It's like some medieval *Descent from the Cross* or *Holy
Burial*: the slumping Christ between two
ministering Angels—
　　　　　　but inside out, inverted, a negative
of the Passion. Passion here only—and nothing
but—passion. Perhaps
not even passion.

This ancient post card: cracked; corners broken; edges
frayed; worn and fragile

from use.

How many has it gratified; disappointed;
hurt? In whose horny fingers has it

been gripped (and did that hand
know what the other was doing)?

Not innocent—

but nothing about them
hard, or hardened yet;

not yet past taking pleasure
in whatever pleasure they

receive, or give.

1994

The Death of the Shah

◇   ◇   ◇

Here I am, not a practical man,
But clear-eyed in my contact lenses,
Following no doubt a slightly different line than the others,
Seeking sexual pleasure above all else,
Despairing of art and of life,
Seeking protection from death by seeking it
On a racebike, finding release and belief on two wheels,
Having read a book or two,
Having eaten well,
Having traveled not everywhere in sixty-seven years but far,
Up the Eiffel Tower and the Leaning Tower of Pisa
And the World Trade Center Twin Towers
Before they fell,
Mexico City, Kuala Lumpur, Accra,
Tokyo, Berlin, Teheran under the Shah,
Cairo, Bombay, L.A., London,
Into the jungles and the deserts and the cities on the rivers
Scouting locations for the movie,
A blue-eyed white man with brown hair,
Here I am, a worldly man,
Looking around the room.

Any foal in the kingdom
The Shah of Iran wanted
He had brought to him in a military helicopter
To the palace.
This one was the daughter of one of his ministers, all legs, a goddess.
She waited in a room.
It was in the afternoon.

I remember mounds of caviar before dinner
In a magnificent torchlit tent,
An old woman's beautiful house, a princess,
Three footmen for every guest,
And a man who pretended to get falling-down drunk
And began denouncing the Shah,
And everyone knew was a spy for the Shah.

A team of New York doctors (mine among them)
Was flown to Mexico City to consult.
They were not allowed to examine the Shah.
They could ask him how he felt.

The future of psychoanalysis
Is a psychology of surface.
Stay on the outside side.
My poor analyst
Suffered a stroke and became a needy child.
As to the inner life: let the maid.

How pathetic is a king who died of cancer
Rushing back after all these years to consult more doctors.
Escaped from the urn of his ashes in his pajamas.
Except in Islam you are buried in your body.
The Shah mounts the foal.
It is an honor.
He is in and out in a minute.
She later became my friend
And married a Texan.

I hurry to the gallery on the last day of the show
To a line stretching around the block in the rain—
For the Shah of sculptors, sculpture's virile king,
And his cold-rolled steel heartless tons.
The blunt magnificence stuns.
Cruelty has a huge following.
The cold-rolled steel mounts the foal.

The future of psychoanalysis is it has none.

I carry a swagger stick.
I eat a chocolate.
I eat brown blood.

When we drove with our driver on the highways of Ghana
To see for ourselves what the slave trade was,
Elmina was Auschwitz.
The slaves from the bush were marched to the coast
And warehoused in dungeons under St. George's Castle,
Then FedExed to their new jobs far away.

One hotel kept a racehorse as a pet.
The owner allowed it the run of the property.
Very shy, it walked standoffishly
Among the hotel guests on the walkways and under the palms.
The Shah had returned as a racehorse dropping mounds of caviar
Between a coconut grove and the Gulf of Guinea.

An English royal is taught to strut
With his hands clasped behind his back.
A racehorse in West Africa kept as a pet
Struts the same way the useless royals do,
Nodding occasionally to indicate he is listening.
His coat has been curried until he is glistening.

Would you rather be a horse without a halter
Than one winning races being whipped?
The finish line is at the starting gate, at St. George's Castle.
The starting gate is at the finish line for the eternal life.
God rears and whinnies and gives a little wave.
He would rather be an owner than a slave.

Someone fancy says
How marvelous money is.
Here I am, an admirer of Mahatma Gandhi,
Ready to praise making pots of money
And own a slave.
I am looking in the mirror as I shave the slave.
I shave the Shah.
I walk into the evening and start being charming.

A counterfeiter prints me.
(The counterfeiter *is* me.)
He prints Mohammad Reza Shah Pahlavi.

I call him Nancy.
He is so fancy.
It is alarming.
He is so charming.
It is the thing he does and knows.
It is the fragrance of a rose.
It is the nostrils of his nose.
It is the poetry and prose.
It is the poetry.
It is a horse cab ride through Central Park when it snows.
It is Jackie Kennedy's hairpiece that came loose,
That a large Secret Service agent helped reattach.

I remember the Duck and Duckess of Windsor.
You could entertain them in your house.

Here I am, looking around the room
At everyone getting old except the young,
Discovering that I am lacking in vanity,
Not that I care, being debonair,
Delighted by an impairment of feeling
That keeps everything away,
People standing around in a display case
Even when they are in bed with you,
And laser-guided bombs destroy the buildings
Inside the TV, not that I care,
Not that I do not like it all,
Not that I am short or tall,
Not that I do not like to be alive,
And I appeal to you for pity,
Having in mind that you will read this
Under circumstances I cannot imagine
A thousand years from now.

Have pity on a girl, perdurable, playful,
And delicate as a foal, dutiful, available,
Who is waiting on a bed in a room in the afternoon for God.

His Majesty is on his way, who long ago has died.
She is a victim in the kingdom, and is proud.
Have pity on me a thousand years from now when we meet.
Open the mummy case of this text respectfully.
You find no one inside.

2007

ALAN SHAPIRO

Country Western Singer

◊　◊　◊

I used to feel like a new man
After the day's first brew.
But then the new man I became
Would need a tall one too.

As would the new man he became,
And the new one after him.
And so on and so forth till the new men made
The dizzy room go dim.

And each one said, I'll be your muse,
I'll trade you song for beer:
He said, I'll be your salt lick, honey,
If you will be my deer.

He said, I'll be your happy hour,
And you, boy, you'll be mine
And mine won't end at six or seven
Or even at closing time.

Yes, son, I'll be your spirit guide;
I'll lead you to Absolut,
To Dewar's, Bushmills, and Jameson,
Then down to Old Tangle Foot.

And there I'll drain the pretense from you
That propped you up so high;
I'll teach you salvation's just
Salivation without the I.

To hear his sweet talk was to think
You'd gone from rags to riches,
Till going from drink to drink became
Like going from hags to bitches,

Like going from bed to barroom stool,
From stool to bathroom stall,
From stall to sink, from sink to stool,
From stool to hospital.

Now the monitors beep like pinball machines
And coldly the IV drips;
And a nurse runs a moistened washcloth over
My parched and bleeding lips,

And the blood I taste, the blood I swallow,
Is as far away from wine
As 5:10 is for the one who dies
At 5:09.

2007

Country Fair

◊   ◊   ◊

If you didn't see the six-legged dog,
It doesn't matter.
We did, and he mostly lay in the corner.
As for the extra legs,

One got used to them quickly
And thought of other things.
Like, what a cold, dark night
To be out at the fair.

Then the keeper threw a stick
And the dog went after it
On four legs, the other two flapping behind,
Which made one girl shriek with laughter.

She was drunk and so was the man
Who kept kissing her neck.
The dog got the stick and looked back at us.
And that was the whole show.

1991

At the Pool

◇   ◇   ◇

The lifeguard, asleep,
                slumps forward, at ease,
As if the Red Sea could be depended upon to part,
As if the waters themselves
                      would save the drowning.
My friend's wife has died
                  and as he tells how the thought

Of her having died,
                being dead, her death and deadness
Being nothing he can stop now and that goes on and on,
He seems as he talks to be
                his own Orpheus,
His own Eurydice
             turning back on the stair each time

He calls her name,
             turning around to climb
Back up, back down, the dead like a film
                    run backwards, forwards,
Forever approaching,
             gliding away . . . My friend at 83
Still calling on his wife to come back to him,
                    making her

Climb up into the light—
             the lifeguard's chiseled
Abdomen, rising,
           falling, makes the pool water

Seem quieter, calmer in the shifting illuminations
And shadows wavering
                    of the underwater lights

That my friend,
                who used to swim but can't now,
Once floated in front of
                    while we talked, taking
A break from doing laps,
                        his old man's
Muscles making his body seem somehow small

And huge, small in relation
                        to the pool bottom
Staring up through itself
                    like an oblivious, blank eye;
Huge in how his arms stretched out
                            made the whole pool's water
Seem to concentrate its buoyancy
                        just to float him.

2009

Building

◇   ◇   ◇

We started our house midway through the Cultural Revolution,
The Vietnam war, Cambodia, in our ears,
   tear gas in Berkeley,
Boys in overalls with frightened eyes, long matted hair, ran
   from the police.
We peeled trees, drilled boulders, dug sumps, took sweat baths
   together.
That house finished we went on
Built a schoolhouse, with a hundred wheelbarrows,
   held seminars on California paleo-indians during lunch.
We brazed the Chou dynasty form of the character "Mu"
   on the blacksmithed brackets of the ceiling of the lodge,
Buried a five-prong vajra between the schoolbuildings
   while praying and offering tobacco.
Those buildings were destroyed by a fire, a pale copy rebuilt
   by insurance.

Ten years later we gathered at the edge of a meadow.
The cultural revolution is over, hair is short,
   the industry calls the shots in the Peoples Forests.
Single mothers go back to college to become lawyers.

Blowing the conch, shaking the staff-rings
   we opened work on a Hall,
Forty people, women carpenters, child labor, pounding nails,

Screw down the corten roofing and shape the beams
   with a planer,
The building is done in three weeks.
We fill it with flowers and friends and open it up to our hearts.

Now in the year of the Persian Gulf,
Of Falsehoods and Crimes in the Government held up as Virtues,
    this dance with Matter
Goes on: our buildings are solid, to live, to teach, to sit,
To sit, to know for sure the sound of a bell—

This is history. This is outside of history.
Buildings are built in the moment,
    they are constantly wet from the pool
        that renews all things
    naked and gleaming.

The moon moves
Through her twenty-eight nights.
Wet years and dry years pass;
Sharp tools, good design.

1989

Asphodel

◇ ◇ ◇

(after the words of Penny Turner, Nymphaion, Greece)

Our guide turned in her saddle, broke the spell:
"You ride now through a field of asphodel,
The flower that grows on the plains of hell.

Across just such a field the pale shade came
Of proud Achilles, who had preferred a name
And short life to a long life without fame,

And summoned by Odysseus he gave
This wisdom, 'Better by far to be a slave
Among the living, than great among the grave.'

I used to wonder, how did such a bloom
Become associated with the tomb?
Then one evening, walking through the gloom,

I noticed a strange fragrance. It was sweet,
Like honey—but with hints of rotting meat.
An army of them bristled at my feet."

2000

The Latest Hotel Guest Walks Over Particles That Revolve in Seven Other Dimensions Controlling Latticed Space

◊   ◊   ◊

It is an old established hotel.
She is here for two weeks.
Sitting in the room
toward the end of October,
she turns on three lamps
each with a sixty watt bulb.
The only window opens
on a dark funnel of brick and cement.
Tiny flakes of paint glitter
between the hairs on her arms.
Paint disintegrates from a ceiling
that has surely looked down on the bed beneath it
during World War Two,
the Korean War, Vietnam,
the Cuban Crisis, little difficulties
with the Shah, Covert Action and, presently,
projected Star Wars.
In fact, within that time,
this home away from home, room 404,
probably now contains the escaped molecules,
radiation photons and particulate particles
of the hair and skin of all its former guests.

It would be a kind of queeze mixture of body fluids
and polyester fibers which if assembled,
might be sculptured into an android,
even programmed to weep and beat its head
and shout, "Which war? . . . How much?"
She feels its presence in the dim artificial light.
It is standing in the closet.
There is an obsolete rifle, a bayonet.
It is an anti-hero composed of all the lost neutrinos.
Its feet are bandaged with the lint of old sheets.
It is the rubbish of all the bodies who sweated here.
She hears it among her blouses and slacks
and she knows at this moment it is, at last,
counting from ten to zero.

1988

From Dark Harbor

◇   ◇   ◇

I

Out here, dwarfed by mountains and a sky of fires
And round rocks, in the academy of revelations
Which gets smaller every year, we have come

To see ourselves as less and do not like
Shows of abundance, descriptions we cannot believe,
When a simple still life—roses in an azure bowl—does fine.

The idea of our being large is inconceivable,
Even after lunch with Harry at Lutèce, even after
Finishing *The Death of Virgil*. The image of a god,

A platonic person, who does not breathe or bleed,
But brings whole rooms, whole continents to light,
Like the sun, is not for us. We have a growing appetite.

For littleness, a piece of ourselves, a bit of the world,
An understanding that remains unfinished, unentire,
Largely imperfect so long as it lasts.

II

Is it you standing among the olive trees
Beyond the courtyard? You in the sunlight
Waving me closer with one hand while the other

Shields your eyes from the brightness that turns
All that is not you dead white? Is it you
Around whom the leaves scatter like foam?

You in the murmuring night that is scented
With mint and lit by the distant wilderness
Of stars? Is it you? Is it really you

Rising from the script of waves, the length
Of your body casting a sudden shadow over my hand
So that I feel how cold it is as it moves

Over the page? You leaning down and putting
Your mouth against mine so I should know
That a kiss is only the beginning

Of what until now we could only imagine?
Is it you or the long compassionate wind
That whispers in my ear: alas, alas?

III

I recall that I stood before the breaking waves,
Afraid not of the water so much as the noise,
That I covered my ears and ran to my mother

And waited to be taken away to the house in town
Where it was quiet, with no sound of the sea anywhere
    near.
Yet the sea itself, the sight of it, the way it spread

As far as we could see, was thrilling.
Only its roar was frightening. And now years later
It is the sound as well as its size that I love

And miss in my inland exile among the mountains
That do not change except for the light
That colors them or the snows that make them remote

Or the clouds that lift them, so they appear much higher
Than they are. They are acted upon and have none
Of the mystery of the sea that generates its own changes.

Encounters with each are bound to differ,
Yet if I had to choose I would look at the sea
And lose myself in its sounds which so frightened me
    once,

But in those days what did I know of the pleasures of loss,
Of the edge of the abyss coming close with its hisses
And storms, a great watery animal breaking itself on the
    rocks,

Sending up stars of salt, loud clouds of spume.

1993

Forty

◇　◇　◇

(for Daniel Pearl, in memoriam)

When did numbers hijack my life of words?
Until today words were everything; numbers nothing.
All changed at 40
when numbers exploded like nails from a suicide bomber.
1 life.
1 lunch hour, 5-mile run, 40 minutes;
10-minute shower; board meeting at 2.
200 dollars per month at 11 percent x 20 years = retirement.
Drop off child at 8; pick up child before 7.
600 thousand dollars of life insurance.
One life.
One dream of trees, tall sycamores perforated by light;
children as trees, inhaling, exhaling light,
and trees the only thing that matters.
One dream carrying my grandmother in my arms
and she weighs exactly the same as my child.
One beloved child.
123 trees in Independence Square Park.
100 thousand fragments of glass in the Parrish-Tiffany Mosaic;
260 colors.
One hawk perched on the weathervane—
rapacious, free.
One Colossus consecrated to the sun;
one Rome, thousands of Visigoths.
911
2 towers 101 stories 2 planes
3 thousand dead.
One evening in Florida the sun, hand over hand, drags notes

from doves' throats like strands of tears.
1 evening after the news, 5-mile run, 40 minutes,
24-hour deadline: one journalist: Pearl.
Palm fronds clatter and shift in the porous light:
clockwise; counter-clockwise.

2009

Bounden Duty

◇   ◇   ◇

I got a call from the White House, from the
President himself, asking me if I'd do him a personal
favor. I like the President, so I said, "Sure, Mr.
President, anything you like." He said, "Just act
like nothing's going on. Act normal. That would
mean the world to me. Can you do that, Leon?" "Why,
sure, Mr. President, you've got it. Normal, that's
how I'm going to act. I won't let on, even if I'm
tortured," I said, immediately regretting that "tortured"
bit. He thanked me several times and hung up. I was
dying to tell someone that the President himself called
me, but I knew I couldn't. The sudden pressure to
act normal was killing me. And what was going on
anyway. I didn't know anything was going on. I
saw the President on TV yesterday. He was shaking
hands with a farmer. What if it wasn't really a
farmer? I needed to buy some milk, but suddenly
I was afraid to go out. I checked what I had on.
I looked "normal" to me, but maybe I looked more
like I was trying to be normal. That's pretty
suspicious. I opened the door and looked around.
What was going on? There was a car parked in front
of my car that I had never seen before, a car that
was trying to look normal, but I wasn't fooled.
If you need milk, you have to get milk, otherwise
people will think something's going on. I got into
my car and sped down the road. I could feel those
little radar guns popping behind every tree and bush,
but, apparently, they were under orders not to stop
me. I ran into Kirsten in the store. "Hey, what's

going on, Leon?" she said. She had a very nice smile. I hated to lie to her. "Nothing's going on. Just getting milk for my cat," I said. "I didn't know you had a cat," she said. "I meant to say coffee. You're right, I don't have a cat. Sometimes I refer to my coffee as my cat. It's just a private joke. Sorry," I said. "Are you all right?" she asked. "Nothing's going on, Kirsten. I promise you. Everything is normal. The President shook hands with a farmer, a real farmer. Is that such a big deal?" I said. "I saw that," she said, "and that man was definitely not a farmer." "Yeah, I know," I said, feeling better.

2004

Elegy

◇　◇　◇

for my father

I think by now the river must be thick
    with salmon. Late August, I imagine it

as it was that morning: drizzle needling
    the surface, mist at the banks like a net

settling around us—everything damp
    and shining. That morning, awkward

and heavy in our hip waders, we stalked
    into the current and found our places—

you upstream a few yards, and out
    far deeper. You must remember how

the river seeped in over your boots,
    and you grew heavy with that defeat.

All day I kept turning to watch you, how
    first you mimed our guide's casting,

then cast your invisible line, slicing the sky
    between us; and later, rod in hand, how

you tried—again and again—to find
    that perfect arc, flight of an insect

skimming the river's surface. Perhaps
        you recall I cast my line and reeled in

two small trout we could not keep.
        Because I had to release them, I confess,

I thought about the past—working
        the hooks loose, the fish writhing

in my hands, each one slipping away
        before I could let go. I can tell you now

that I tried to take it all in, record it
        for an elegy I'd write—one day—

when the time came. Your daughter,
        I was that ruthless. What does it matter

if I tell you I *learned* to be? You kept casting
        your line, and when it did not come back

empty, it was tangled with mine. Some nights,
        dreaming, I step again into the small boat

that carried us out and watch the bank receding—
        my back to where I know we are headed.

2011

Counterman

◇   ◇   ◇

—What'll it be?

Roast beef on rye, with tomato and mayo.

—Whaddaya want on it?

A swipe of mayo.
Pepper but no salt.

—You got it. Roast beef on rye.
You want lettuce on that?

No. Just tomato and mayo.

—Tomato and mayo. You got it.
. . . Salt and pepper?

No salt, just a little pepper.

—You got it. No salt.
You want tomato.

Yes. Tomato. No lettuce.

—No lettuce. You got it.
. . . No salt, right?

Right. No salt.

—You got it.—Pickle?

No, no pickle. Just tomato and mayo.
And pepper.

—Pepper.

Yes, a little pepper.

—Right. A little pepper.
No pickle.

Right. No pickle.

—You got it.
Next!

Roast beef on whole wheat, please,
With lettuce, mayonnaise, and a center slice
Of beefsteak tomato.
The lettuce splayed, if you will,
In a Beaux Arts derivative of classical acanthus,
And the roast beef, thinly sliced, folded
In a multifoil arrangement
That eschews Bragdonian pretensions
Or any idea of divine geometric projection
For that matter, but simply provides
A setting for the tomato
To form a medallion with a dab
Of mayonnaise as a fleuron.
And—as eclectic as this may sound—
If the mayonnaise can also be applied
Along the crust in a Vitruvian scroll
And as a festoon below the medallion,
That would be swell.

—You mean like in the Cathedral St. Pierre in Geneva?

Yes, but the swag more like the one below the rosette
At the Royal Palace in Amsterdam.

—You got it.
Next!

2006

Necrophiliac

◊ ◊ ◊

More marrow to suck, more elegies
to whistle through the digestive tract. So help
me God to another dollop of death,
come on strong with the gravy and black-eyed peas,
slop it all in the transcendental stew
whose vapors rise and shine in the nostrils of heaven.
Distill the belches, preserve the drool as ink:
Death, since you nourish me, I'll flatter you
inordinately. Consumers both, with claws
cocked and molars prompt at the fresh-dug grave,
reaper and elegist, we collaborate
and batten in this strictest of intimacies,
my throat an open sepulchre, my tongue
forever groping grief forever young.

1992

Time Pieces

◇　◇　◇

Eden time

They spent every day,
blissfully ignorant, in
amorous delay.

Temp time

Will I be alive
when the twelve-headed jailer
announces it's five?

In a parched time

Clouds make this appeal:
the more you wait, the wetter
the water will feel.

Intermission time

Guilty admission:
this plunge from art to life's a
painful transition.

Sleep time

Quick nap—but it seemed
an ocean of joys, a sea
of griefs that I dreamed.

Reunion time

Days passed like drugged snails.
I met you at the station,
laughed at their faint trails.

Just give it time

Though I frankly feel
better, there's nothing sadder
than starting to heal.

Retronym time

Cheering: it was done.
But soon the Great War would be
renamed World War One.

Lately I haven't had the easiest time

Overcathexis
has me asking clouds if they
know where my ex is.

The Marschallin returns for the third and final time

Ja, ja, so it goes:
I've got memories, but she's
got the silver rose.

Ahab time

Though I do not thrive,
I confess I've never felt
so purely alive.

You get lucky from time to time

Once, in a mad rush,
I painted a blizzard that
blew away my brush.

2011

A Filial Republic

◊   ◊   ◊

And out on the plaza, there were more people
Than had been expected: the aviators, with their
Thick dark muffs; the women in red, clapping
For Coca-Cola; the small trumpet player,
Leaning on the fender of the car which was not his;
The mechanics, spreading flat the manuals
For timing and for gaps; the blue majorettes;
The mother, who wished so hard she broke in two;
Those divided against the rule; Mick Jagger;
The security-green police; the gentle inquisitor;
The woman who had not yet found the voice for tragedy;
The exercise cadet, with Adidas and cassettes;
The deaf man, elegant, who bends to tie
His shoe; the grocery clerks, hanging back,
Aloof; the girls who clutched their T-shirts
From behind; the model with the cordless telephone;
The guests of honor, in their limousine;
The *New Yorker* hack; the derelicts, smitten with their
Own advice; the shampooer; the plasterer; the
Dishwasher; the drunk; the man so sodden with sex
He reeled; the crook; the benevolent sister;
The priest, wistfully; Allen Funt;
The father, crying with desire; the great
Conquistadors; the dreamers, who looked past the crowd
As it rolled in the sun; and the children:
Exclaiming together, as one hut and then another,
South, on the horizon, burst into fire.
Rise up, from where you are seated, smoking,

At a wooden desk. There has been a terrible dream
In the apartment above you, and the tenant is pacing.

1993

RICHARD WILBUR

This Pleasing Anxious Being

◇   ◇   ◇

I

In no time you are back where safety was,
Spying upon the lambent table where
Good family faces drink the candlelight
As in a manger scene by de La Tour.
Father has finished carving at the sideboard
And Mother's hand has touched a little bell,
So that, beside her chair, Roberta looms
With serving bowls of yams and succotash.
When will they speak, or stir? They wait for you
To recollect that, while it lived, the past
Was a rushed present, fretful and unsure.
The muffled clash of silverware begins,
With ghosts of gesture, with a laugh retrieved,
And the warm, edgy voices you would hear:
Rest for a moment in that resonance.
But see your small feet kicking under the table,
Fiercely impatient to be off and play.

II

The shadow of whoever took the picture
Reaches like Azrael's across the sand
Toward grownups blithe in black-and-white, encamped
Where surf behind them floods a rocky cove.
They turn with wincing smiles, shielding their eyes
Against the sunlight and the future's glare,
Which notes their bathing caps, their quaint maillots,

The wicker picnic hamper then in style,
And will convict them of mortality.
Two boys, however, do not plead with time,
Distracted as they are by what?—perhaps
A whacking flash of gull wings overhead—
While off to one side, with his back to us,
A painter, perched before his easel, seeing
The marbled surges come to various ruin,
Seeks out of all those waves to build a wave
That shall in blue summation break forever.

III

Wild, lashing snow, which thumps against the windshield
Like earth tossed down upon a coffin lid,
Half clogs the wipers, and our Buick yaws
On the black roads of 1928.
Father is driving; Mother, leaning out,
Tracks with her flashlight beam the pavement's edge,
And we must weather hours more of storm
To be in Baltimore for Christmastime.
Of the two children in the back seat, safe
Beneath a lap robe, soothed by jingling chains
And by their parents' pluck and gaiety,
One is asleep. The other's half-closed eyes
Make out at times the dark hood of the car
Plowing the eddied flakes, and might foresee
The steady chugging of a landing craft
Through morning mist to the bombarded shore,
Or a deft prow that dances through the rocks
In the white water of the Allagash,
Or, in good time, the bedstead at whose foot
The world will swim and flicker and be gone.

1999

C. K. WILLIAMS

A Hundred Bones

◇   ◇   ◇

In this mortal frame of mine, which is made of a hundred bones and nine orifices, there is something, and this something can be called, for lack of a better name, a windswept spirit . . .

—Bashō

And thus the hundred bones of my body plus various apertures plus that thing
      I don't know yet
to call spirit are all aquake with joyous awe at the shriek of the fighter planes that
      from their base
at Port Newark swoop in their practice runs so low over our building that the
      walls tremble.

Wildcats, they're called, *Thunderbolts* or *Corsairs,* and they're practicing *strafing,*
      which in war means
your machine guns are going like mad as you dive down on the enemy soldiers
      and other bad people,
Nips, Krauts, trying to run out from under your wings, your bullet-pops leaping
      after their feet.

It's a new word for us, *strafing.* We learn others, too: *blockbusters,* for instance,
      which means
bombs that smash down your whole block: not our block, some *Nip* block, or
      Nazi—
some gray block in the newsreel. B-24 is the number of my favorite bomber:
      the *Liberator.*

My best fighter: *Lightning.* The other kind of lightning once crashed on an eave
      of our building
and my mother cried out and swept me up in her arms: *The war is here,* she must
      have thought,

the war has found me. All her life I think she was thinking: *The war is here, the war has found me.*

Some words we don't know yet—*gas chamber, napalm*—children our age, in nineteen forty-four, say,
say Arnold Lilien and I, who're discussing how we'll torture our treacherous enemy-friends
who've gone off to a ball game without us. They're like enemies, Japs or Nazis: so of course torture.

Do children of all places and times speak so passionately and knowledgeably about torture?
Our imaginations are small, though, Arnold's and mine. Tear out their nails. Burn their eyes.
Drive icicles in their ear so there's no evidence of your having done it except they're dead.

Then it was Arnold who died. He was a doctor; out West; he learned to fly "Piper Cubs,"
and flew out to help Navajo women have babies. He'd become a good man. Then he was dead.
But right now: victory! V-Day! Clouds like giant ice creams over the evil Japanese empire.

Cities are burning. Some Japanese cities aren't even there. *The war is here! The war has found me!*
Japanese poets come later. We don't know we need them until they're already buffing the lens.
Bashō. Issa. Buson. Especially Bashō: ah, that *windswept spirit;* ah, that hardly there frog.

Atom bomb, though: Bashō as shadow burned into asphalt. House torn by mad burning wind.
Poets in coats of straw, burning. What is our *flaw,* we human-beings? What is our *error*?
Spikes in your tushy, ice in your brain. That frog invisibly waiting forever to make its leap.

2011

The Mill-Race

◊   ◊   ◊

Four-fifty. The palings of Trinity Church
Burying Ground, a few inches above the earth,
are sunk in green light. The low stones
like pale books knocked sideways. The bus so close to the curb
that brush-drops of ebony paint stand out wetly, the sunlight
seethes with vibrations, the sidewalks
on Whitehall shudder with subterranean tremors. Overhead, fain
       flickers

crackle down the window-paths: limpid telegraphy of the
late afternoon July thunderstorm unfurling over Manhattan.
Its set and luminous velocity, the long stalks of stormlight, and then
       the first drops
strike their light civic stripes on the pavement.
Between the palings, oat-panicles sift a few bright
grains to the stonecourse. Above it, at shoulder height,
a side door is flung open; a fire-exit; streaming from lobbies

come girls and women, black girls with ripples of cornrows and plaits,
ear-hoops, striped shadowy cotton-topped skirts, white girls in gauzy-
       toned nylons,
one girl with shocked-back ash hair, lightened eyebrows;
one face from Easter Island, mauve and granitic;
thigh on thigh, waist by waist; the elbow's curlicue and the fingers';
       elbow-work, heel-work,
are suddenly absorbed in the corduroyed black-rubber stairs of the bus.
       Humid
sighs, settlings, each face tilts up to the windows'
shadowless yards of mercuric green plateglass. In close-up
you can see it in the set and grain of each face,

despite the roped rainlight pouring in the bus-windows—
it's the strain of gravity itself, life-hours cut off and offered
to the voice that says, "Give me this day your
life, that is LABOR, and I'll give you back
one day, then another. For mine are the terms."
It's gravity, spilling in capillaries, cheek-tissue trembling
despite the makeup, the monograms, the mass-market designer
       scarves,
the army of private signs disowning the workplace and longing for
       night . . .

But this, at least, is the interspace. Like the slowing of some rural
water mill, a creaking and dipping pause
of black-splintered paddles, the irregularly
dappled off-lighting—bottle-green—the lucid slim sluice
falling back in a spittle-stream from the plank-edge. It won't take us
altogether, we say, the mill-race—it won't churn us up, altogether.
    We'll keep
this glib stretch of leisure-water, like our self's self—to reflect the sky.
But we won't (says the bus-rider, slumped, to herself). Nothing's
left over, really, from labor. They've taken it all for the mill-race.
    Even now.

as the driver flicks off the huge felt-edged wipers,
the rain slackening, lifting, labor
lengthens itself along Broadway. Fresh puddles
mirror in amber and crimson the night signs
that wit has set up to draw money: O'Donnell's,
Beirut Café, Yonah's Knish . . . People dart out from awnings.
The old man at the kiosk starts his late shift, whipping off rain-
       streaked
Lucite sheets from his new stacks of newsprint.

If there is leisure, bus-riders, it's not for you,
not between here and uptown or here and the Bronx. . . .
Outside Marine Midland, the black sea of unmarked corporate hire-cars
waits for the belated office-lights, the long rainy run to the exurbs.
Somewhere it may be, on a converted barn-roof in Connecticut,
leisure silvers the shingles, somewhere the densely packed
labor-mines running a half-mile down from the sky
to the Battery's bedrock rise, metamorphic, in water-gardens,

lichened windows where the lamp lights Thucydides or Gibbon.
It's not a water mill really, work. It's like the nocturnal
paper-mill pulverizing, crushing each fiber of rag into atoms,
or the smooth-lipped workhouse
treadmill, that wore down a London of doxies and sharps,
or the paper-mill, faërique, that raised the cathedrals and wore out hosts
        of dust-demons,
but it's mostly the miller's curse-gift, forgotten of God yet still grinding,
        the salt-
mill, that makes the sea, salt.

                                1996

American Twilight

◇   ◇   ◇

Why do I love the sound of children's voices in unknown games
So much on a summer's night,
Lightning bugs lifting heavily out of the dry grass
Like alien spacecraft looking for higher ground,
Darkness beginning to sift like coffee grains
                              over the neighborhood?

Whunk of a ball being kicked,
Surf-suck and surf-spill from traffic along the by-pass,
American twilight,
                    Venus just lit in the third heaven,
Time-tick between "Okay, let's go," and "This earth is not my home."

Why do I care about this? Whatever happens will happen
With or without us,
                    with or without these verbal amulets.
In the first ply, in the heaven of the moon, a little light,
Half-light, over Charlottesville.
Trees reshape themselves, the swallows disappear, lawn sprinklers do the wave.

Nevertheless, it's still summer: cicadas pump their boxes,
Jack Russell terriers, as they say, start barking their heads off,
And someone, somewhere, is putting his first foot, then the second,
Down on the other side,
                    no hand to help him, no tongue to wedge its weal.

1999

A Happy Thought

◇　◇　◇

Assuming this is the last day of my life
(which might mean it is almost the first),
I'm struck blind but my blindness is bright.

Prepare for what's known here as death;
have no fear of that strange word *forever*.
Even I can see there's nothing there

to be afraid of: having already been
to forever I'm unable to recall
anything that scared me, there, or hurt.

What frightened me, apparently, and hurt
was being born. But I got over that
with no hard feelings. Dying, I imagine,

it will be the same deal, lonesomer maybe,
but surely no more shocking or prolonged—
It's dark as I recall, then bright, so bright.

2006

Religion

◇   ◇   ◇

The last thing the old dog brought home
from her pilgrimages through the woods
was a man's dress shoe, a black, still-shiny wing tip.

I feared at first a foot might be in it.
But no, it was just an ordinary shoe.
And while it was clear it had been worn,

and because the mouth of the dog—
a retriever skilled at returning ducks and geese—
was soft, the shoe remained a good shoe,

and I might have given it
to a one-legged friend,
but all of them dressed their prostheses too,

so there it was. A rescued
or a stolen odd shoe. Though in the last months
of the dog's life, I noticed

how the shoe became her friend, almost,
something she slept on or near
and nosed whenever she passed,

as though checking it to see if,
in her absence, that mysterious, familiar,
missing foot might not have come again.

2006

Vespers

◇　◇　◇

Clarendon, Jamaica

Because it was a pilgrimage,
we left during the fifth hour of daylight
like the children in our textbooks

marching off to fight with devils.
Not yet women but no longer girls, my sisters and I
marched behind our mother to the river

where a secret society of women holding white sheets
waded into reflections of rose-apple blossoms,
into the icy, black morning water.

We watched our mother drowning sheets,
then men's shirts, her back bending, straightening,
her arms lifting the white cloth into the air,

a benediction, her arms as fluid as water,
as fluid as a Chancery *f* written in fresh ink.
I would pull the white shirts from the water

—embarrassed at touching my father, my uncles—
and drape them across rocks to bleach in the sunlight.
Walking home, arms filled with laundry

sweet with the smell of the sun now dissolving in the hills,
I would remember my mother in the dark water.
I would pray motherhood would never find me there.

1996

No Forgiveness Ode

◇　◇　◇

The husband wants to be taken back
into the family after behaving terribly,
but nothing can be taken back,
not the leaves by the trees, the rain
by the clouds. You want to take back
the ugly thing you said, but some shrapnel
remains in the wound, some mud.
Night after night Tybalt's stabbed
so the lovers are ground in mechanical
aftermath. Think of the gunk that never
comes off the roasting pan, the goofs
of a diamond cutter. But wasn't it
electricity's blunder into inert clay
that started this whole mess, the I-
echo in the head, a marriage begun
with a fender bender, a sneeze,
a mutation, a raid, an irrevocable
fuckup. So in the meantime: epoxy,
the dog barking at who knows what,
signals mixed up like a dumped-out tray
of printer's type. Some piece of you
stays in me and I'll never give it back.
The heart hoards its thorns
just as the rose profligates.
Just because you've had enough
doesn't mean you wanted too much.

2008

KEVIN YOUNG

Lime Light Blues

◊ ◊ ◊

I have been known
   to wear white shoes
beyond Labor Day.
   I can see through
doors & walls
   made of glass.
I'm in an anger
   encouragement class.
When I walk
   over the water
of parking lots
   car doors lock—
When I wander
   or enter the elevator
women snap
   their pocketbooks
shut, clutch
   their handbags close.
Plainclothes
   cops follow me in stores
asking me to holler
   if I need any help.
I can get a rise—
   am able to cause
patrolmen to stop
   & second look—
Any drugs in the trunk?
   Civilian teens
beg me for green,
   where to score

around here.
    When I dance,
which is often,
    the moon above me
wheels its disco lights—
    until there's a fight.
Crowds gather
    & wonder how
the spotlight sounds—
    like a body
being born, like the blare
    of car horns
as I cross
    the street unlooking,
slow. I know all
    a movie needs
is me
    shouting at the screen
from the balcony. From such
    heights I watch
the darkness gather.
    What pressure
my blood is under.

2010

CONTRIBUTORS' NOTES AND COMMENTS

SHERMAN ALEXIE was born in 1966 and grew up on the Spokane Indian Reservation. His first collection of stories, *The Lone Ranger and Tonto Fistfight in Heaven* (1993), won a PEN/Hemingway Award. In collaboration with Chris Eyre, a Cheyenne / Arapaho Indian filmmaker, Alexie adapted a story from that book, "This Is What It Means to Say Phoenix, Arizona," into the screenplay for the movie *Smoke Signals*. His most recent books are the poetry collection *Face,* from Hanging Loose Press, and *War Dances,* a volume of stories and poems from Grove Press. He is lucky enough to be a full-time writer and lives with his family in Seattle.

Of "Terminal Nostalgia," Alexie writes: "For such a young country, the United States is intensely nostalgic. And Internet culture—with its endless remixes of pop culture—is even more nostalgic. As for the particular brand of nostalgia that afflicts Native Americans? Well, it has a lot to do with romanticizing pre-Columbian culture. Thinking about all this, I thought I'd write a ghazal (a seventh-century Arabic poetic form) that combined American pop culture nostalgia with Native American cultural nostalgia. The result is, I believe, funny and sad at the same time, although, when I've performed it live, it seems that people are afraid to laugh."

A. R. AMMONS was born outside Whiteville, North Carolina, in 1926. He started writing poetry aboard a U.S. Navy destroyer escort in the South Pacific in World War II. After his discharge, "Archie"—everyone who knew him called him Archie—attended Wake Forest University, where he studied the sciences. He took a class in Spanish, married the teacher, and went on to work as an executive in his father-in-law's biological glass company before he began teaching poetry at Cornell University in 1964. Ammons wrote nearly thirty books of poetry, many published by W. W. Norton, including *Glare* (1997); *Garbage* (1993), which won the National Book Award and the Library of Congress's Rebekah Johnson Bobbitt National Prize for Poetry; *A Coast of Trees* (1981), which received the National Book Critics Circle Award for Poetry; *Sphere* (1974), which was awarded the Bollingen Prize; and *Collected Poems 1951–1971* (1972), which won the National Book Award. He lived in Ithaca, New York, where he was Goldwin Smith Professor of Poetry at Cornell University until his retirement in 1998. He received a MacArthur Fellowship in 1981, the year the award was established. He was the guest editor of *The Best American Poetry 1994*. He died on February 25, 2001.

"I write for love, respect, money, fame, honor, redemption," Ammons told his *Paris Review* interviewer. "I write to be included in a world I feel rejected by. But I don't want to be included by surrendering myself to expectations. I want to buy my admission to others by engaging their interests and feelings, doing the least possible damage to my feelings and interests but changing theirs a bit. I think I was not aware early on of those things. I wrote early on because it was there to do and because if anything good happened in the poem I felt good. Poems are experiences as well as whatever else they are, and for me now, nothing, not respect, honor, money, seems as supportive as just having produced a body of work, which I hope is, all considered, good."

One day in 1987, Archie and his wife, Phyllis, were driving north on the I-95 in Florida when a gigantic mound of rubble came into view. The sight hit Ammons like an epiphany: "I thought maybe that was the sacred image of our time," he said. In *The Best American Poetry 1993*, Ammons commented: "I wrote 'Garbage' in the late spring of 1989. Because of some medical problems that developed soon after the poem was written, I didn't send it anywhere for a long time. *The American Poetry Review* very generously accepted it but because of a backlog had to delay publication for a while. By Capote's view, the poem is typing, not writing. I wrote it for my own distraction, improvisationally: I used a wide roll of adding machine tape and tore off the sections in lengths of a foot or more. The whole poem is over eighty pages long, so I sent only the first five sections to *APR*. Norton will publish the whole poem as a book in 1993. I've gone over and over my shorter poems to try to get them right, but alternating with work on short poems, I have since the sixties also tried to get some kind of rightness into improvisations.

"The arrogance implied by getting something right the first time is incredible, but no matter how much an ice skater practices, when she hits the ice it's all a one-time event: there are falls, of course, but, when it's right, it seems to have been right itself."

RAE ARMANTROUT was born in Vallejo, California, in 1947. She teaches writing at the University of California, San Diego. *Just Saying,* her latest book of poems, is forthcoming from Wesleyan University Press in 2013. "Soft Money" is from her collection *Money Shot* (Wesleyan, 2011). Her previous book, *Versed,* also from Wesleyan, won the 2010 Pulitzer Prize.

Armantrout writes: "I started 'Soft Money' after hearing an old Duran Duran song, called either 'Rio' or 'Rio Dancer,' on the radio. Some of the verses I could make out were, 'Rio, Rio dancer 'cross the Rio Grande,' and 'She don't need to understand.' The poem spins out of that standard depiction of an exoticized erotic object. It proceeds to run some changes on the always complex relationship between sex and power."

JOHN ASHBERY was born in Rochester, New York, in 1927. His *Notes from the Air: Selected Later Poems* (Ecco, 2007) won the 2008 Griffin International Prize for Poetry. *The Landscapist,* his collected translations of the poetry of Pierre Martory, was published in 2008 by Sheep Meadow Press in the United States and by Carcanet in the United Kingdom. The Library of America published the first volume of his *Collected Poems* in fall 2008; his most recent collections are *Quick Question* (2012) and *Planisphere* (2009), both from Ecco, and a new translation of Arthur Rimbaud's *Illuminations* (W. W. Norton, 2011). In 2006, the City Council of New York declared April 7 to be John Ashbery Day in perpetuity in the five boroughs that constitute New York City. "Wakefulness," the poem selected for this volume, is the title poem of Ashbery's seventeenth book, which was published by Farrar, Straus and Giroux in 1998.

In 1973, Elizabeth Bishop read Ashbery's *Three Poems* and wrote to the book's author: "At first I felt extremely baffled—only a sense of 'motion' and the extremely good writing led me on—but now after many re-readings I think I am getting to understand them better—especially 'The Recital'—and some of 'The System.' Actually, when I do enjoy passages or pages most, they remind me very oddly of Kierkegaard (whose name I don't remember how to spell right, I think). Although no theologian, probably no Christian, I've always been able to read him with the greatest pleasure—and your THREE POEMS have now begun to give me the same sort of pleasure. I hope you don't mind my saying this—that I shd. be saying something like they remind me of Yeats! Whatever—you have really arrived at a personal, purely logical, and deep—as well as beautiful way of saying things. I'm not a critic and have difficulties expressing myself about poems—but I'm sure this book is very important—as they say all the time, of course—but really, as well." Ashbery was the guest editor of the inaugural volume in this series, *The Best American Poetry 1988.*

MARGARET ATWOOD was born in Ottawa, Ontario, in 1939. She was educated at Victoria College, the University of Toronto, Radcliffe College, and Harvard University. She is the author of numerous books of poetry, fiction, and nonfiction. Her novels include *The Blind Assassin,* which won the Booker Prize in 2000; *The Robber Bride* (Doubleday, 1993); and *The Handmaid's Tale* (1985), which was adapted for the screen by Harold Pinter. The film was directed by Volker Schlöndorff and released in 1990. *Oryx and Crake,* a dystopic novel, was published in 2003. Both *The Tent* (mini-fictions) and *Moral Disorder* (short stories) appeared in 2006. Her most recent volume of poetry, *The Door,* was published in 2007. An alliterative children's book, *Princess Prunella and the Purple Peanut,* a paean to a particular letter, was published by Workman in 1995. Atwood has edited *The New Oxford Book of Canadian Verse in English* (1982), *The Best American Short Stories* (1989), and *The Oxford Book of Canadian Short Stories in English* (1986). She lives in Toronto, Canada.

Of "Bored," Atwood writes: "This is one of a series of poems on my father and his death—published in *Morning in the Burned House.* The details are from my assistant wood-sawing, house-building, etc., as a child in northern Quebec."

FRANK BIDART was born in Bakersfield, California, in 1939. In 1957 he entered the University of California, Riverside. In 1962 he began graduate work at Harvard, where he studied with Reuben Brower and Robert Lowell. His books include *Star Dust* (2005) and *Desire* (1997), both from Farrar, Straus and Giroux, and a chapbook, *Music Like Dirt* (2002). *Desire* received the 1998 Bobbitt Prize for poetry from the Library of Congress and the Theodore Roethke Memorial Poetry Prize. Bidart is the coeditor of Robert Lowell's *Collected Poems* (Farrar, Straus and Giroux, 2003). He has taught at Wellesley College since 1972. His long poem "The Second Hour of the Night" appeared in the 1998 edition of *The Best American Poetry.* He lives in Cambridge, Massachusetts.

Bidart writes: "Think of 'Injunction' as the injunction heard by an artist faced with the forever warring elements of the world that proceed from the forever unreconciled elements of our nature. It is not meant to stand alone, but to be part of the tapestry of *Music Like Dirt.*"

STEPHANIE BROWN was born in 1961 in Pasadena, California, and grew up in Newport Beach. She has degrees from Boston University, the University of Iowa Writers' Workshop, and the University of California, Berkeley. She is the author of two books of poetry, *Domestic Interior* (University of Pittsburgh Press, 2008) and *Allegory of the Supermarket*

(University of Georgia Press, 1998). She is the recipient of fellowships from the National Endowment for the Arts and the Bread Loaf Writers' Conference. Her poems have been published in *The American Poetry Review* (including covers in 1996 and 2005), *Ploughshares, Green Mountains Review,* and other print and online journals. She was a curator of the Casa Romantica Reading Series for poets and fiction writers in San Clemente, California, from 2004 to 2010. She has taught creative writing at the University of California, Irvine, and the University of Redlands, but has primarily made her living as a librarian and library manager. She is currently a regional branch manager for Orange County Public Libraries in Southern California. She is a book review editor for the online journal *Connotation Press: An Online Artifact* and poetry editor for the *Zócalo Public Square* website.

Of "Feminine Intuition," Brown writes: "A couple of notes: The three parts of the poem are meant to suggest the three parts (Kore, Demeter, Hecate) of the female life story. 'A Woman Clothed with the Sun' is another name for the Virgin Mary. The more I try to write about this poem, the more it resists me . . . so I'll leave it at that."

CHARLES BUKOWSKI was born in Andernach, Germany, in 1920, the only child of an American soldier and a German mother. At the age of three, he came with his family to the United States and grew up in Los Angeles. He attended Los Angeles City College from 1939 to 1941, then left school and moved to New York City to become a writer. He gave up writing in favor of drinking in 1946. After a ten-year binge, he developed a bleeding ulcer and decided to take up writing again. "That's the problem with drinking, I thought, as I poured myself a drink," he wrote in *Women*. "If something bad happens you drink in an attempt to forget; if something good happens you drink in order to celebrate; and if nothing happens you drink to make something happen." He worked a wide range of jobs to support his writing, including mail carrier and postal clerk, dishwasher, guard, elevator operator, gas station attendant, stock boy, warehouse worker, and shipping clerk. His first story appeared when he was twenty-four. At the age of thirty-five he began writing poetry. He wrote, he once said, for "the defeated, the demented, and the damned." His first book of poetry was published in 1959. He went on to publish more than forty-five books of poetry and prose, including *The Last Night of the Earth Poems* (Black Sparrow Press, 1992), *Post Office* (Black Sparrow, 1980), *Sifting Through the Madness for the Word, the Line, the Way: New Poems* (Ecco, 2003), and *Come On In!* (HarperCollins, 2006). Bukowski's poems swagger and boast—they are "in your face" with boozy breath and unabashed braggadocio; they win you over with their feigned artlessness and candor that conceal artistry and calculation. According to unofficial bookstore records, shoplifters favor Bukowski over any other writer. He died of leukemia on March 9, 1994.

Bukowski wrote: "The more said about a poem, the less it becomes."

ANNE CARSON was born in Toronto, Canada, in 1950. She teaches ancient Greek at various places, now at New York University. Her most recent books are *NOX* (New Directions, 2011) and *Red Doc>* (Knopf, 2013).

Of "The Life of Towns," Carson writes: "The poem is part of an ongoing war with punctuation; we fought to a standstill here."

HENRI COLE was born in Fukuoka, Japan, in 1956. He has published eight collections of poetry, including *Middle Earth*. He has received the Kingsley Tufts Award, the Rome Prize, the Berlin Prize, a Guggenheim Fellowship, and the Lenore Marshall Award. His most recent collection is *Touch* (Farrar, Straus and Giroux, 2011). He teaches at Ohio State University and is poetry editor of *The New Republic*. He lives in Boston.

Cole writes: "I wrote 'Self-Portrait as Four Styles of Pompeian Wall Painting' over a period of a year while living in Rome. I saw many paintings during this time, most of them religious and violent. My goal was not so much to put pictures into words, but to take something of their naked realism and project it into the realm of the abstract, where the lyric poem exists. Yet it was in the secular Pompeian wall paintings (200 BC–100 AD) that I found the simplest trope for autobiography. At first I saw the four styles as chronological representations of four stages in my life. But as I began to write and scrutinize myself, the four styles became mixed up and seemed to coexist metaphorically in me.

"In the first style there are vivid stucco reliefs made to look like Greek mortar and drafted blocks; it is more a plastic than a painted style; there is rarely a presence of figures. The second style substituted stucco work with illusionistic representations of architectural elements, colonnades, podia, views of gardens and landscapes. The third style abandoned perspective and flattened out into unified fields with inserted figurative scenes and portraits, often erotic. Ornamentation is clean and subtly calligraphic. And the fourth style is eclectic and fantastic. It continued after the eruption of Mt. Vesuvius (79 AD). Unexpectedly, by writing in the imaginary voice of Pompeian wall paintings, I came closer than ever before to the truths of my life. I am indebted to the classical scholar Malcolm Bell for guiding me aesthetically through the Pompeian ruins."

BILLY COLLINS was born in the French Hospital in New York City in 1941. He was an undergraduate at Holy Cross College and received his PhD from the University of California, Riverside. His books of poetry include *Horoscopes for the Dead* (Random House, 2011), *Ballistics* (Random House, 2008), *The Trouble with Poetry and Other Poems* (Random House, 2005), a collection of haiku titled *She Was Just Seventeen* (Modern Haiku Press, 2006), *Nine Horses* (Random House, 2002), *Sailing Alone Around the Room: New and Selected Poems* (Random House, 2001), *Picnic, Lightning* (University of Pittsburgh Press, 1998), *The Art of Drowning* (University of Pittsburgh Press, 1995), and *Questions About Angels* (William Morrow, 1991), which was selected for the National Poetry Series by Edward Hirsch and reprinted by the University of Pittsburgh Press in 1999. He is the editor of *Poetry 180: A Turning Back to Poetry* (Random House, 2003) and *180 More: Extraordinary Poems for Every Day* (Random House, 2005). He is a distinguished professor of English at Lehman College (City University of New York) and Senior Distinguished Fellow of the Winter Park Institute of Rollins College. A frequent contributor to and former guest editor of *The Best American Poetry* series, he was appointed United States Poet Laureate 2001–2003 and served as New York State Poet 2004–2006. He also edited *Bright Wings: An Anthology of Poems About Birds,* illustrated by David Sibley (Columbia University Press, 2010).

In his introduction to *The Best American Poetry 2006,* Collins wrote: "If you are anything like me, you do not turn to poetry because you are interested in the author; you go there because you are interested in yourself and you see poetry as a means of stimulating your sense of being. If you are a poet, you read other poets for inspiration, that is, for opportunities to steal, or for the possibility that another poet will open a door for you that you never knew existed. But the primary reason for reading is pleasure, and, dry as it sounds to say so, the primary source of poetic pleasure is form. The content may be personal to the point of narcissism, self-involved to the point of autism, but its form—that is, any feature that gives the poem cohesion and keeps it from drifting into chaos—is communal, inclusive, even cordial."

Of "Dharma," Collins writes: "For years I had no dog. Or, as I liked to think of it, I was 'between dogs.' Nonetheless, every so often a dog would appear in one of my poems. I might be writing about taking a walk or spending the day at home, and a dog would unexpectedly lope onto the scene. If anyone would ask me about the dog, I would always admit that it was just a 'poetry dog.' But now I have the real thing, a little collie mix, who was the inspiration for the poem and whose name, by the way, is not Dharma, but Jeannine after the title of a very upbeat tune by Cannonball Adderley. The poem itself, I think, is about as self-explanatory as they come—almost as self-explanatory as the dog herself."

ROBERT CREELEY was born in Arlington, Massachusetts, in 1926. Educated at Harvard University (1943–1946), he went on to study at Black Mountain College, where he formed a close alliance with Charles Olson and edited the *Black Mountain Review*. Key books by Creeley were published by Scribner in the 1960s and 1970s: *For Love* (1962), *Words* (1967), *Pieces* (1969), and the *Selected Poems* of 1976. *The Collected Poems of Robert Creeley, 1945–1975* was published by the University of California Press in 1982. Other collections include *So There: Poems 1976–1983* (1998) and *Just in Time: Poems 1984–1994* (2001), both from New Directions. *Tales Out of School,* a book of selected interviews, came out in the University of Michigan Press's Poets on Poetry series in 1993. Creeley edited Charles Olson's *Selected Writings* (New Directions, 1967) as well as volumes devoted to Walt Whitman (Penguin, 1973) and Robert Burns (Ecco, 1989). He held a titled professorship at the State University of New York at Buffalo for twenty-five years beginning in 1978 and later accepted an appointment at Brown University.

Creeley described himself as "a New Englander by birth and disposition, who spent much of his life in other parts of the world," including stints in Guatemala, Finland, British Columbia, France, and Spain. He was the guest editor of *The Best American Poetry 2002*. In his introduction to that volume he brought up the vexing question of "whether or not there is finally the 'best' of anything." He decided that the poems he had chosen were "*better* than the best, each and every one of them. If you don't agree, then go find your own—which is not offered as a challenge. Rather as fact of what, one has to recognize, is the point of any of this to begin with, that we are 'instructed, moved, and delighted' by poetry, as Pound said, quoting Agricola, who had said it centuries before him." Robert Creeley died on March 30, 2005.

Of "En Famille," Creeley noted: "This poem was written expressly for a collaboration with the photographer Elsa Dorfman. In fact, you can see what came of it at this site: www.granarybooks.com/books/dorfman/dorfman2.html.

"It all began when Ellie gave me a great batch of her portraits—from which I first made a selection of ten for the so-called narrative of the poem, then an additional six for either end, making twelve—so twenty-two in all. I was up in Maine by myself, and I put the whole sequence on our big kitchen table, and then just sat and looked at them. Outside our place there's a big hayfield sloping down, with woods going off on all sides. I guess that's how Wordsworth got in there, with that opening line—and then, later, the wind. I would write two quatrains for each portrait, then move to the next—closing with old friend Bill Alfred's wise look (now gone, alas) and his dear friend Faye Dunaway. Perhaps because I was alone there, these dear people all became my company. They certainly made me recognize that I, like all, much needed it."

OLENA KALYTIAK DAVIS was born in Detroit in 1963. She is the author of *And Her Soul Out of Nothing* (University of Wisconsin Press, 1997), *Shattered Sonnets, Love Cards, and Other Off and Back Handed Importunities* (Tin House/Bloomsbury, 2003), and *On the Kitchen Table From Which Everything Has Been Hastily Removed* (Hollyridge Press, 2009). She is tentatively working on a manuscript titled *The Poem She Didn't Write and Other Poems*. She lives in Anchorage, Alaska.

Of "You Art A Scholar, Horatio, Speak To It," Davis writes: "According to the evidence in my commonplace book of the time (September 1998) I had in fact recently reread *Hamlet,* but was most immediately responding to this tripartite (unattributed in my tablet) description: 'brow-hanging, shoe-contemplative, strange.' The thought was to make the seemingly and semi-educated-literateandry-detached part of myself try and understand, reason with, and perhaps even exorcise, the undying doppelganger of my unreasonable, obsessive, and totally unrequited (?!?!) feelings for/about, let's call them/it, X. Or at least attribute some adjectives to it. To descry by describing and describe by decrying, or so the notes say. Turns out no part of me wasn't complicit, was up for/ to it. (And turns out that was Coleridge describing Hazlitt.) I can still recognize in the poem some stuff stolen from Emily and Susan Dickinson's bickering with each other, but the rest fell/falls on deaf ears, eyes, lips. . . ."

CARL DENNIS was born in St. Louis, Missouri, in 1939. In 1966 he received his PhD in English from the University of California, Berkeley. He has lived since then in Buffalo, New York, where he is writer-in-residence at the State University of New York. He has also served on the faculty of the Warren Wilson low-residency MFA program. He has written eleven books of poetry, including *Unknown Friends* (Penguin, 2007), in which "Our Generation" is included, and *New and Selected Poems 1974–2004* (Penguin, 2004). *Practical Gods* (Penguin, 2001) won the Pulitzer Prize for poetry in 2002.

Dennis writes: " 'Our Generation' comes out of my reaching my mid-sixties and wondering what kind of distinct contribution, if any, my generation has made to the country. In particular, I wondered how well my contemporaries and I have filled the places left by our elders, and what more than filling those places, if anything, might be expected of us."

Susan Dickman was born in Chicago, Illinois, in 1963. She majored in English at the University of Illinois, Urbana-Champaign, and received an MFA in writing at the University of California, Irvine. In 1998 she received an Illinois Arts Council Award in fiction. Much of her subject matter derives from her years of travel, physical and psychic, spiritual and political, within and among Israel's multilayered, intersecting diasporas of cultural longing, language, history, and myth. She has received three Illinois Arts Council awards, is working on two novels, and teaches in Chicago.

Dickman writes: " 'Skin' came to me in one draft in the form of a meditation or prayer, as a way to contain the horror and drama of what is now rather casually known as a suicide bombing. What struck me each time I watched the television coverage of a bombing were the religious men in the background working quickly and diligently, searching for bits of skin in accordance with the biblical edict that no human flesh be left unburied. It is strange to consider that minutes after a bomb explodes, a corps of men arrives to begin the work of picking up every shred of human biological evidence; once the bomb has gone off, flesh is merely flesh and cares nothing for nationality, ethnic identity, or argument over homeland. I often wonder what the men are thinking—are they thinking? are they praying?—as they gather for burial the mixed flesh of bombers and victims, all children of God. The repetition of ritual and the focus on the physical—the skin itself—was my way of mediating the reality that horror, particularly when viewed through the lens of the media, rapidly becomes banal. I wrote the poem simply in order to remember that on some level, if present only as a television viewer and a lover of one blessed and cursed region on this earth, I was a witness."

Stephen Dobyns was born in Orange, New Jersey, in 1941. He has published thirteen books of poems, twenty novels, a book of short stories, and two books of essays on poetry, including *Next Word, Better Word* (Palgrave, 2011). His most recent book of poems is *Winter's Journey* (Copper Canyon Press, 2010). *The Burn Palace,* a new novel, will be published by Blue Rider early in 2013. His new and selected poems appeared under the title *Velocities* from Penguin in 1994. Several of his works have been made into movies. A Guggenheim Fellow who has thrice received fellowships from the National Endowment for the Arts, he teaches in the MFA program at Warren Wilson College and lives with his wife in Westerly, Rhode Island.

Of "Desire," Dobyns writes: "Although I don't write autobiographical poems, this one began just as the first stanza relates. I like poems that are aggressive and full of surprise, and the sound and content are sculpted to that end. This poem I think of as an aggressive meditation. I also feel that the increased sensitivity to gender issues has tended to make men feel overly apologetic, timorous, and hypocritical. As the poem says, 'What good does it do to deny desire . . . ?' The poem argues that it is better to embrace and analyze our natures than to deny them. Nietzsche writes someplace, 'A more complete human being is a human being who is more completely bestial.' The truth of that sentence needs to be celebrated and understood, not whined about."

MARK DOTY was born in Maryville, Tennessee, in 1953. *Fire to Fire: New and Selected Poems* (HarperCollins, 2008), the most recent of his eight books of poems, won the National Book Award for poetry in 2009. His work has been honored by the National Book Critics Circle Award, the T. S. Eliot Prize, and the *Los Angeles Times* Book Prize. He has also received a Whiting Writers' Award, fellowships from the Guggenheim and Ingram-Merrill Foundations, a Lila Wallace–Reader's Digest Writers' Award, and a grant from the National Endowment for the Arts. He is the author of four volumes of nonfiction prose, the most recent of which, *Dog Years* (HarperCollins, 2007), won the Israel Fishman Nonfiction Award from the American Library Association. After ten years of teaching at the University of Houston, he joined the faculty at Rutgers University in New Brunswick, New Jersey. He has taught in writing programs around the country, including the University of Iowa Writers' Workshop, New York University, Stanford, Columbia, and Princeton. He is working on two books, *Deep Lane,* a collection of poems, and a book-length prose meditation on Walt Whitman, desire, and the ecstatic, *What Is the Grass?* He lives in New York City and on the east end of Long Island.

Doty was the guest editor of *The Best American Poetry 2012.* In his introduction he quoted George Eliot's "remarkable, entirely disruptive aside in *Middlemarch:* 'If we had a keen vision and feeling of all ordinary human life, it would be like hearing the grass grow and the squirrel's heart beat, and we should die of that roar which lies on the other side of silence.' Poetry is an attempt to move closer to the other side of silence."

Of "Difference," Doty writes: "After wrestling all morning with a poem that just wouldn't come right, I went for a walk along the shore, where I encountered a whole flotilla of jellyfish, a lesson in mutability and grace. When I got home I found that they'd replaced whatever poem it was I had been trying to shape, and over the course of a day or two 'Difference' seemed to write itself. It's a poem that tries to think about the slippery, shapeshifting nature of words themselves, which can only be metaphors for what they represent. Language itself is as slippery, undulant, and unreliable as the uncapturable world it attempts to fix. I hope my poem suggests that this unreliability might be cause for celebration—and perhaps reason to work all the harder at the project of making meaning in language, instead of giving up on the idea altogether."

RITA DOVE was born in Akron, Ohio, in 1952. A 1970 Presidential Scholar, she received her BA summa cum laude from Miami University of Ohio and her MFA from the University of Iowa Writers' Workshop. She served as United States Poet Laureate from 1993 to 1995 and is the author of nine collections of poetry, including *Thomas and Beulah,* winner of the 1987 Pulitzer Prize. Other publications include a collection of short stories, a novel, and the drama *The Darker Face of the Earth.* She received the 2011 National Medal of Arts (from President Barack Obama) and the 1996 National Humanities Medal (from President Bill Clinton). Her latest book, *Sonata Mulattica* (W. W. Norton, 2009), is a poetic treatise on the life of nineteenth-century violinist George Polgreen Bridgetower. She edited *The Penguin Anthology of Twentieth-Century American Poetry* (2011). She is Commonwealth Professor of English at the University of Virginia.

Dove was guest editor of *The Best American Poetry 2000.* "My method was simple," she wrote in the introduction to that volume. "Read the poems without looking at the author's name, if possible, and put aside for further consideration only those pieces which made me catch my breath. The final criterion was Emily Dickinson's famed description— if I felt that the top of my head had been taken off, the poem was in."

Of "All Souls'," she writes: "Our house burned down after a lightning strike in 1998. During the subsequent rebuilding and refurnishing, I didn't have much inclination to write at all; it took about six months before the poems began to reappear—shy, erratic blossoms poking their heads up through the ashes—and always without warning or, as far as I could tell, logic. The beginnings of 'All Souls'' arose at this time, the first scribbled entry in a brand-new notebook. I liked what was there—the cadences and authorial distance—but I didn't yet understand its urgency, its raison d'être, so I put the draft away in a drawer. Then came 9/11, and somehow its haunting images of catastrophe sent me back to those abandoned lines. Endings, beginnings; to linger in regret or to move on: I found myself turning back to the front of that notebook, reconsidering what had been jotted down years before, in haste and incomprehension . . . and I finished the poem."

DENISE DUHAMEL was born in Providence, Rhode Island, in 1961. She is the author, most recently, of *Ka-Ching!* (University of Pittsburgh Press, 2009), *Two and Two* (Pittsburgh, 2005), *Mille et un Sentiments* (Firewheel, 2005), and *Queen for a Day: Selected and New Poems* (Pittsburgh, 2001). A professor at Florida International University in Miami, she has received a National Endowment for the Arts Fellowship and has appeared in *The Best American Poetry* nine times since Louise Glück chose her poem "Feminism" for the 1993 volume.

Duhamel writes: " 'How It Will End' was written following a walk on the beach very much like the one described in this poem. I was interested in the way the speaker and her husband were able to observe and judge another couple in crisis—poor things!—rather than look at their own relationship. Or alternately, looking at the young couple gave the speaker and her husband a way to talk about their failing relationship. This is a poem of witness and of admission."

STEPHEN DUNN was born in Forest Hills, New York, in 1939 and is a distinguished professor (emeritus) of creative writing at Richard Stockton College of New Jersey. He is the author of sixteen books of poetry, including the recent *Here and Now* (W. W. Norton, 2011). His *Different Hours* (Norton, 2000) was awarded the Pulitzer Prize. He has also received the Paterson Prize for Sustained Literary Achievement, and an Academy Award in Literature from the American Academy of Arts and Letters. In 2014 Syracuse University Press will bring out a book of essays about his life and work, edited by Laura McCullough.

Dunn writes: "I began 'The Imagined' at Yaddo in the summer of 2010, and 'finished' it a few weeks later. At this point the poem consisted of its first half, with which I was somewhat but not fully pleased. A few days later I gave an 'imagined man' to the woman. This seemed not only fair, but finally truer to the likelihood of my concerns. For a while, the poem ended with 'just the two of you,' which I still believe could be a satisfactory ending. But on revisiting the poem, I added the last three lines, then crossed them out, then put them back in again.

"When I've read this poem at readings, very solemn-faced women in the audience seem to be registering disapproval with the first half of the poem. Their demeanor changes in the second half—many seem delighted that their secret man has been acknowledged and identified."

ALICE FULTON was born in Troy, New York, in 1952. She received a MacArthur Fellowship in 1991 and an American Academy of Arts and Letters Award in Literature in 2011. Her books include *Cascade Experiment: Selected Poems* (W. W. Norton, 2004); *Felt* (Norton, 2001), which received the 2002 Bobbitt Prize for Poetry from the Library of Congress; and *The Nightingales of Troy: Connected Stories* (Norton, 2008). In 2004 she was the Holloway Poet at University of California, Berkeley, and in 2010 she was the George Elliston Poet at University of Cincinnati. She has taught at Cornell University since 2002.

Fulton writes: "'Powers of Congress' is more regular in form than some of my poems. Most lines contain seven syllables and four or five stresses, creating a strong-stress, almost sprung-sounding rhythm. Thus language has been subjected to considerable pressure in the making of this poem. Meaning resists such distillation, and this resistance gives the lines a bursting, combustible quality. One of the poem's concerns is union: the unthinking meshes of nature and the lawful forging of lives in wedlock. Couplings can involve a violent chemistry, as when trees and fire meet to form ashes in a stove. On the other hand, some unions, like the marriages sketched in the last few lines, are the products of stasis. Most broadly, then, this is a poem about change and resistance to change. I hoped the muscular language would underscore the images of molten steel cast into solid stoves and trees transformed to heat. The tightly constructed lines are meant to convey the energy released or contained when objects or people are enmeshed in mutual sway; the poem describes the emotional and physical outcomes of such powerful congress."

ALLEN GINSBERG was born in Newark, New Jersey, in 1926. He attended Columbia College, where he studied with Lionel Trilling and Meyer Schapiro. When Ginsberg wrote the words "fuck the Jews" in the dust of his dormitory windowsill, the dean of the college summoned Trilling to his office and, too aghast to utter the words, wrote them on a slip of paper. In *On the Road,* Jack Kerouac based the character of Carlo Marx on Ginsberg. When the poet read *Howl* at San Francisco's North Beach in 1956, he uttered the battle cry of the Beat movement. *Howl* was banned, a court case followed, and the poem and its author became a cause célèbre. Other poems of this period, such as "America" ("America I'm putting my queer shoulder to the wheel") and "Kaddish," his elegy for his mother ("Get married Allen don't take drugs"), were among the most seminal works in the countercultural literary uprisings of the 1960s. In that decade, Ginsberg chanted mantras, sang poems, advocated peace and pot, and fused the influences of William Blake, William Carlos Williams, Eastern mysticism, and Hebrew prophecy in his work. Crowned May King in Prague in 1965, Ginsberg was promptly expelled by Czech police. To a Senate subcommittee investigating the use of LSD in 1966, he said, "If we want to discourage use of LSD for altering our attitudes, we'll have to encourage such changes in our society that no-one will need it to break through the common sympathy." Once, at a reading, a heckler shouted, "What do you mean, nakedness?" Ginsberg stripped off his clothes in response. "Under all this self-revealing candor is purity of heart," says the narrator of Saul Bellow's *Him with His Foot in His Mouth*. "And the only living representative of American Transcendentalism is that fat-breasted, bald, bearded homosexual in smeared goggles, innocent in his uncleanness." Ginsberg traveled to and taught in the People's Republic of China, the former Soviet Union, Scandinavia, and Eastern Europe. His later books include *Collected Poems 1947–1980* (Harper & Row, 1984), *White Shroud: Poems, 1980–1985* (Harper & Row, 1985), and *Cosmopolitan Greetings: Poems 1986–1992* (HarperCollins, 1994). Several volumes of his photographs have been published, including *Snapshot Poetics* (Chronicle Books, 1993). Ginsberg was diagnosed with liver cancer in April 1997. He died on April 5, 1997.

LOUISE GLÜCK was born in New York City in 1943. She lives in Cambridge, Massachusetts, and teaches at Yale University. Her most recent book, *Poems, 1962–2012,* was published by Farrar, Straus and Giroux in 2012. She has won the Bollingen Prize, the Pulitzer Prize, the Bobbitt National Poetry Prize, and the National Book Critics Circle Award. She was appointed United States Poet Laureate from 2003 to 2004 and served as the judge of the Yale Series of Younger Poets from 2003 until 2010. Her collection of essays, *Proofs and Theories* (Ecco, 1995), won the PEN/Martha Albrand Award.

Glück was the guest editor of *The Best American Poetry 1993*. "A great work of art is an absolute," she wrote in a subsequent volume. "In its presence, all experience seems to adhere to it, to be included in it; the world conforms to its terms as though there need be no other terms. We feel, as readers, something like electric satiation, and a sense of majestic order: *this* is what was lacking, this poem. Which is to say, we feel something of what Copernicus may have felt staring at the heavens."

JORIE GRAHAM was born in New York City in 1950. She received the 1996 Pulitzer Prize in poetry. Her books include *The Dream of the Unified Field: Selected Poems 1974–1994* (1995), *Never* (2002), *Overlord* (2005), *Sea Change* (2008), and *Place,* all from Ecco Press. She taught at the University of Iowa Writers' Workshop for many years and succeeded Seamus Heaney as the Boylston Professor of Rhetoric and Oratory at Harvard University.

Graham was the guest editor of *The Best American Poetry 1990.* In her introduction she raised the question of contemporary poetry's alleged "difficulty or inaccessibility." Some of this difficulty "dissipates as one opens up to the experience of poetry. To comprehend poetry one must, after all, practice by reading it. As to 'see' modern dance, one must at least know its vocabulary, its texture, what the choreographer chose *not* to do. As to understand good carpentry one must be able to grasp what the maker's options were, what the tradition is, what the nature of wood is, what the structural necessities were: what is underpinning, what flourish and passion, what *décor.* Of course, with woodworking or ballet, one can still enjoy what one barely grasps. And such pleasure would also be possible with poetry if intimidation didn't set in: intimidation created by its apparently close relation to the normal language of discourse; fear that one is missing the point or, worse, that one is stupid, blind." Another reason for the real or apparent difficulty of poetry, she wrote, is that "much of it attempts to render aspects of experience that occur outside the provinces of logic and reason, outside the realm of narrative realism."

Of "Manifest Destiny," Graham writes: "I don't know if this has much to do with the poem as it stands, but Fabrice Helion was my first lover, and when I received news of his death (an apparent suicide) by drug overdose, I happened to be unpacking books I'd kept in storage for twenty-two years—many of them inscribed to me by him—tattered Gallimard editions of German and French philosophers. Notes in my fifteen-year-old hand (in French) all over Marx and Engels and Spinoza and Schopenhauer and Kierkegaard and Nietzsche took me aback—especially the earnestness and seriousness of them, and the great, helplessly imperial desire to *know* inscribed in them tonally. As I was holding these books in my hand—reading the notes in his eighteen-year-old hand alongside mine (corrective, instructive)—the phone rang with the news of his death. All of our time together had been in Rome during my early and midteens. He was shooting heroin on and off then. In case anyone should care, the restaurant and bar in question are Il Bolognese and Rosati—then rather inexpensive. The opening scene takes place on a dirt road in Wyoming where, driving to town, I recalled the rest. As far as I can tell, it's all, though layered over time, true."

LINDA GREGERSON's fifth book of poetry is *The Selvage* (Houghton Mifflin Harcourt, 2012). Her previous volume, *Magnetic North,* was a finalist for the National Book Award, and *Waterborne* won the 2003 Kingsley Tufts Poetry Award. She is also the author of two books of criticism and coeditor of *Empires of God: Religious Encounters in the Early Modern Atlantic.* Gregerson teaches Renaissance literature and creative writing at the University of Michigan, where she is the Caroline Walker Bynum Distinguished University Professor.

Of "Safe," she writes: "As to the verse form: I've taken to using these tercets in an effort to vary the pacing of the poem on the page. When the block stanzas I used in earlier poems began to seem airless and static, overcompressed, I tried a new template: two longer lines (usually four or five feet) divided by a one- or two-foot pivot line. Syntax is probably the closest thing I've got to a habit of mind, or voice, and I needed some means of rendering the tension between lineation and syntax, the syncopated tug of war between unfolding argument and the argument latent in syntactical form.

"The poem's larger argument is with loss. I'm not sure it's possible to write an elegy, or to talk about one, without wronging the dead. Grief is shamefully self-absorbed. And grief-in-verse has a thousand ways of turning exploitative, especially when death has been accompanied by violence. Elegy tries to console us with a failed rescue attempt. The paradox is a stark one, it seems to me, even when people can agree to believe in an afterlife. 'Safe' was written for my friend Karin Strand, who died in Rochester, New York, just before Christmas 1986."

LINDA GREGG was born in Suffern, New York, in 1942, but grew up in Marin County, California. Her books of poetry include *All of It Singing: New and Selected Poems* (Graywolf Press, 2008), which won the 2009 Lenore Marshall Poetry Prize and the Poetry Society of America's William Carlos Williams Award; *In the Middle Distance* (2006); *Things and Flesh* (1999); *Chosen by the Lion* (1994); *The Sacraments of Desire* (1991); *Alma* (1985); and *Eight Poems* (1982). Her first two books, *Too Bright to See* and *Alma,* were republished jointly by Graywolf in 2002. She has won a Guggenheim Fellowship and has taught at the University of Iowa, Columbia, Princeton, and the University of California, Berkeley. She spent six months in Nicaragua, where she wrote "The War."

THOM GUNN was born in Gravesend, Kent, England, in 1929. He enrolled at Trinity College, Cambridge, in 1950, and *Fighting Terms,* his first book, was published to acclaim in 1954. He arrived in California in 1954 and studied with Yvor Winters at Stanford. He lived in San Francisco and taught at Berkeley for many years. His books include *My Sad Captains* (1961), *Moly* (1971), *The Man with Night Sweats* (1992), *Collected Poems* (1994), and *Boss Cupid* (2000). In 1993 he won the Lenore Marshall Poetry Prize and was named a MacArthur Fellow. *The Occasions of Poetry,* comprising essays in criticism and autobiography, was published in England in 1982 and was reprinted in 1999 by the University of Michigan Press. He was a poet of skill and wit ("Their relationship consisted / In discussing if it existed"), who increasingly addressed intimate subjects. He endorsed Edmund White's view that "coming out in public was good for any writer's work. It was for mine, because the subject matter is so much greater." He died on April 25, 2004.

Of "Cafeteria in Boston," Gunn wrote: "People love talking about how they wrote poems; it is so much easier than writing new ones. I am no exception.

"The cafeteria in this poem actually had another name, but it was also the name of someone I had been in love with, so I changed it, as I didn't want to confuse my associations.

"The poem is about what I really ate and what really happened, but to start with there was other stuff in it, things I had on my mind, but I realized (as so often) in revising and rewriting what I truly wanted to write about, so I cut out what I had originally emphasized, and what had started as a couple of details became the poem I ended up with.

"The first friend I showed it to said that the poem just gave him a stomachache, so I almost didn't print it. I still don't know if it is any good or not. It is one of those poems where I don't clearly see what I have done."

DONALD HALL was born in New Haven, Connecticut, in 1928. He has published sixteen books of poetry, most recently *The Back Chamber* in 2011 by Houghton Mifflin Harcourt. In 2006 he published a volume of selected poems, *White Apples and the Taste of Stone.* Besides poetry, he has written books on baseball, the sculptor Henry Moore, and the poet Marianne Moore; children's books, including *Ox-Cart Man* (1979), which won the Caldecott Medal; short stories; and plays. He has edited more than two dozen textbooks and anthologies, including *The Oxford Book of Children's Verse in America* (1990), *The Oxford Book of American Literary Anecdotes* (1981), *New Poets of England and America* (with Robert

Pack and Louis Simpson, 1957), and *Contemporary American Poetry* (1962; revised 1972). He served as poetry editor of *The Paris Review* from 1953 to 1962. From 2006 to 2007 Hall was Poet Laureate of the United States. In 2011 President Obama awarded him the National Medal of Arts. Hall writes: "I live in a New Hampshire house where my grandmother and mother were born. I taught for some years at the University of Michigan, but in 1975 resigned my job and moved with Jane Kenyon to this house and to a life of freelance writing. Jane died in 1995." Hall was guest editor of *The Best American Poetry 1989*. His introduction to the volume was published separately, and reprinted, under the title "Death to the Death of Poetry."

In his textbook *To Read Poetry* (Holt, Rinehart and Winston, 1981), Hall writes: "Many people assume that poetry's medium is emotions and ideas. Emotions and ideas exist *in* poems or *through* poems, and we must account for them in paraphrase when we explicate, but they are not poetry's medium. If we argued that emotions and ideas are poetry's medium, we would have to claim that trees and mountains are the medium of landscape painting. Canvas and paint make the painter's medium, and poems are made of words."

Hall writes: " 'Prophecy' is one of 'Four Classic Texts' (together with 'Pastoral,' 'History,' and 'Eclogue') that make the middle of a long poem, *The One Day*, which Ticknor & Fields (then an imprint of Houghton Mifflin) published in September 1988. The whole poem began in the fall of 1971, when I was subject to long and frequent attacks of language. I wrote as rapidly as I could write, page after page, loose free verse characterized by abundance and strangeness rather than by anything else, certainly not by art. After a month or two the onslaught stopped. Every now and then over the next few years, lines would occur that announced themselves as part of this work. In 1979 and 1980 I tried to find a form. In 1981 the poem began to shape itself.

"Not that I knew what I was doing. If *The One Day* (or 'Prophecy') is intended, it is intended by not being crossed out. I wrote with excitement but without judgment; afterward I concentrated to decide whether to keep what I wrote down. If it succeeds, this poem is impulse validated by attention."

MARK HALLIDAY was born in Ann Arbor, Michigan, in 1949. Educated at Brown and Brandeis Universities, he has taught at Indiana University, Western Michigan University, and Ohio University. His honors include the Rome Fellowship in Literature from the American Academy of Arts and Letters, a Lila Wallace–Reader's Digest Writers' Award, and a Guggenheim Fellowship. His five books of poems are *Little Star* (William Morrow, 1987), *Tasker Street* (University of Massachusetts, 1992), *Self-wolf* (University of Chicago, 1999), *Jab* (University of Chicago, 2002), and *Keep This Forever* (Tupelo Press, 2008). His critical study, *Stevens and the Interpersonal,* was published by Princeton University Press in 1991.

Halliday writes: "Poetry is always about saying what can't be said— that beguiling hypnotic paradox. As a poet who usually places a high value on clarity and readability, I'm naturally troubled by the infinity of what my poems don't catch. In 'The Opaque' I experiment with dwelling in the gnarly otherness of what I haven't been able to interpret. But I find (humanly) that I can't live there."

ROBERT HASS was born in San Francisco in 1941. He is the author of *The Apple Trees at Olema: New and Selected Poems* (Ecco, 2010) and *What Light Can Do: Essays on Art, Imagination, and the Natural World* (Ecco, 2012). A professor of English at the University of California, Berkeley, he has won the National Book Critics Circle Award in poetry for *Sun Under Wood* (1996) and for criticism, *Twentieth Century Pleasures: Prose on Poetry* (1984).

Hass was the guest editor of *The Best American Poetry 2001.* He writes in his introduction to that volume that when David Lehman asked him to choose the seventy-five poems of 2000 most worthy of perpetuation, he "pointed out that there were whole centuries in which there weren't seventy-five good poems" but that, as we neared the end, he was arguing in favor of "a format that included eighty-five poems, or eighty, or, my last pitch, seventy-eight, just three more, why not? What's the difference? It didn't happen. A form is a form." His essay also includes this cogent insight into generational change: "It is an interesting time for young poets. They've inherited an aesthetic, or set of aesthetics, in which the basic relationship to language has become the central problem and it has given their work, so far, its particular forms of playfulness and tortuousness, interest and opacity and risk. Partly they're reacting against what has come to seem effortless and therefore indulgent in a previous generation, the poem of incident in plain language, which aims at a certain sincerity of address and tone, as if life was exactly the size of the self and consisted of a set of serial epiphanies. Some of this echoes the influence of the critical tradition in European philosophy in the universities, some of it is the ground-clearing required of any oppositional art. In this case, because it's suspicious of subject matter as such, suspicious, as I've seen it described, of the 'aboutness' of poetry, it's preoccupied with issues of style, with the relationship therefore between language and perception.

It also goes largely on instinct and the instinct is that some right, cool, strange, or estranged ferocity of language would catch the instability of things and undo, in its utopian versions, if not the whole global economy at least the self-satisfied clichés which present that vision of power in the world as triumphant and inevitable."

Of "Bush's War," Hass writes: "I was completely taken by the experience of Berlin, especially the leafy western suburbs where I was living. I tried to get some of the feel of it into this poem. Living in Berlin one thinks incessantly about the Holocaust, about violence, mass hypnosis, fear and hatred, scapegoating, political consent. One of the things I came to feel, living there, reading histories of the war and books like W. G. Sebald's *Air War and Literature* and Sven Lindqvist's *A History of Bombing*, is that we are not sufficiently horrified by the sheer extent of the butchery in the twentieth century, that the human race had found ways not to absorb it. I came to think that the second most evil thing that Hitler and the German people did, after the Holocaust, was, through the Holocaust, to keep the idea of a good war afloat. Coming back to the United States, watching how easily my own countrymen were stampeded into a war based on claims about Iraq that most informed people knew to be untrue was—and remains—a shock to me. I was also outraged by the moral and political arguments made to justify the war by the president and the war's apologists. Had they said that they were willing to be responsible for the death of thirty to a hundred thousand Iraqis, most of them innocent civilians caught in the multiple crossfires, because they knew what was good for them and had decided to sacrifice their lives, and had the American people consented to that, things would at least have been clear. Commentators in all of our media repeated the other high-minded arguments about freedom and democracy without blinking and ignored the dead. So another of my impulses was to state, to try to state plainly, the counter-argument. 'Bush's War' may be too frontal. It tries to weave these things—and some others—together fairly directly. And one hopes that the stuff of poetry—the complexity of a particular tone of voice, the subterranean pull of metaphor, the feel that poetry can convey a mind alive in time—will also do their work."

TERRANCE HAYES was born in Columbia, South Carolina, in 1971. He won the 2010 National Book Award in poetry for his book *Lighthead* (Penguin). His other books are *Wind in a Box* (Penguin, 2006), *Muscular Music* (Carnegie Mellon University Classic Contemporary, 2005, and Tia Chucha Press, 1999), and *Hip Logic* (Penguin, 2002). He has won a Whiting Writers' Award, a National Endowment for the Arts Fellowship, a USA Zell Fellowship, and a Guggenheim Fellowship. He is a professor of creative writing at Carnegie Mellon University and lives in Pittsburgh, Pennsylvania.

Of "A House Is Not a Home," Hayes writes: "Though this poem runs fairly close to an autobiographical experience, it's the fictitious/fanciful moments that ring truest for me. I read where Franz Kafka worked for a while at the 'Worker's Accident Insurance Institute for the Kingdom of Bohemia.' That sounds like the *real* in sur*real*. Where, in a parallel universe, would the black Kafka work, if not the African-American Acoustic and Audiological Accident Insurance Institute? And this poem is of course an elegy for crooner Luther Vandross, who I know was more complicated than his music let on. . . . And an apology. This poem is an apology to Ron. He didn't actually punch me. But he should have."

LYN HEJINIAN was born in the San Francisco Bay Area in 1941. In 2013 Wesleyan University Press reprinted her best-known book, *My Life,* in an edition that includes her related work, *My Life in the Nineties.* She is also the author of *The Book of a Thousand Eyes* (Omnidawn Books, 2012), *The Language of Inquiry* (University of California Press, 2000), and *The Wide Road,* written in collaboration with Carla Harryman (Belladonna, 2010). In addition to literary writing, editing, and translating, she has in recent years been involved in anti-privatization activism at the University of California, Berkeley, where she teaches.

Hejinian was the guest editor of *The Best American Poetry 2004.* In her introduction she wrote: "It is precisely in its being an ongoing *series* that *The Best American Poetry* undertaking has, to my mind, its particular interest and value. Implicit in its being a series is an awareness that the story of American poetry is never, in any single period of its activity, complete, and no set of examples from a single year of it can possibly reveal all that is under way in its unfolding. Dynamic, ever-changing, poetry (and American poetry in particular) is a site of perpetual transitions and unpredictable metamorphoses."

Hejinian writes: " 'The Polar Circle' is from a long work entitled *Sleeps.* The initial impetus for *Sleeps* was the *Thousand and One Nights,* from which I extrapolated a notion of my own: to the degree one can say that dreams are an interpretation of waking experience, then by extension one might say that night interprets day—which is, in fact, one of the functions of the tales Scheherazade tells. 'The Polar Circle,' like the other sections of *Sleeps,* is a night work; it was written just after I returned from some weeks spent within the Arctic Circle in Finland and Norway, summer weeks without any night at all (the sun's lower rim would touch the ocean but never sink), and it occurred to me that the poem might serve as a night to that very long day."

Bob Hicok was born in Grand Ledge, Michigan, in 1960. His most recent collection is *Words for Empty and Words for Full* (University of Pittsburgh Press, 2010). *This Clumsy Living* (University of Pittsburgh Press, 2007) won the Rebekah Johnson Bobbitt National Prize for Poetry from the Library of Congress and was published in a German translation by Luxbooks in 2011. He has received a Guggenheim Fellowship and two grants from the National Endowment for the Arts. He is an associate professor at Virginia Tech.

Of "Having Intended to Merely Pick on an Oil Company, the Poem Goes Awry," Hicok writes: "This poem was written before the Gulf oil spill. Had it been written after the oil spill, it would have had dead fish and pelicans in it, though some of the cows in the poem have died since the poem was written. You may have eaten some of the cows who have died. 'Died' is obviously a euphemism, as 'you' are in some sense a euphemism. While the poem suggests I know things about the foreskins of seraphim, I do not. In the spirit of full disclosure, I don't know anyone who knows much about the foreskins of seraphim. Most of the people I know are generalists, in that they are generally hungry or sleepy or hoping to be understood as essential to the endeavor. By the way, gas prices are going back up, which means interest in alternative sources of energy will go up, until gas prices go down, when interest in alternative energy will go down. The graph of this cycle should be called the Laugher Curve, for obvious reasons."

Brenda Hillman was born in Tucson, Arizona, in 1951. She was educated at Pomona College and received her MFA at the University of Iowa Writers' Workshop. Her books include *Pieces of Air in the Epic* (Wesleyan University Press, 2005), *Cascadia* (2001), *Loose Sugar* (1997), *Bright Existence* (1993), and *White Dress* (1985). She has edited an edition of Emily Dickinson's poetry for Shambhala Publications. She is on the faculty of Saint Mary's College in Moraga, California, where she is the Olivia C. Filippi Professor of Poetry. She is involved with antiwar activism as a member of CODEPINK in the San Francisco Bay Area.

Hillman writes: " 'Phone Booth' accretes lines that might be thought of as independent smaller poems. I'd drafted it in much longer form (at Squaw Valley Community). It derives from certain ideas about emotion. I'm interested in feeling-seeds for lyric collage that are hybrids—like sadness that is full of bemusement or dread-excitement etc. in this case a mix of Gnostic sorrow/empathy for obsolescent things like the noble, retired phone booths and aspects of expression like the interpunct, plus a hatred of soulless fetishized objects (cellphones) and a firm and permanent adoration of Rimbaud."

EDWARD HIRSCH was born in Chicago, Illinois, in 1950. He has published several books of poems with Alfred A. Knopf, including *For the Sleepwalkers* (1981); *Wild Gratitude* (1986), which won the National Book Critics Circle Award; *The Night Parade* (1989); *Earthly Measures* (1994); *On Love* (1998); *Lay Back the Darkness* (2003); and *Special Orders* (2008). He is the author of three prose books centering on a passion for poetry: *How to Read a Poem: And Fall in Love with Poetry* (Harcourt, 1999); *Responsive Reading* (University of Michigan Press, 1999); and *The Demon and the Angel: Searching for the Source of Artistic Inspiration* (Harcourt, 2002). He has received the Prix de Rome, a Guggenheim Fellowship, an American Academy of Arts and Letters Award for Literature, and a MacArthur Fellowship. After teaching in the creative writing program at the University of Houston for seventeen years, he became the fourth president of the John Simon Guggenheim Memorial Foundation, which was founded in 1925.

Of "Man on a Fire Escape," Hirsch writes: "This poem is an attempt to explore the literal and metaphorical possibilities of its dramatic situation: a man on a fire escape on a late day in the empire. There are a couple of things I had it in mind to do. To send a man out of his empty room onto iron stairs overlooking a city, and then to reel him back in. To describe a moment that is both ordinary and extraordinary, inside and outside of time. To invoke dusk, the hour of changes, as vividly as possible. To imagine and dwell upon an extended apocalyptic moment, the world being destroyed, and then to see that visionary moment transfigured and withdrawn, the twilight seeping into evening, the world continuing on as before. What has the man seen and what has he envisioned? Nothing. That resonating answer bears the full burden of meaning in the poem."

JANE HIRSHFIELD was born in New York City in 1953. She received her BA at Princeton as a member of the first graduating class to include women. Her most recent book of poetry is *Come, Thief* (Alfred A. Knopf, 2011). Earlier books include *After* (HarperCollins, 2006) and *Given Sugar, Given Salt* (HarperCollins, 2001). She is also the author of a book of essays, *Nine Gates: Entering the Mind of Poetry* (HarperCollins, 1997) and four books collecting and cotranslating the work of poets from the past, including *The Heart of Haiku* (Amazon Kindle Single, 2011) and *The Ink*

Dark Moon: Love Poems by Ono no Komachi and Izumi Shikibu, Women of the Ancient Japanese Court (Vintage Classics, 1990). She has received fellowships from the Guggenheim and Rockefeller Foundations. In 2012 she was elected a chancellor of the Academy of American Poets and given the third annual Donald Hall–Jane Kenyon Poetry Award. Seven of her poems have appeared in *The Best American Poetry* series. She has lived in Northern California since 1974.

Of "In Praise of Coldness," she writes: "It has long seemed to me that one of the defining qualities in a human life is the tension between the path of the passions and that of a certain nonattachment to one's own fate. The advice the poem quotes (from one of Chekhov's letters) strikes me as somehow related to a solution: 'If you want to move your reader, write more coldly.' The underbelly of that sentence is what interests: the point is not the coldness, but the way that a restraining coldness can in fact contain heat, can move the reader more than would a simple explosive outpouring. In art, in life, a certain coldness (the emotional distance of classical tragedy, the technical use of perspective in a Renaissance canvas, the capacity a person might have to step back sometimes from the pulse's racing) allows, paradoxically, greater feeling, greater range, increase of compassion, but it cannot so dominate as to deny human feeling, human life. Heat alone is narcissism; coldness alone is fatal. And so a dying man daydreams of travel, of eating, knowing all the while that he dreams the contemplation of Chekhov's allegiance to the world of the living, right to the end, both breaks and awakens the heart.

"The Japanese call the human realm 'the world of the middle,' or 'the world of betweeness.'" One task then of a human life is to find a way of being that seats itself between—that falls neither into a plummeting, arid coldness nor into unrestrained heat. (It is only because we humans lean by nature toward warmth that the title of this poem leans toward the cold.) What I've written here, I must add, are the thoughts that came to mind while looking at the poem in retrospect. In writing it, one line simply followed the next onto the page, and I only discovered in the reading and revising of those lines what the poem was exploring in its words and musics. That discovering, and its consequent clarifying, are the reason I write."

TONY HOAGLAND was born in Fort Bragg, North Carolina, in 1953, though in this series his birthplace has been identified as Tucson, Arizona, and he notes that he "has moved so many times that he can't remember where he's from." His books include *Sweet Ruin* (University of Wisconsin Press, 1992), which Donald Justice chose for the Brittingham Prize; *Donkey Gospel* (Graywolf Press, 1998); *What Narcissism Means to Me* (Graywolf, 2003); and *Unincorporated Persons in the Late Honda Dynasty* (2010). He has received a Guggenheim Fellowship and teaches at the University of Houston and in the low-residency MFA program at Warren Wilson College.

Hoagland writes: "When 'In a Quiet Town by the Sea' was chosen for *BAP,* I was, at first, dismayed, and considered declining the privilege of being published here. The poem was written a few years ago, and its subject matter, masculinity and sex, is sort of in my rearview mirror now. Craftwise, too, the poem seems a little hacked-out to me. What, really, does it discover? Yet the poem does represent several of my ongoing poetic interests: the art of rudeness, the bafflements of gender, and the dialectical play of multiple tones and voices in a poem. Although 'In a Quiet Town by the Sea' did indeed arise from experience—listening one night to two of my married friends talk about temptation and infidelity—I value more the en route rhetorical transformations and ornaments of the poem. Maybe this poem is taking a look at the fossil record, and in some of its movements, maybe there is evidence of life."

JOHN HOLLANDER was born in New York City in 1929. He has published eighteen books of poetry, including *Picture Window* (Alfred A. Knopf, 2003) and a reissue of his *Reflections on Espionage* with added notes and commentary (Yale University Press, 1999). His books of criticism include *The Work of Poetry* (Columbia University Press, 1999) and *The Poetry of Everyday Life* (University of Michigan Press, 1998). *Rhyme's Reason: A Guide to English Verse* (Yale University Press, rev. ed. 1989), a manual on set forms, rhetorical figures, and metrical arrangements, is in every sense exemplary—with seeming effortlessness Hollander illustrates the rules of a villanelle or a triolet in the specified form. (Thus the tanka, an elaboration of the haiku with two additional lines of seven syllables each: "Like a *haiku* that, / Awaking from dreams, dreams on / From sleep's closing door, / The *tanka*'s vision lives on / For seven syllables more.")

Hollander's dedication to literature has manifested itself not only in his writing but in his admirable editorial efforts. He has edited volumes of sonnets, war poems, Ben Jonson's poetry, *American Short Stories since 1945,* critical essays on modern poetry, the textbook *Literature as Experience,* and the Library of America's comprehensive two-volume anthology of nineteenth-century American poetry. Under his general editorship, the Signet Classic Poetry Series issued selected editions of canonical figures introduced by contemporary critics: David Kalstone on Sir Philip Sidney, for example, and W. H. Auden on Lord Byron. A MacArthur Fellow, Hollander lives in Connecticut and is Sterling Professor Emeritus of English at Yale University. He was the guest editor of *The Best American Poetry 1998*.

Of "The See-Saw," Hollander writes: "This 'mad song' grew out of two germs. The first was the note of Hegel's now preserved in the epigraph, which seemed to me the silliest thing I'd read in months. I'd jotted it down, together with a reminder of the old nursery rhyme 'See-saw, / Margery Daw, / Jack shall have a new master,' etc. The idea of confounding it with an idée fixe of see-sawing itself seemed inevitable. The other was the *dah-di-di-dah* rhythm of the words 'Margery Daw,' which I'd scrawled right under Hegel's note; being that of a sort of sapphic-stanza short line (with the final unstressed syllable missing), it seemed to belong at the end of a stanza of three longer lines. But I started out with it in 'Margery Daw,' and then it wandered crazily through subsequent stanzas, even as the name metamorphosed. I hadn't planned for the speaker to break out into German, but he suddenly did, perhaps because of Hegel, perhaps because I was remembering the voices of German refugee nannies in Central Park playgrounds in my early childhood."

RICHARD HOWARD was born in Cleveland, Ohio, in 1929. He lives in New York City and teaches in the writing division of Columbia University's School of the Arts. He is the author of a landmark work of poetry criticism, *Alone with America* (1969). He won the Pulitzer Prize for poetry in 1970 for *Untitled Subjects,* one of several volumes in which he makes innovative use of the dramatic monologue in the Browning manner. In *Two-Part Inventions* (1974) he brilliantly renders unlikely encounters of historical personages—Oscar Wilde and Walt Whitman, for example. Many younger poets owe a debt to Howard for his encouragement and support; at one time or another he served as the poetry editor of such magazines as *The Paris Review, New American Review, The New Republic, Shenandoah,* and *Western Humanities Review.*

Howard continues to translate works of literature from the French. He has translated Stendhal, Robbe-Grillet, Cocteau, Genet, Gide, Roland Barthes, Simone de Beauvoir, Henri Michaux, Emil Cioran, Jules Verne, Michel Foucault, Maurice Nadeau's *The History of Surrealism,* Camus, and Charles de Gaulle. His translation of Baudelaire's *Les Fleurs du mal* (1982) won a National Book Award. A few months before that book appeared, he wrote from Los Angeles, to a friend who had remarked on his itinerant ways, that he was "waiting for the Baudelaire production to make me, literally, effete: having given up the fetus—did you know that? You ask about my moving around—I am, and believe one must be, a born refugee, easily adapting to the comforts of whatever offers itself as the Next Home. No trouble at all when the trees out the window are palms, and the sun keeps at itself." The most recent of his fifteen books of poems, *Without Saying,* was published in 2008 by Turtle Point Press. He was the guest editor of *The Best American Poetry 1995.*

Of "Like Most Revelations," Howard writes: "The paintings of Morris Louis were created, for the most part, by tilting the canvas so that the paint could slide across the surface, staining it according to the artist's determination. The poem attempts to respond to the exigencies of this novel fashion of producing an image."

FANNY HOWE was born in Buffalo, New York, in 1940. She studied at Stanford University, graduating in 1962, and has lived mostly in New England and California. She taught literature at the University of California, San Diego. Her novels include *The Lives of a Spirit, The Deep North, Saving History,* and *Nod,* all from Sun and Moon Books, and *Indivisible* from Semiotext(e)/MIT Press. Some of her poetry (appearing from small presses for many years) was published as *Selected Poems* by the University of California Press (2000) and was awarded the 2001 Lenore Marshall Poetry Prize from the Academy of American Poets and *The Nation* magazine. *Come and See,* her most recent poetry collection, was published by Graywolf Press in 2011. In 2009 she won the Ruth Lilly Lifetime Achievement Award for poetry.

Of "9-11-01," Howe writes: "This poem was drawn from notes and an earlier poem written during the Gulf War, when I lived in San Diego, and watched the military planes flying out from Miramar Air Force base to the Pacific. The sense of there being no difference between one desert and another, given the magnitude of attacks by air, was revived by the events of September 11, 2001, as was the end game of strict materialism."

MARIE HOWE was born in Rochester, New York, in 1950. Her books of poetry are *The Good Thief* (Persea Books, 1988), *What the Living Do* (W. W. Norton, 1997), and *The Kingdom of Ordinary Time* (Norton, 2008). She has taught at Sarah Lawrence College, Columbia, and New York University. She lives in New York City.

Of "Magdalene—The Seven Devils," Howe writes: "It occurred to me, walking through the city one day, that Mary Magdalene, who has been so often depicted and characterized by men, was a woman bedeviled—and then a woman clarified, integrated. What might have been the seven devils she was said to have been possessed by? And then, what are the devils we are possessed by? Then the poem began to speak."

MAJOR JACKSON was born in Philadelphia, Pennsylvania, in 1968. He is the author of three poetry collections: *Holding Company* (W. W. Norton, 2010), *Hoops* (Norton, 2006), and *Leaving Saturn* (University of Georgia Press, 2002), winner of the Cave Canem Poetry Prize. He received a Whiting Writers' Award and spent a year as a creative arts fellow at the Radcliffe Institute for Advanced Study at Harvard University. He is the Richard Dennis Green and Gold Professor at the University of Vermont and a core faculty member of the Bennington Writing Seminars. He is the poetry editor of the *Harvard Review*.

Of "Urban Renewal," Jackson writes: "For all of my life, I have been asked if I am (or when I was younger was my father) a member of the military. In my family tree, 'Major' appears thrice, dating back four generations to pre–Civil War times. To some extent, the poem pays homage to the long and great naming practices of African Americans, whereby enterprising parents sought to endow their children with enchanting names that when uttered evoked power, prestige, and glory, despite their lack of physical or economic empowerment.

"The battle for respect is continual for black people in America. Of late, I have been appalled by the derisive response to names that are plainly 'ethnic' in sound. Against this tide of mockery, I wanted to write about the strength in such names as Kareem, Amari, and Mustafa. Then, like a drowned corpse, an early memory surfaced of a substitute teacher assigned to my class for the week who called out the roll on the first day with extreme difficulty and wonder and returned the following day with new names for all of us. Although it was cloaked as part of her curriculum for the week, I recognized even then the arrogance and disrespect behind that kind of erasure. The revulsion, so representative of the average American toward their immigrant and native-born brothers and sisters, lay on her tongue. But these considerations fall short of the pleasures of composition. Normally, composing a poem is an exercise in failed play which makes the process fun. This was the first time I experienced a palpable pain in my gut as I was writing the poem through various drafts. I am normally not in favor of the didactic in poetry, but I am growing older and the urgency to change the world around me seems starker."

RODNEY JONES was born in Hartselle, Alabama, in 1950. He grew up on a farm near Falkville, Alabama, then studied at the University of

Alabama and the University of North Carolina at Greensboro. Most recently he has published *Imaginary Logic* (Houghton Mifflin Harcourt, 2011) and *Salvation Blues: One Hundred Poems, 1985–2005* (Houghton Mifflin, 2007), which won the Kingsley Tufts Award. His previous volumes include *Elegy for the Southern Drawl* (1999), *Things That Happen Once* (1996), *Apocalyptic Narrative* (1993), and *Transparent Gestures* (1989), winner of the 1990 National Book Critics Circle Award. He has won a Guggenheim Fellowship and the Jean Stein Award from the American Academy of Arts and Letters. He has taught for many years at Southern Illinois University, Carbondale, as well as at Virginia Intermont College, the University of Cincinnati, and in the low-residency MFA program at Warren Wilson College.

LAWRENCE JOSEPH was born in Detroit, Michigan, in 1948. He attended the University of Michigan, the University of Cambridge, and the University of Michigan Law School. He is the author of five books of poetry: *Into It* (Farrar, Straus and Giroux, 2005), *Codes, Precepts, Biases, and Taboos: Poems 1973–1993* (FSG, 2005), *Before Our Eyes* (FSG, 1993), *Curriculum Vitae* (University of Pittsburgh Press, 1988), and *Shouting at No One* (University of Pittsburgh Press, 1983), which received the Agnes Lynch Starrett Poetry Prize. He has also written *Lawyerland* (FSG, 1997), a book of prose, and *The Game Changed: Essays and Other Prose* (University of Michigan Press, 2011). He is Tinnelly Professor of Law at St. John's University School of Law, where he teaches courses on labor, employment, and tort and compensation law, legal theory, jurisprudence, and law and interpretation. He has won a fellowship from the Guggenheim Foundation and has taught creative writing at Princeton University. Married to the painter Nancy Van Goethem, he lives in downtown Manhattan.

Joseph writes: "There's a couplet in the opening poem of Wallace Stevens's late work *The Rock*: 'The self and the earth—your thoughts, your feelings, / Your beliefs and disbeliefs, your whole peculiar plot.' The whole of my work is my 'whole peculiar plot.' I see myself—as Stevens and as Eugenio Montale and Louis Zukofsky did—writing, plotting, one long poem.

" 'So Where Are We?' is the title poem of my next book. My last book, *Into It*, contains poems, or parts of poems, which touch on the 9/11 World Trade Center attacks. My reaction to the terrorist bombings has an intensely personal dimension. My wife and I live a block from Ground Zero. Shortly before the first plane hit on the morning of September 11, I left her to go to St. John's University in Queens, where I teach. Nancy spent that night in our apartment. More than twenty-four hours went by before I saw her again. We were evacuated from our apartment for over two months.

"Before I write a poem, I usually try to imagine the form or shape it will take. I feel the form or shape visually ('conversation as design' was one of William Carlos Williams's definitions of poetry). Then, in effect, I load the shape or form with parts of the entire world of my subjects—with my 'whole peculiar plot.' I imagined 'So Where Are We?' in couplets. I also envisaged it as the second part of a diptych, the first part being 'Unyieldingly Present,' a poem in couplets in *Into It* written as a compressed, collective portrayal of the terrorist attacks."

Jane Kenyon was born in Ann Arbor, Michigan, in May 1947. She died of leukemia in New Hampshire on April 22, 1995. She had published a book of translations and four books of poems, all from Graywolf Press: *The Boat of Quiet Hours* (1986), *Let Evening Come* (1990), *Constance* (1993), and *Otherwise: New & Selected Poems* (1996). She had received fellowship grants from the National Endowment for the Arts and the Guggenheim Foundation. She lived with her husband, Donald Hall, on Eagle Pond Farm.

In "April, New Hampshire," an elegy published in *The American Poetry Review,* Sharon Olds wrote:

> Don said, *This is it, this*
> *is where we lived and died.* To the center of the dark
> painted headboard—sleigh of beauty,
> sleigh of night—there was an angel affixed
> as if bound to it with her wings open.
> The bed spoke, as if to itself,
> it sang. The whole room sang,
> and the house, and the curve of the hill, like the curve
> between a throat and a shoulder, sang, in praising
> grief, and the earth, almost, rang,
> hollowed-out bell waiting for its tongue
> to be lowered in.

Speak, Memory is the book by Nabokov quoted in Kenyon's "Reading Aloud to My Father."

Donald Hall wrote (in 1996): "Jane wrote many poems about her father's illness and death, of which 'Reading Aloud to My Father' is the latest and last. Reuel Kenyon died of cancer in Michigan in 1981; Jane and I stayed with him for much of his illness, helping Jane's mother care for him. When Jane was dying I thought of this poem. Music was her passion, as it was her father's; at the end, she could not bear to hear it, because it tied her to what she had to leave. In her last twenty-four hours, her hands remained outside the bedclothes, lightly clenched. I touched them from time to time, but I did not try to hold tight."

KENNETH KOCH was born in Cincinnati, Ohio, in 1925. After serving in the United States Army in World War II, seeing action as a rifleman in the Philippines, he went to Harvard on the G.I. Bill. Following graduation in 1948 he moved to New York City, where he became a central figure in the New York School of poets. He received his doctorate at Columbia University and taught there for forty years. His course in imaginative writing proved a college highlight for many future writers. *Ko, or A Season on Earth,* a long poem in ottava rima, appeared in 1960; *Thank You and Other Poems* followed two years later. He adapted his teaching techniques to the needs of elementary school children and elderly residents of nursing homes, and worked a minor revolution in pedagogy through such influential books as *Rose, Where Did You Get That Red?* (1973) and *I Never Told Anybody: Teaching Poetry Writing to Old People* (1977). His later collections of poetry include *One Train* (1994), *On the Great Atlantic Rainway: Selected Poems 1950–1988* (1996), *Straits* (1998), *New Addresses* (2000), and the posthumous *A Possible World* (2002), all from Alfred A. Knopf. Also published in the 1990s were two books about poetry: *The Art of Poetry* (University of Michigan Press, 1996) and *Making Your Own Days: The Pleasures of Reading and Writing Poetry* (Scribner, 1998). A volume of "comics, mainly without pictures," was published by Soft Skull Press as *The Art of the Possible* in 2004.

"When I first read [Koch's] poems I felt as though I had been standing for a very long time and that someone had just pushed a big comfortable chair behind me for me to sit in, where I could relax and take notes on what was going on around me," John Ashbery said, introducing Koch at a poetry reading in the 1960s. "In other words I feel his poems give the world back to you; you always had it but somehow from reading works of literature you felt that there must be some difference between it and what you thought it was, with what your experience offered up to you, which always seems like such a miserable thing in comparison with what everybody else has." At another New York reading from that era, Ashbery quoted three lines from his friend's poem "Lunch": "Do you see that snowman tackled over there / By summer and the sea? The boardwalk went to Istanbul / And back under his left eye." Ashbery commented, "This seems at first to be a random enumeration of impossible relationships and events. But all poetry contains these, a fact the lines casually remind us of as they are hurrying to make their point, which is that all kinds of fantastic and dull exchanges are going on in the air around us all the time, that the world is a wonderful and horrible place, that we are all existing at a very fast pace, that things like love and death and old age and platonic love are important things and full of interest. The final result of Koch's releasing so much hitherto classified information, which we already knew without being able to experience it, is a new kind of energy that is very real and precious, which will stimulate anyone who lets himself come in contact with it." Kenneth Koch died on July 6, 2002.

JOHN KOETHE was born in San Diego on December 25, 1945. A Princeton graduate, he received his doctorate in philosophy at Harvard University. His nine poetry books include *ROTC Kills* (HarperCollins, 2012). He received the Lenore Marshall Prize for *Ninety-fifth Street* (2009), the Kingsley Tufts Award for *Falling Water* (1997), and the Frank O'Hara Award for *Domes* (1973). *North Point North: New and Selected Poems* appeared in 2002. He is also the author of *Scepticism, Knowledge, and Forms of Reasoning* (2005) and *The Continuity of Wittgenstein's Thought* (1996), both from Cornell University Press. He has received a Guggenheim Fellowship and an award in literature from the American Academy of Arts and Letters. He is distinguished professor of philosophy (emeritus) at the University of Wisconsin–Milwaukee. The poem in this book is the title poem of Koethe's 2006 volume *Sally's Hair*.

Koethe writes: "'Sally's Hair' was the first of a group of recollective poems I've written over the last few years and which make up the last section of my most recent book, of which it's the title poem. The poem is pretty much self-explanatory: the intense blue and gold colors of a summer day made me remember a woman I met when I was a junior in college, and I simply wrote the encounter down. Some of the other poems in the group are centered upon memories of a track meet in high school, reading through all of *Remembrance of Things Past* (appropriately enough), watching Secretariat win the Triple Crown in 1973, and seeing Richard Burton portray Hamlet when I was a college freshman. I had a lot of fun writing them."

YUSEF KOMUNYAKAA was born in Bogalusa, Louisiana, on April 29, 1947. His thirteen books of poetry include *I Apologize for the Eyes in My Head* (1986); *Dien Cai Dau* (1988); *Neon Vernacular: New and Selected Poems 1977–1989* (1993), for which he received the Pulitzer Prize and the

Kingsley Tufts Poetry Award; and *Pleasure Dome* (2001), all published by Wesleyan University Press; and *Talking Dirty to the Gods* (2000), *Taboo* (2004), and *Warhorses* (2008), all published by Farrar, Straus and Giroux. His many honors include the William Faulkner Prize (Université de Rennes, France), the Ruth Lilly Poetry Prize, and the 2011 Wallace Stevens Award. His plays, performance art, and libretti have been performed internationally and include *Saturnalia, Testimony,* and *Gilgamesh.* He teaches at New York University. He was the guest editor of *The Best American Poetry 2003.*

When Komunyakaa won the Wallace Stevens Award from the Academy of American Poets in 2012, Mark Doty wrote an appreciation for *American Poet,* the Academy's journal. Doty characterized "Facing It" as a "poem of both national grief and nearly overwhelming personal sorrow," adding: "The black speaker's image dissolves in the black wall of Maya Lin's memorial, and indeed the speaker is both stone and flesh because he is literally a body and its reflection and because he must be both steeled and vulnerable in order to continue. The wall of names intersects with the world around it, as it was surely meant to do. The memory won't stay out of the present, the war won't remain in the past, the living and the lost can't leave each other alone."

Of "Facing It," Komunyakaa wrote (in 1990): "Now, as I think back to 1984 when I wrote 'Facing It,' with the humidity hanging over New Orleans (a place raised by the French out of the swampy marshes) in early summer, I remember that it seemed several lifetimes from those fiery years in Vietnam. I lived at 818 Piety Street, and was in the midst of renovating the place: trekking up and down a twelve-foot ladder, scribbling notes on a yellow pad. I had meditated on the Vietnam Veterans Memorial as if the century's blues songs had been solidified into something monumental and concrete. Our wailing, our ranting, our singing of spirituals and kaddish and rock anthems, it was all captured and refined into a shaped density that attempted to portray personal and public feelings about war and human loss. It became a shrine overnight: a blackness that plays with light—a reflected motion in the stone that balances a dance between the grass and sky. Whoever faces the granite becomes a part of it. The reflections move into and through each other, dance between the dead and the living. Even in its heft and weight, emotionally and physically, it still seems to defy immediate description, constantly incorporating into its shape all the new reflections and shapes brought to it: one of the poignant shrines of the twentieth century.

"Today, I have attempted to journey from that blues moment of retrospection that produced 'Facing It' to this moment, now, when I am a member of the advisory council for the My Lai Peace Park Project in Vietnam. This project is also connected to the reflective power of that granite memorial in DC. Joined in some mysterious and abiding way, we can hope that the two can grow into a plumb line or spirit level etched with names and dates that suggest where we are and the distance we have journeyed—something instructive that we can measure ourselves against."

STANLEY KUNITZ was born in Worcester, Massachusetts, in 1905. He discovered poetry at the local public library, and at age fourteen, when a teacher read Robert Herrick's poem "Upon Julia's Clothes," the boy raised his hand and said how much he liked the word *liquefaction* in "the liquefaction of her clothes." He attended Harvard. At thirty-seven, he was drafted into the army, where, declaring himself a pacifist, he cleaned latrines. After the war he received a Guggenheim Fellowship and taught at Bennington College. His *Selected Poems, 1928–1958,* won the Pulitzer Prize in 1959. He also received the Bollingen Prize, the Brandeis Medal, the Lenore Marshall Prize, and the National Medal of Arts presented at the White House by President Clinton in 1993. He was New York State's first official poet laureate. Other books include *The Poems of Stanley Kunitz: 1928–1978* (Little Brown and Co., 1979), *Next-to-Last Things* (Atlantic Monthly Press, 1985), and *Passing Through: The Later Poems* (W. W. Norton), which received the National Book Award in 1995. He lived with his wife, the artist Elise Asher, in New York City and Provincetown, Massachusetts. "In youth, poems come to you out of the blue," Kunitz, an inveterate gardener, told Mary B. W. Tabor of *The New York Times* (November 30, 1995). "They're delivered at your doorstep like the morning news. But at this age, one has to dig." In 2000 he was named United States Poet Laureate. He died at the age of one hundred on May 14, 2006.

Kunitz noted: "I began writing 'Touch Me' in the midst of a furious late August storm on Cape Cod that marked for me the turning-point of summer and the conclusion of my eighth decade. The opening line is recalled from 'As Flowers Are,' a poem I wrote in the mid-fifties at the MacDowell Colony."

DAVID LEHMAN was born in New York City in 1948. His books of poetry include *Yeshiva Boys* (2009), *When a Woman Loves a Man* (2005), *The Evening Sun* (2002), *The Daily Mirror* (2000), and *Valentine Place* (1996), all from Scribner, and *Operation Memory* (1990) and *An Alternative to Speech* (1986), both from Princeton University Press. He is the author of six nonfiction books, including *A Fine Romance: Jewish Songwriters, American Songs* (Schocken/Nextbook, 2009), which won ASCAP's Deems Taylor Award in 2010. He is the editor of *The Oxford Book of American Poetry* (2006) and *Great American Prose Poems* (2003), among other books. He launched *The Best American Poetry* series in 1988. He teaches in the graduate writing program of The New School and lives in New York City and in Ithaca, New York.

Of "Operation Memory," Lehman writes: "I've long been fascinated by military code names, such as Operation Torch for the Allied invasion of North Africa in World War II. 'Operation Memory' suggested a military metaphor for an autobiographical reflection. Or was memory (or its loss) a metaphor for a military experience? Perhaps both. I set out to write a poem about the war in Vietnam. (An undeclared war, Vietnam is nowhere mentioned in the poem.) 'Operation Memory' is a sestina with a variable. Ordinarily, there are six repeating end-words in a sestina. Here there are five fixed end-words and a sequence of numbers where the sixth would go. It's a downward progression (hundred, fifty, eighteen, ten, one) plus a year (1970) and an age (38, the age I was when I wrote the poem). I thought of Abraham trying to persuade God to spare the sinful cities: if there were fifty righteous men, would he do it? If there were twenty righteous men? Ten? I was recently asked whether the speaker commits suicide at the end of the poem ('a loaded gun on my lap'). That's one possibility; a second is that he is about to shoot somebody else; a third is that it's 'a loaded gun' in metaphor only."

PHILIP LEVINE was born in Detroit, Michigan, in 1928. At age twenty-six he left Detroit for other pastures (he writes), and the city slowly collapsed (there is "no connection although I also slowly collapsed"). He has received two Pulitzer Prizes, two National Book Awards, two National Book Critics Circle Awards, the Lenore Marshall Poetry Prize, and the Ruth Lilly Award, and was named United States Poet Laureate in 2011. His eighteenth book of poetry, *News of the World,* appeared in 2009. His other books include *Breath* (2004), *The Mercy* (1999), *The Simple Truth* (1994), and *What Work Is* (1991), all from Alfred A. Knopf, and *Unselected Poems* (Greenhouse Review Press, 1997). In 1994 Knopf published *The Bread of Time: Toward an Autobiography.* He lives half the year in Fresno, California, where he taught for twenty-two years at California State, and half in Brooklyn, New York.

Of "The Return," Levine writes: "I believe the poem was born out of the experience of turning seventy, twice the age of my father when he died. During my years as a boy and a young man growing up in Detroit

I went back again and again to places I knew he'd frequented, in an effort to find some trace or hint of his nature. I must have failed, for I kept repeating the search. A few years ago my mother—knowing she was nearing the end (she was over ninety)—presented me with a thick packet of letters he'd written her in the late twenties and early thirties. Most of them were on hotel stationery from such cities as New York, Philadelphia, and Chicago where he'd gone repeatedly on business. It was the first time since he'd died in 1933 that I encountered his actual words and got a precise sense of how he expressed himself. To my surprise he was in the letters not the tall, austere, mysterious figure my memory had created out of the scraps of detail it contained; he was a man alone missing his home, his wife, his children. Did I ever make the actual trip I describe in the poem? No. The poem relies for its specificity on several other trips with the same or similar purposes, some real, some imagined."

AMIT MAJMUDAR was born in New York City in 1979. Having earned his MD in 2003, he works as a diagnostic nuclear radiologist in Dublin, Ohio. His books of poetry are *0°, 0°* (TriQuarterly/Northwestern University Press, 2009) and *Heaven and Earth* (Story Line Press), which received the 2011 Donald Justice Award. His novels are *Partitions* (Holt/Metropolitan, 2011) and *The Abundance* (forthcoming from Holt/Metropolitan).

Of "The Autobiography of Khwaja Mustasim," Majmudar writes: "Khwaja Mustasim is an elderly Afghan schoolteacher, Mustasim Muja-hid Rahman. He currently lives in Herat, which Word's spellcheck function insists on switching to 'Heart.' Mustasim's (Sufi Muslim) name happens to be an uncanny near-rearrangement of my own (Hindu) full name, Amit Himanshu Majmudar. (The extra *s* is the serpent in the garden.) Mustasim likes to joke about this anagrammatical connection between us—he calls me his 'infidel amanuensis.' I call him my 'dapple-dawn-drawn doppelganger.' We are good friends, Mustasim and I.

"Khwaja Mustasim dictated his 'Autobiography' to me in a form derived either from the Holy Qur'an or the Book of Taliesin. To this day I am uncertain which. I notice that he tells his life *as a series of past lives,* though he does not, as a Muslim, believe in rebirth—while *I,* as a Hindu, do. Might this 'Autobiography' be a kind of metaphysical joke? And if so, at whose expense?

"I tried to pin old Mustasim down on this question, and he explained to me (in Sanskrit, no less) that a man of faith embodies his faith—and the whole history of his faith. 'So when anyone, martyr or murderer, speaks Islam, he speaks me,' said Mustasim. 'I figured I should fight back like your long-lined poet Whitman: By singing myself.'"

SARAH MANGUSO was born in Newton, Massachusetts, in 1974. Educated at Harvard and the Iowa Writers' Workshop, she is the author, most recently, of two book-length essays, *The Guardians* (Farrar, Straus and Giroux, 2012) and *The Two Kinds of Decay* (Picador, 2008). Her other books include the story collection *Hard to Admit and Harder to Escape* (2007), published as one of three volumes in McSweeney's *One Hundred and Forty-Five Stories in a Small Box,* and the poetry collections *Siste Viator* (2006) and *The Captain Lands in Paradise* (2002). She has received a Guggenheim Fellowship, a Hodder Fellowship from Princeton University, and the Rome Prize from the American Academy of Arts and Letters. She holds dual citizenship (the United States and Ireland), lives in Brooklyn, New York, and currently teaches literature and writing at New York University.

Of "Hell," Manguso writes: "The music I refer to in the fourth section (per my journal entry of 11/3/01, the day I wrote this poem) is the sound of Will Oldham singing 'I See a Darkness.'"

J. D. MCCLATCHY was born in Pennsylvania in 1945. He is the author of seven books of poetry, most recently *Mercury Dressing* (Alfred A. Knopf, 2009). A prolific librettist, whose work has been performed in opera houses around the world, including the Metropolitan, Covent Garden, and La Scala, he has also written four books of prose and edited dozens of books and anthologies. With Stephen Yenser he edited James Merrill's *Collected Poems* (2001) and his *Collected Novels and Plays* (2002). In 2011, Norton published McClatchy's verse translations of *Seven Mozart Librettos,* including *The Magic Flute* and *The Abduction from the Seraglio* from the German and *The Marriage of Figaro, Così Fan Tutte,* and *Don Giovanni* from the Italian. He has served as president of the American Academy of Arts and Letters and as a chancellor of the Academy of American Poets. He teaches at Yale and is the editor of *The Yale Review.* He lives in Stonington, Connecticut.

Of "My Mammogram," McClatchy writes: "I *did,* a year ago, have a mammogram, but my description of the procedure itself—in the second of the poem's five sonnets—is the only part of the poem that is 'true.' The rest was exaggerated or invented or colored in such a way as to make (or at least this was my intention) the 'experience' seem both more vivid and more substantial, and also perhaps less scary, than it was in fact. The formal distractions of the sonnet form seemed the best way to prompt and control material that could too easily turn sensational or sentimental; the sequence of sonnets as well discourages a plodding or overdetailed narrative. The tone of the poem was hardest to get right.

What I tried for was this: a nervous humor about the incongruities at the start that gradually gives way to a darker, more serious meditation."

HEATHER MCHUGH was born in San Diego, California, in 1948. She was raised in Virginia and educated at Harvard University. She is Pollock Professor of Creative Writing at the University of Washington in Seattle, and a core faculty visitor at the low-residency MFA program at Warren Wilson College in Asheville, North Carolina. Her most recent books of poems, essays, and translation are, respectively, *Upgraded to Serious* (Copper Canyon Press, 2009), *Broken English: Poetry and Partiality* (Wesleyan University Press, 1993), and *Glottal Stop: 101 Poems by Paul Celan* (with cotranslator Nikolai Popov, Wesleyan, 2004). A former chancellor of the Academy of American Poets, she was awarded a John D. and Catherine T. MacArthur Fellowship in 2009. In 2012 she started caregifted.org, a nonprofit organization giving vacations to long-term full-time caregivers of severely disabled family members.

McHugh was the guest editor of *The Best American Poetry 2007.* "My lifelong romance with literary objects began not with the wish to say some*thing* but with the hope to say some*how,*" she wrote in the introduction to the volume, adding: "I'm a logic-and-structure addict but I'm also swayable by a passage's sonic architectonics. I hope my heart is smart; my brain knows braille. I bring six senses to the enterprise, or seven: because poetry is (as Poe said) not a purpose, but a passion."

Of "Past All Understanding," which first appeared under the title "Flap Copy," McHugh writes: "Dog driven by fear and love. Man driven by fear and love. Earth driven by God. (The rest is singing.)"

JAMES MCMICHAEL was born in Pasadena, California, in 1939. His most recent books of poems are *The World at Large: New and Selected Poems, 1971–1996* and *Capacity,* which was a finalist for the National Book Award in 2006. He has written two books of prose, *The Style of the Short Poem* and *"Ulysses" and Justice.* He has won a Guggenheim Fellowship, a Whiting Writers' Award, the Arthur O. Rense Prize from the American Academy of Arts and Letters, the Shelley Memorial Prize, and an Academy of American Poets Fellowship. He recently retired from the University of California, Irvine, where he taught for forty-six years. "The Person She Is," the original title of the sequence from which the excerpt in *The Best American Poetry 1993* was taken, was changed to *Each in a Place Apart* when it appeared as a book.

McMichael writes: "The selection is from the early-middle of a book-length sequence. Written in the first person, these lines rehearse one segment of a twenty-year relationship between the writer and the woman he loves, a woman to whom he is not married."

JAMES MERRILL (1926–1995) was born in New York City. He was the son of the financier Charles Merrill, who founded the brokerage firm Merrill Lynch, and his second wife, Hellen Ingram. He interrupted his studies at Amherst College to serve in the infantry for a year during World War II. Returning to Amherst, he impressed his professor, Reuben Brower, with his analysis of the relation of rhetoric to emotion in the writings of Marcel Proust. He graduated summa cum laude, spent a year teaching at Bard College, then went to Europe, to Paris and Venice mostly, for a two-and-a-half-year journey of self-discovery. This is the subject of Merrill's memoir, *A Different Person* (1993). *First Poems* came out in 1951, *The Country of a Thousand Years of Peace* eight years later. Already in these elegantly crafted poems, Merrill pursued visions of angelic transcendence. "There are moments when speech is but a mouth pressed / Lightly and humbly against the angel's hand," he wrote in "A Dedication." He used sonnets as narrative building blocks in poems determined "to make some kind of house / Out of the life lived, out of the love spent," as he put it in *Water Street* (1962), his watershed volume. In such poems as "A Tenancy" and "An Urban Convalescence," he developed the relaxed conversational style that he perfected in *Nights and Days* (1966), *The Fire Screen* (1969), and *Braving the Elements* (1972).

Sometimes dismissed as an opera-loving aesthete, Merrill was able to identify himself with history and could handle subjects that defeat most poets (the anarchist's bomb, the space traveler's capsule, the shopping mall, and the alcoholic's recovery program). He had grown up in the Manhattan brownstone that was blown up by a radical fringe group in 1970. In "18 West 11th Street" he writes about that incident, as if his own life were passing before him in the slow-motion replay of the blast. His books received two National Book Awards, the Pulitzer Prize, and the Bollingen Prize. The epic poem begun in *Divine Comedies* (1976) and extended in two subsequent volumes was published in its entirety (and with a coda) as *The Changing Light at Sandover* (1982), which won the National Book Critics Circle Award. His last books of poetry were *Late Settings* (Atheneum, 1985), *The Inner Room* (Alfred A. Knopf, 1988), and *A Scattering of Salts* (Knopf, 1995). *Recitative,* a collection of Merrill's critical prose edited by J. D. McClatchy, appeared from North Point Press in 1986. Merrill owned homes in Stonington, Connecticut, and New York City, and spent many winters in Key West, Florida. He died Monday, February 6, 1995, while on holiday in Tucson, Arizona.

On four consecutive weekday evenings in May 1990, the Metropolitan Opera in New York City staged the four operas that constitute "The 'Ring' Cycle," thus providing the occasion for Merrill's poem of that title.

W. S. MERWIN was born in New York City in 1927. He was educated at Princeton. From 1949 to 1951 he worked as a tutor in France, Portugal, and Majorca, later earning his living by translating from the French, Spanish, Latin, and Portuguese. *A Mask for Janus,* Merwin's first volume of poems, was chosen by W. H. Auden for the Yale Series of Younger Poets in 1952. His recent collections, published by Copper Canyon Press, include *Migration: New & Selected Poems* (2005), recipient of the National Book Award; *Present Company* (2007); and *The Shadow of Sirius,* which received the Pulitzer Prize. Merwin was named United States Poet Laureate in 2010.

Of "The Stranger," Merwin notes that he found a prose summary of the legend in question "and tried to tell it as the Guarani would tell it." The Guarani are rainforest Indians from the central section of South America, where Paraguay, Brazil, and Bolivia meet. "They are to South America what the Hopi are to the American Southwest: the museum, compendium, and storehouse for the spiritual life of that region."

THYLIAS MOSS was born in Cleveland, Ohio, in 1954. A graduate of Oberlin College, she has taught at Brandeis University, the University of New Hampshire, and Phillips Academy in Andover, Massachusetts, and is a professor of English at the University of Michigan. In 1996 she won fellowships from the Guggenheim and MacArthur Foundations. Her books include *Tokyo Butter: Poems* (Persea Books, 2006), *Slave Moth: A Narrative in Verse* (Persea, 2004), *Last Chance for the Tarzan Holler* (Persea, 1998), *Tale of a Sky-Blue Dress,* a memoir (Avon, 1998), *Small Congregations* (Ecco, 1993), *Rainbow Remnants in Rock Bottom Ghetto Sky* (Persea, 1991), and *Pyramid of Bone* (Callaloo/University of Virginia Press, 1989). Her work was chosen for the 1989, 1990, 1991, 1992, and 1998 editions of *The Best American Poetry.* She also was included in *The Best of the Best American Poetry 1988–1997,* edited by Harold Bloom. Since 2004, when she developed Limited Fork Theory, she has taught limited fork with a limited fork in the department of English and in the School of Art & Design at the University of Michigan. She lives in Ann Arbor.

Of "There Will Be Animals," Moss writes: "I am a small woman full of doubts, full because being small means that what might be normal, reasonable quantities and doses for someone else are excesses for me. I fill quickly. Yet there is room for something else: faith in ideals. Not paradise—I don't want or need paradise, because I don't think it will teach us anything but pride (some have too much of that) and haughtiness, belief that what we did was right, that the ultimate good was achieved through what we did, no matter how recklessly performed. No; I mean those other ideals, the 'no man is an island' theory, the idea that no human is complete, self-contained, entirely self-providing, absolved from need altogether. Understand from this that I believe that struggling will in fact change us, that the form of paradise we do eventually have will not be permanent, immutable, or total (a part of existence might become ideal while other parts lag in destitute hellishness—most lagging is a form of poverty). We will have to work at the maintenance of our ideals; the attainable paradise will always be threatened as we work to control and curb (only occasionally successfully) instincts and passions that are part of our design, that therefore must accompany us wherever we go, even to paradise. Recognizing then—and this is easy recognition, for it is how we know ourselves—that we have limitations, that what makes us human, keeps us human, keeps us hungry; we cannot hope to discover the answers by ourselves. But since hunger demands feeding and what we want to be are gluttons, I have every faith that we will seek answers to eat. And they are going to come from the unlikely source, from what we have dominion over—licensed dominion, if one defers to biblical entitlement—from what is below us, inferior, subjugated and all that, because we need humbling first before we can alter our evolution and move toward becoming marvelous beings. The animals, the residents of that parallel world, the one that watches ours, that already realizes it is our teacher since we learned from it the survival tactics of hunt, kill, maim, attack, consume, and destroy, that on our higher human level become systems of cruelty; that world, that natural world can certainly teach us something else just as effectively as it taught us war. Judging from how well we learned that first lesson, who can then doubt that any other lesson would be as perfectly learned, perfectly implemented even into our very definition of ourselves? So, elimination of doubt is what that poem says to me. An insistence on hope despite everything, a belief that hope is rational is what I am trying to prove to myself in that poem, and to anyone else who needs convincing. Accomplishing that, this small woman has room to live."

PAUL MULDOON was born in County Armagh, Northern Ireland, in 1951 and was educated in Armagh and at the Queen's University of Belfast. He is Howard G. B. Clark '21 Professor at Princeton University and chair of the Peter B. Lewis Center for the Arts. His main collections of poetry are *New Weather* (1973), *Mules* (1977), *Why Brownlee Left* (1980),

Quoof (1983), *Meeting the British* (1987), *Madoc: A Mystery* (1990), *The Annals of Chile* (1994), *Hay* (1998), *Poems 1968–1998* (2001), *Moy Sand and Gravel* (2002), which won the Pulitzer Prize, *Horse Latitudes* (2006), and *Maggot* (2010). In 2007 he succeeded Alice Quinn as poetry editor of *The New Yorker*.

Muldoon was the guest editor of *The Best American Poetry 2005*. "The editing of this anthology began as something akin to a chore and ended as something akin to a cherishing, a cherishing of the heart of American poetry," he wrote in his introduction.

Muldoon writes: "'The Loaf' is set in a house on the bank of the Delaware and Raritan canal, a canal built in the 1830s by Irishmen, many of whom were lost to cholera, many more to the severity of their lives."

HARRYETTE MULLEN is the author of several poetry collections, including *Sleeping with the Dictionary* and *Recyclopedia: Trimmings, S⋆PeRM⋆⋆K⋆T, and Muse & Drudge*. Her poems have been translated into Spanish, Portuguese, French, Polish, German, Swedish, Danish, Turkish, and Bulgarian. She teaches American poetry, African American literature, and creative writing at UCLA. A collection of her essays and interviews, *The Cracks Between What We Are and What We Are Supposed to Be,* was published in 2012 by the University of Alabama Press.

Mullen writes: "*Muse & Drudge* is a praise-song to the women of Africa, to their daughters and sisters of the diaspora. It is also dedicated to bluesmen, poets and singers, who are fond of saying, 'If it wasn't for women, we wouldn't have the blues.' *Muse & Drudge,* a book-length work, signaled a return to verse after two books of prose poetry. For me it marks a crossroads where Sappho meets the blues lyric. My poetry would not be here if not for some praiseworthy people. I thank them: A. R. Ammons and Stephen Yenser, for unbounded generosity. Thomas Sayers Ellis, of the Dark Room Collective, for choosing to excerpt *Muse & Drudge* in *AGNI* and *Muleteeth*. Leslie Scalapino, whose Boston poetry reading, among other delights, allowed me to meet Tom Ellis, Barbara Henning, and David St. John, who have encouraged me by publishing parts of the poem. Diane Rayor, whose American language translations of Sappho and other divine dead Greeks reminded me so much of the blues, I couldn't wait to start a new poem in verse. Gwendolyn Brooks, pathbreaker. Ted Pearson, the most lyrical poet alive. For what they have given, I praise them!"

CAROL MUSKE-DUKES was born in St. Paul, Minnesota, in 1945. She is a professor at the University of Southern California and has also taught at Columbia, the University of Iowa Writers' Workshop, the University of Virginia, and the University of California, Irvine. She is the author of eight books of poetry, four novels, and two essay collections. Her most recent books are *Twin Cities* (Penguin, 2011) and two anthologies: *Crossing State Lines: An American Renga,* coedited with Bob Holman (Farrar, Straus and Giroux, 2011) and *The Magical Poetry Blimp Pilot's Guide,* coedited with Diana Arterian (Figueroa Press, 2011). Her other books of poetry include *Sparrow* (Random House, 2003), *An Octave Above Thunder, New and Selected Poems* (Penguin, 1997), and *Red Trousseau* (Viking/Penguin, 1991). *Women and Poetry: Truth, Autobiography, and the Shape of the Self,* her collection of reviews and critical essays, was published in the Poets on Poetry series of the University of Michigan Press in 1997. She has received a Guggenheim Fellowship, a National Endowment for the Arts Fellowship, an Ingram-Merrill Foundation Award, the Witter Bynner Award from the Library of Congress, and the Castagnola Award from the Poetry Society of America. For many years she was poetry columnist for the *Los Angeles Times Book Review.* On November 13, 2008, Governor Schwarzenegger appointed her as California's Poet Laureate.

Of "Hate Mail," Muske-Dukes writes: "I am (and have always been) an outspoken woman. Thus I've acquired a lot of friends and also a few enemies. Someone in the latter group began sending me anonymous 'hate' email not long ago. If you have ever received hate mail, you know that it is quite scary—especially if the unknown correspondent has 'facts' about your life, and appears to have some familiarity with your day-to-day life and your family and friends. The emails I received were somewhat threatening, but they were mostly just rantings by an odd, not-very-intelligent, very angry person who did not like me at all. (My webmaster and others tried to track the emails, but the author had disappeared into cyberspace, impossible to trace.)

"At one point, I realized that this mail was kind of funny. The ability to reread the emails and laugh at them gave me the idea of writing a parody: writing hate mail to myself. Of course, the bizarre insulting perspective and nutzoid observations of my poem are original, are mine—but the 'spirit' of the disturbed correspondent inspired my 'voice' in the poem.

"Goethe said, 'A poet must know how to hate.' I've always written poems of love and loss. I must say that I found it absolutely exhilarating to write a 'hate' poem, especially a hate poem to myself. It was cathartic, but it was also kind of inspiring—I think I may have a talent for this! I experienced the 'freeing' of a reckless voice, the freedom of (faux) anonymity. Perhaps I'll crank out a couple more."

SHARON OLDS was born in San Francisco, California, in 1942. By nature "a pagan and a pantheist," she grew up in California in a "hellfire Episcopalian religion." After receiving her doctorate at Columbia in 1972, she vowed, for the sake of her poems, to renounce all she had learned in graduate school. *The Dead and the Living,* her 1984 collection, won the Lamont Poetry Prize and the National Book Critics Circle Award. She was New York State Poet Laureate for 1998–2000. Her most recent books are *Stag's Leap* (Alfred A. Knopf, 2012), *One Secret Thing* (Knopf, 2008), and *Strike Sparks: Selected Poems, 1980–2002* (Knopf, 2004). She has organized writing workshops for the disabled at Goldwater Hospital. She teaches at New York University and lives in New York City.

Olds offers this "Short Biography of 'Q'": "During the W. administration, I was looking at *The New York Times* one day and felt sorry for the letter q—the qarrier of so much war news.

"Then I went to the dictionary, to find words in the q family.

"I knew it was going to be a punch-line poem—whether it worked or no—and I knew that was cheesy but could I be forgiven the shoq value for what it was trying to convey: if one feels sorry for a letter of the alphabet, how much more for a person, one of the hourly rising number of fatalities and severe injuries in an invasion so many Americans had been against? (And are we as helpless to affect policy as a piece of movable type being dropped into the composing stick?)

"When I include this poem in a reading, I feel a little mean—about to jump out and say Boo!—and hope the playfulness and the swerve and protest seem OK together.

"I was so happy when Paul Muldoon accepted 'Q' for *The New Yorker,* and Jenna Krajeski and I had a fun flurry of emails: Q & A became Q. & A.; quinoa lost its underline; the fact-checker found not 28 but 29 pages of k's, and not 18 but 13 pages of q's; and I was happy to get those 8's (infinities up on their hind legs) out of there, and the odd and sharp-pointed 3 and 9 in instead. Especially I was happy with the glorious long-tailed Q's *The New Yorker* has at hand—more devolved, more lemur.

"(And again, now, so happy to be between these covers in this company.)"

• • •

"Results of round-robin between the capital letters in the paragraphs above:

Tied for last place, with 1 each: A, D, E, J, K, M, O, P, S
Tied for 5th place, with 2 each: B, N, W
4th place, with 3: Y

3rd place, with 4: T
2nd place, with 5: Q
1st place, with 11: I (surprise!)"

MEGHAN O'ROURKE was born in New York City in 1976. A graduate of Yale University, she has worked as culture editor and literary critic for *Slate* as well as poetry editor and advisory editor for *The Paris Review*. She is the author of the poetry collections *Halflife* (W. W. Norton, 2008) and *Once* (Norton, 2011), and the memoir *The Long Goodbye* (Riverhead, 2011). She has taught at Princeton, The New School, and New York University. She lives in Brooklyn, where she grew up, and in Marfa, Texas.

O'Rourke writes: "'The Window at Arles' was an attempt to investigate the proximity between creation and destruction. It was also originally part of a larger series that interwove fragments of biographical material (letters, diaries) with imagined situations; the aim was to exploit the gap between what was 'real' and what was patently invented, and, in fragmenting what might otherwise be a narrative account of 'making,' to examine, somehow, the failure of language (or any form of representation) to communicate without slippage. The evolving quotation (which begins as Van Gogh's language and then morphs into something else) was meant to provide a destabilizing friction, one that would call into question the integrity of the whole."

MICHAEL PALMER was born in Manhattan in 1943 and has lived in San Francisco since 1969. He has worked with the Margaret Jenkins Dance Company for more than thirty-five years and has collaborated with many visual artists and composers. His poetry collections include *Codes Appearing: Poems 1979–1988* (New Directions, 2001) and *Company of Moths* (New Directions, 2005). His selected essays and talks, *Active Boundaries,* was published by New Directions in 2008. In 2006 he received the Wallace Stevens Prize from the Academy of American Poets. He has taught at various universities in the United States and Europe, and his writings have been translated into more than thirty languages. A new collection of poetry, *Thread,* was published by New Directions in 2011, and in 2012 the American Academy of Arts and Letters honored him for excellence in literature.

Palmer writes: "Some time ago, the French poet Emmanuel Hocquard sent me his reprint of Georges Hugnet's preface to Hugnet's 1922 translation of selected passages from Gertrude Stein's *The Making of Americans*. The preface begins with the following two sentences:

Je ne sais pas l'anglais.

Je ne sais pas l'anglais mais j'ai traduit lettre par lettre et virgule par virgule.

Immediately I felt that I was being given both the start of a poem (poem as natural home of Monsieur, or is it Madame, Paradoxe) and its essential prose-poetry cadence, one that would carry me through to the end, though I couldn't of course envision that end. The 'war' mentioned is our renewed bombing of Iraq, with the usual, tightly controlled images supplied to an ever-gullible and/or servile media. For the Antioch College 'protocol' (the 'Antioch Ruling') on sexual conduct, I am indebted to an anecdote in the novelist Siri Hustvedt's cogent and engaging essay, 'A Plea for Eros,' from her collection *Yonder* (Henry Holt, 1998). And so the hall of mirrors constructs itself, fragment by fragment, necessity and chance doing their dance."

CARL PHILLIPS was born in Everett, Washington, in 1959. He is the author of twelve books of poetry, most recently *Silverchest* (forthcoming from Farrar, Straus and Giroux, 2013) and *Double Shadow* (Farrar, Straus and Giroux, 2011), which won the *Los Angeles Times* Book Prize. He has received the Kingsley Tufts Poetry Award, the Thom Gunn Award for Gay Male Poetry, a Lambda Literary Award, and fellowships from the Guggenheim Foundation, the Academy of American Poets, and the Library of Congress. Phillips teaches at Washington University in St. Louis.

Of "Fretwork," Phillips writes: "When is enough enough? At that point when we realize that 'what will suffice' not only will, but may have to suffice? The body is restive, or I don't want it. Rough country. *Briar, clover, thorn—all three shall figure.* I woke with more or less those words in my head. Like waking from a mistake better off forgotten. I stayed in bed all morning, and wrote the poem. Unexpectedly, a love poem. And a valediction—briefly—to all the struggling against those parts of love that bring with them only peace."

ROBERT PINSKY was born in Long Branch, New Jersey, in 1940. His *Selected Poems* was published in paperback in March 2012 by Farrar, Straus and Giroux. His CD *PoemJazz,* with the pianist Laurence Hobgood, has been released by Circumstantial Productions. He has won the Italian Premio Capri, the Korean Manhae Prize, and the *Los Angeles Times* Book Prize for his best-selling translation *The Inferno of Dante.* He served as Poet Laureate of the United States from 1997 until 2000. He is also the author of several critical books (such as *The Situation of Poetry*, 1977), an interactive computer game (*Mindwheel*, 1984), and a prose book about King David (*The Life of David*, 2006). He lives in Cambridge, Massachusetts, and teaches in the MFA program at Boston University.

Pinsky writes: " 'Samurai Song' was inspired by a poem I heard read at one of the many Favorite Poem Project readings I have attended. The project, as well as the anthology *Americans' Favorite Poems* and the website at www.favoritepoem.org, has involved many readings in communities around the country. In Salina, Kansas, the readers, as I remember, included the mayor, some schoolchildren, and other citizens including a welder who read a fourteenth-century Japanese poem based on the formula 'When I . . . then I . . .'

"In the plane on the way back to Boston I kept thinking about the formula, and it evoked familiar, tangled memories of my mother's head injury, her persistent inner-ear problems, the years of disarray that required each member of the family to devise a kind of code for survival. I thought about how those years were my version of universal trials: loneliness and deprivation that in different ways and degrees are part of every life. I had always found this material difficult to write about without self-pity in one direction, or a kind of existential grandiloquence in the other. The Japanese formula, stylizing both directions, seemed to give me a way out of the clichés of personal narrative in poetry. So I stole the formula, and wrote the poem on my flight home."

CLAUDIA RANKINE was born in Kingston, Jamaica, in 1963. She is the author of four collections of poetry, including *Don't Let Me Be Lonely* (Graywolf Press, 2004); *PLOT* (Grove Press, 2001); *The End of the Alphabet* (Grove, 1998); and *Nothing in Nature is Private* (1994), which received the Cleveland State University Poetry Prize. She has edited (with Juliana Spahr) *American Women Poets in the 21st Century: Where Lyric Meets Language* (Wesleyan University Press, 2002) and (with Lisa Sewell) *American Poets in the 21st Century: The New Poetics* (Wesleyan, 2007). Her other works include *Provenance of Beauty: A South Bronx Travelogue*, commissioned by the Foundry Theatre, and *Existing Conditions*, written jointly with Casey Llewellyn. She has also produced a number of videos in collaboration with John Lucas, including "Situation One." A recipient of fellowships from the Academy of American Poets and the National Endowment for the Arts, she is the Henry G. Lee Professor of English at Pomona College.

Rankine writes: "Katie Couric of the *Today* show on NBC interviewed a doctor who argued that women were intended to have children and that, because more and more women were choosing not to have them, all kinds of things were going awry in their bodies. He contended that a childless woman should stay on birth control pills all the time, including the week she normally bleeds. I forget now what this was supposed to achieve. Another doctor—Doctor Love from Santa Cruz perhaps, beamed into the studio via satellite—was outraged. This five-minute interview remained with me in the form of a warning to those women and had something to do with my writing 'A short narrative of breasts and wombs.'"

ADRIENNE RICH was born in Baltimore, Maryland, in 1929. She went to Radcliffe College. In 1951, the year she graduated, W. H. Auden chose her book *A Change of World* for the Yale Series of Younger Poets. In the 1960s, her poetry underwent a signal change; she outgrew her attachment to traditional formal structures and became increasingly committed to political and feminist causes. From 1984 until her death on March 27, 2012, she lived in California. She published more than twenty collections of poetry and several books of nonfiction prose, and achieved an international reputation. She received a MacArthur Fellowship, the Dorothea Tanning Prize from the Academy of American Poets, and the Ruth Lilly Poetry Prize. Her recent books, all from W. W. Norton, include *Midnight Salvage: Poems 1995–1998* (1999), *Arts of the Possible: Essays and Conversations* (2000), *Fox: Poems 1998–2000* (2001),*The Fact of a Doorframe: Poems 1950–2001* (2002), *A Human Eye: Essays on Art in Society, 1997–2008* (2009), and *Tonight No Poetry Will Serve: Poems 2007–2010* (2011).

David Lehman writes: "Rich was the guest editor of *The Best American Poetry 1996*. Her poems had been picked by Jorie Graham and Charles Simic, respectively, for the 1990 and 1992 books in the series, and when Adrienne and I corresponded on the latter occasion, it turned out that she admired the anthology and its aims and had very definite opinions on how to make it even better and more inclusive. I decided to ask her to serve as the guest editor of a volume and courted her to this end for more than a year before she accepted. I met with her in New York in September 1993 and we sealed the deal with a handshake.

"In *The Best American Poetry 1996,* Adrienne broke with precedent in more ways than one. She was the first editor to include more than one poem by a given poet. Her edition includes four poems by high school students and four poems by men and women incarcerated in prison. Reading for the anthology, she said, 'I always felt I was panning for gold.' Among the poems she wanted to include were several by authors that, in spite of our assiduousness, we (Maggie Nelson and I) failed to track down in that winter of 1995–1996 when email was still a novelty. Adrienne named the authors in her introduction to the volume, and eventually we heard from them. 'A poem often becomes a kind of commodity in the competitive world of curriculum vitae, though I deplore the fact,' she wrote to a disappointed poet. 'I would be very sorry if either this mischance, or your numerous recognitions, were to get between you and the life of poetry, which is an art, not a competition, an art demanding self-discipline and apprenticeship, often through very unencouraging circumstances, for stakes which have nothing to do with the market. I hope you will consider this, unfashionable idea though it is.'"

Of "Ends of the Earth," Rich wrote: "Writing in an artists' residence in New Mexico, in a season of high winds and forest fires, my predecessor in the house a photographer of extreme landscapes whom I had and have never met; spectral intimacy of solitude shared with absent presence—the roots of the poem."

DAVID RIVARD was born in Fall River, Massachusetts, in 1953. He is the author of five books of poetry: *Otherwise Elsewhere, Sugartown, Bewitched Playground, Wise Poison,* winner of the James Laughlin Award from the Academy of American Poets in 1996, and *Torque.* In 2006 he was awarded the O.B. Hardison Jr. Poetry Prize from the Folger Shakespeare Library in Washington, DC. He has won fellowships from the Guggenheim Foundation, the Civitella Ranieri Foundation, and the National Endowment for the Arts. He teaches in the MFA program at the University of New Hampshire.

Rivard writes: "'The Rev. Larry Love Is Dead' was one of the earliest poems written for my most recent book, *Sugartown.* Formally, I was interested in collaging together a set of image fragments, floating them along a line of highly enjambed syntax. I also wanted to have rhythmic resistances, catches, pauses to counterpoint the flow of the speech. The sound of the place where Issa meets George Oppen, if you will. The refrain in the first half of the poem is adapted from W. C. Williams.

"There was an actual Rev. Larry Love, a street character in Cambridge. Born Lawrence Hinkson, he had had a minor hit in the 1950s with a doo-wop band called the Lovenotes. In the early '90s, he would roller-skate between Harvard and Central Square, dressed in legwarmers, an orange crossing guard's vest or drum-major's jacket, a police hat, and sometimes (in my mind's eye, anyway) shorts and twirler's baton. Comically charming, cosmic and flirtatious, but with enough crankiness in him to guarantee that he was nobody's clown. He passed in 2001, a native of the old Cambridge (and a citizen of 'the old, weird America,' as Greil Marcus would say), a stranger in the culture of gentrified amnesia."

J. ALLYN ROSSER was born in Bethlehem, Pennsylvania, in 1957. Her most recent collection of poems is *Foiled Again*. She has received awards and fellowships from the Guggenheim Foundation, the Poetry Foundation, the Lannan Foundation, the National Endowment for the Arts, and the Ohio Arts Council. She teaches in the creative writing program at Ohio University and edits *New Ohio Review*.

Of "Discounting Lynn," Rosser writes: "People frequently confuse hover flies (diptera), which can't sting, with sweat bees (hymenoptera), because through Batesian mimicry hover flies manage to look more like honey bees than sweat bees do. So you, like the speaker, might have heard that sweat bees aren't really bees. They like to lick sweat from people; they are 'solitary'; the female makes its nest in the ground or in rotting wood, then lays an egg on a pollen ball, seals off the nest and forgets about it. This is not what one tends to think of as normal bee behavior. Nonetheless officially it is a bee, so the speaker, who in correcting herself mistakes the sweat bee for the hover fly commonly mistaken for the sweat bee, is even more confused than she supposes.

"I think of this poem as a kind of literary panic attack."

MARY RUEFLE was born in McKeesport, Pennsylvania, in 1952. Her latest book is *Madness, Rack, and Honey*, a collection of lectures on poetry (Wave Books, 2012). Her *Selected Poems* appeared in 2010. She has written a second book of prose, *The Most of It*. She is an artist who erases, treats, and extra-illustrates nineteenth-century books (maryruefle.com). She lives in Vermont.

Of "Middle School," Ruefle writes: "When I reread this poem, two lost memories return. Once I was watching an Italian film (whose name, sadly, I can't recall) and one of its scenes was shot in front of 'Cesare Pavese Middle School.' I loved that! It lodged in my mind long enough to appear in the poem. Another time I was in a Laundromat, staring at the floor. I found a wonderful object there, a little totem figure, a chieftain made entirely out of twist ties twisted together. I took this figure home and for a couple of years he sat on my desk until I gave him to a friend in need of such a thing. I would like to take this opportunity to divulge (now that no one cares) that my principal, in whose office I stood trembling many a time, was later arrested for shoplifting and lost his job. I imagine he must have fallen into a great depression, and come at last to understand those he shepherded. Let us hope."

KAY RYAN was born in California in 1945. She has published eight books of poetry, including *Flamingo Watching* (Copper Beech Press, 1994), and *Elephant Rocks* (1996), *Say Uncle* (2000), *The Niagara River* (2005), and *The Best of It: New and Selected Poems* (2010), all from Grove Press. *The Best of It* was awarded the Pulitzer Prize in 2011. She served as United States Poet Laureate from 2008 to 2010.

Of "Outsider Art," Ryan writes: "I had been looking at a big handsome book of American primitive art, and it dawned gradually and disagreeably upon me that I didn't like it. The work of these isolates felt urgent and obsessed, squeezing me out. I almost never describe actual things in poems and the fact that I have here just goes to show how invaded I felt by this stuff. I don't even want to think about whether they're my spiritual cousins."

MICHAEL RYAN was born in St. Louis in 1946. He is the author of five books of poems, an autobiography, a memoir, and a collection of essays about poetry and writing. He has won the Lenore Marshall Poetry Prize and the Kingsley Tufts Poetry Award. He is director of the MFA program in poetry at the University of California, Irvine, where he lives with his wife and daughter.

Of "Switchblade," Ryan writes: "We tell one another hundreds of stories every day, some more important than others. I'm very interested in how they're shaped, what they do, and why we need them. 'Switchblade' tells part of a story that's important to me, but if it has any significance beyond that it's because of its music: the moment-to-moment manifold relationships of stress, phrasing, and varieties of rhyme to one another and to the syntax of the sentences and to their meaning. I think the most articulate thing you can say about a poem is the way that you read it, and I write my poems to be experienced, to be voiced and heard, so I hope anyone who likes 'Switchblade' will read it aloud."

JAMES SCHUYLER (1923–1991) was born in Chicago, Illinois. His books of poems include *Freely Espousing* (1969), *The Crystal Lithium* (1972), *Hymn to Life* (1974), *The Morning of the Poem* (1980), and *A Few Days* (1985). *The Morning of the Poem* received the Pulitzer Prize. Farrar, Straus and Giroux published both his *Collected Poems* and *Selected Poems*. A mainstay of the New York School of poets, Schuyler collaborated with John Ashbery on a novel (*A Nest of Ninnies*) and was coeditor of *Locus Solus* magazine. Like an expert draftsman who with three or four strokes can suggest a human face, Schuyler wrote "skinny poems"—pastoral in setting, exact in description, terse in expression—that can bring a landscape to life. In other poems, such as the title poem of *A Few Days,* Schuyler favored a conversational style and brought a touching intimacy and exuberance to the depiction of the erotic life. In his novels (such as *Alfred and Guinevere*) and such stories as "Current Events" (in *Locus Solus*) and "Life, Death and Other Dreams" (in *The Paris Review*), he displayed a droll wit and irony that somehow accentuate an underlying tenderness. Selecting "Life, Death and Other Dreams" for *The Poet's Story* (1973), Howard Moss, the anthology's editor, wrote, "Using awareness of the medium in the medium itself can result in parody—like bad movie music signaling the action ahead—but in Mr. Schuyler's sad and funny story, I take it to be a form of ironic honesty, like saying 'Dear reader' to a reader one almost holds dear."

Of "Let's All Hear It for Mildred Bailey!" Schuyler noted: "Among the poems I've written since mid-'85 there are several about entertainers (Duke Ellington, Mildred Bailey, Brook Benton, Simone Signoret), but it wasn't a plan, or even new: 'Beautiful Funerals,' about Libby Holman and a lot of others, was written in '71."

LLOYD SCHWARTZ was born in Brooklyn, New York, in 1941. He is Frederick S. Troy Professor of English at the University of Massachusetts (Boston); he is also classical music editor of *The Boston Phoenix* and a regular commentator on music and the arts for NPR's *Fresh Air.* He is the author of three poetry collections: *These People* (Wesleyan University Press, 1981), and *Goodnight, Gracie* (1992) and *Cairo Traffic* (2000), both from the University of Chicago Press. He edited *Elizabeth Bishop and Her Art* (University of Michigan Press, 1983), *Elizabeth Bishop: Poems, Prose, and Letters* (Library of America, 2008), and *Elizabeth Bishop: Prose* (Farrar, Straus and Giroux, 2011). A three-time winner of ASCAP's Deems Taylor Award for his writing about music, he has also won grants and awards from the National Endowment for the Arts and the Poetry Society of America (for poetry), from the United States Information Agency (for his work on Elizabeth Bishop), and from the Amphion Foundation (for his writing on contemporary music). In 1994 he was awarded the Pulitzer Prize for his "skillful and resonant" music criticism.

"Pornography," Schwartz writes, "is under fire not only from the conservative right but also from the politically correct left. I've always found it fascinating—more often for what it reveals about the participants themselves than for its ability to stimulate the libido (although I'm not puritanical about the latter, either). When a friend of mine, a scholar of noncanonical nineteenth-century Americana, acquired an extensive collection of nineteenth- and early-twentieth-century 'French postcards,'

I was invited to look them over. Three of the images first touched and then haunted me. The figures seemed so convincing in their pleasure, yet so vulnerable. I couldn't get them out of my head. This was the last subject I expected to write a poem about. The year I won an NEA grant, I had to promise not to use it to 'promote, disseminate, or produce materials . . . which, when taken as a whole, do not have serious literary, artistic, political, or scientific value.' Although the poem was published several years after I made this promise, it remains my sincerest intention to comply with this stipulation—in all four categories."

FREDERICK SEIDEL was born in St. Louis, Missouri, in 1936. He attended Harvard College. His books include a trio—*The Cosmos Poems* (2001), *Life on Earth* (2001), and *Area Code 212* (2002)—that were published in a single volume, *The Cosmos Trilogy,* in 2003. Other collections include *Ooga-Booga* (2006) and, most recently, *Nice Weather* (2012). Since 1993 he has been published by Farrar, Straus and Giroux. In a profile of Seidel in *The New York Times Magazine* (April 12, 2009), Wyatt Mason reported that Seidel has been labeled "the Darth Vader of contemporary poetry," which Seidel chalks up to his "calmly unembarrassed tone while saying something 'unacceptable.'" He lives in New York City.

ALAN SHAPIRO was born in Boston, Massachusetts, in 1952. He is the William R. Kenan Jr. Distinguished Professor of English at the University of Carolina at Chapel Hill. His books include *Tantalus in Love* (Houghton Mifflin, 2005) and *Old War,* from the same publisher three years later. Two books were published in 2012: *Night of the Republic* (Houghton Mifflin), poems, and *Broadway Baby* (Algonquin), a novel.
    Shapiro writes: "'Country Western Singer' is from the title sequence of my book *Old War,* which attempts to imagine the last thoughts (not the last words) of a variety of characters and speakers (everyone from the president to the pronoun *I*). The title of each poem identifies the speaker. For each speaker, I choose a different verse form and idiom expressive of his or her or its particular character and situation. In this poem, written as a song, or ballad, a country western singer is dying of alcohol poisoning. It's meant to be a profoundly affectionate parody of a genre of music I love."

CHARLES SIMIC is a poet, essayist, and translator. He was born in Yugoslavia in 1938 and immigrated to the United States in 1954. His first poems were published in 1959, when he was twenty-one. In 1961 he was drafted into the U.S. Army, and in 1966 he earned his bachelor's degree from New York University while working at night to cover the cost of tuition. Since 1967, he has published twenty books of his own poetry, seven books of essays, a memoir, and numerous translations of French, Serbian, Croatian, Macedonian, and Slovenian poetry. He has received many literary awards, including the Pulitzer Prize, the Griffin Prize, the MacArthur Fellowship, and the Wallace Stevens Award. His recent collections of poems are *The Voice at 3:00 A.M.* (Harcourt, 2003), *That Little Something* (Harcourt, 2009), and *Master of Disguises* (Harcourt, 2010). Simic is an emeritus professor at the University of New Hampshire, where he has taught since 1973. He was the Poet Laureate of the United States from 2007 to 2008. He had two other books in 2009, *The Renegade* (George Braziller, Inc.) and *The Monster Loves His Labyrinth* (Copper Canyon Press), selections from notebooks.

Simic was the guest editor of *The Best American Poetry 1992*. In the introduction he wrote, "Just when everything else seems to be going to hell in America, poetry is doing fine. The predictions of its demise, about which we read often, are plain wrong, just as most of the intellectual prophecies in our century have been wrong. Poetry proves again and again that any single overall theory of anything doesn't work. Poetry is always the cat concert under the window of the room in which the official version of reality is being written."

Of "Country Fair," Simic writes: "I witnessed this scene in the mid-1970s at the nearby fair in Deerfield, New Hampshire. What a life, I thought at the time. It's not enough to have six legs, they want you to do tricks, too.

"Then it occurred to me. That's what a poet is: a six-legged dog."

TOM SLEIGH was born in Mount Pleasant, Texas, in 1953. He is the author of eight books of poetry, including *Army Cats* (Graywolf Press, 2012) and *Space Walk*, which won the $100,000 Kingsley Tufts Award in 2008. He has also received the Shelley Prize from the Poetry Society of America, the John Updike Award from the American Academy of Arts and Letters, and a Guggenheim Fellowship. In fall 2011 he was the Anna-Maria Kellen Fellow at the American Academy in Berlin. He teaches in the MFA Program at Hunter College and lives in Brooklyn, New York.

Of "At the Pool," Sleigh writes: "If you're a committed swimmer, one day you'll find yourself swimming long distances in open water—one of my favorite swims takes me from the lighthouse at Long Point clear across the bay of Provincetown harbor, about a mile and a half. Most times, though, I swim in public pools where light scattering across the pool bottom and the way the acoustics distort sound can give the pool an otherwordly quality—not quite an underworld, but like one. I remember meeting an older friend by accident in the pool and thinking how odd our bodies looked, buoyant and heavy at the same time.

"And so in the poem the contrasts between large and small, between heavy and light, reveal the older man's body through shifts in scale. And the younger man, who hasn't yet learned that being old is as new to the old as being young is to the young, tries to comprehend the older man's loss—and discovers that loss is serial, not final: Eurydice glides away from Orpheus only when he turns to look at her, but comes speeding toward him just as soon as he turns away. The long lines and the way they break down the page are in flux, too; the syntax can't resolve into certainty. At the bottom of the pool is time and the end of time: and on the surface is the way time seems to stretch out and out, even as it's coming to an end."

GARY SNYDER was born in San Francisco, California, in 1930. As a youth in the Pacific Northwest, he worked on the family farm and seasonally in the woods. He graduated from Reed College in Portland, Oregon, in 1951. After a semester of graduate study in linguistics at Indiana University, he returned west to attend graduate school at Berkeley in the department of East Asian languages. In the Bay Area, he associated with Kenneth Rexroth, Robert Duncan, Philip Whalen, Allen Ginsberg, Jack Kerouac, and others who were part of the remarkable flowering of West Coast poetry during the fifties. In 1956 he moved to Kyoto, Japan, to study Zen Buddhism and East Asian culture. He has eighteen books of poetry and prose in print. *Turtle Island* (New Directions, 1974) won the Pulitzer Prize for Poetry in 1975, and his book-length poem *Mountains and Rivers Without End* (Counterpoint Press, 1996) won the Bollingen Prize. His recent publications include *Danger on Peaks* (Counterpoint, 2005), *Back on the Fire,* a volume of prose essays (Counterpoint, 2007), *The High Sierra of California,* with prints by Tom Killion (Heyday Press, 2002), and *The Selected Letters of Allen Ginsberg and Gary Snyder* (Counterpoint, 2008). From 1986 until 2002, he taught part-time at the University of California, Davis, in the creative writing and the "Nature and Culture" programs.

A. E. STALLINGS was born in 1968 and studied classics at the University of Georgia and Oxford University. Her first poetry collection, *Archaic Smile,* was chosen by Dana Gioia for the Richard Wilbur Award and was published by the University of Evansville Press (1999). *Hapax* was published by Northwestern University Press in 2006. She has also published a verse translation of Lucretius, *The Nature of Things* (2007). She is a 2011 Guggenheim Fellow and a 2011 MacArthur Fellow. She lives in Athens, Greece.

Of "Asphodel," she writes: "As the epigraph suggests, the poem was triggered by a real moment and conversation, about which began to gather, in my memory, clusters of natural rhymes, and a shape. Our guide, a horsewoman involved in rescuing a native breed of Greek pony (the Skyros pony) from possible extinction, was broadly read, and an expert on local flora and fauna. Nymphaion is in the lush north of Greece, near the Albanian border. This area in no way resembles the Greece of postcards, the Peloponnese and the islands, with their familiar dust-silver olive groves, old women in black, and patient donkeys. The north is green, mountainous, and wild, still home to bears, eagles, wild boars, and wolves, the animals of Homeric similes.

"Some years back, in Atlanta, I was in a Greek reading group that was working through the Homeric Hymn to Demeter. In the opening scene, where Persephone and other nymphs are gathering flowers in a meadow, a number of flowers are named: the orchid, hyacinth, narcissus, iris, crocus, and others (this may not be exact, being from memory). And I made a comment at the time that perhaps this was to symbolize a golden age before seasons, when all flowers bloomed simultaneously; because I could not imagine them all in bloom together. At least in my garden, crocuses came up before narcissuses, and so on. But in these alpine meadows in the north of Greece, I saw all these things blooming together, wild. I was quite startled. But this goes to show that there is always a danger in doubting the literal truth of ancient poetry."

RUTH STONE was born in Roanoke, Virginia, on June 8, 1915. A beloved teacher at Binghamton University, she disproved the notion that a poet's powers decline with age. She won a Guggenheim Fellowship in 1975. She received national recognition for her books *Ordinary Words* (Paris Press, 1999) and *In the Next Galaxy* (Copper Canyon Press, 2002), both published after she turned eighty. She was eighty-seven when *In the Next Galaxy* won the National Book Award. Her later books include *In the Dark* (2004) and *What Love Comes To: New & Selected Poems* (2008), both from Copper Canyon Press. It has been said that the subject of much of her poetry is her widowhood: her second husband, the novelist Walter Stone, committed suicide in 1959. Bianca Stone, whose work was selected for *The Best American Poetry 2011,* points out that her grandmother "explored age and aging in her poems as much as she explored the death of her husband. And she was humorous, innovative, and wrote about science and the human condition." Ruth Stone won the Shelley Memorial Award, the National Book Critics Circle Award, a second Guggenheim Fellowship, and the Wallace Stevens Award from the Academy of American Poets. She lived in a farmhouse in Goshen, Vermont. She died on November 19, 2011, at the age of ninety-six.

MARK STRAND was born in Summerside, Prince Edward Island, Canada, in 1934. His father was an executive with Pepsi-Cola and the family traveled widely. Strand went to Antioch College and then to Yale, where he studied painting with Josef Albers; he has continued to make prints, etchings, and collages, and to write about art and photography. His books of poetry include *Reasons for Moving* (1968), *Elegy for My Father* (1978), *The Continuous Life* (1990), *Dark Harbor* (1993), and *Blizzard of One* (1998), which won the Pulitzer Prize. He has held a MacArthur Foundation Fellowship and has served as United States Poet Laureate from 1990 to 1991. He has taught at the University of Utah, The Johns Hopkins University, the University of Chicago, and Columbia University. *Almost Invisible,* a book of prose poems, appeared from Alfred A. Knopf in 2012.

Strand was the guest editor of *The Best American Poetry 1991.* In the introduction he wrote, "Poetry is language performing at its most beguiling and seductive while being, at the same time, elusive, even seeming to mock one's desire for reduction, for plain and available order. It is not just that various meanings are preferable to a single dominant meaning; it may be that something beyond 'meaning' is being communicated, something that originated not with the poet but in the first dim light of language, in some period of 'beforeness.' It may be, therefore, that reading poetry is often a search for the unknown. Something that lies at the heart of experience but cannot be pointed out without being altered or diminished—something that nevertheless can be contained so that it is not so terrifying."

Strand writes: "*Dark Harbor* is a long poem in forty-five sections. When I sent out the sections for magazine publication, I sent them out in groups of three, not believing at the time that the single sections could stand on their own. Sometimes they were titled, but most often they were called 'from *Dark Harbor.*' Though grouped together for the purpose of magazine publication, the sections are not necessarily together in the long poem, that is, they are taken from different parts of it. The principle by which I grouped them was simply whether or not they seemed right together."

PAMELA SUTTON was born in Ypsilanti, Michigan, in 1960. She holds an MS in journalism from Northwestern University and an MA in creative writing from Boston University, where she was awarded the George Starbuck Fellowship. She taught writing at the University of Pennsylvania for seven years. At present she lives on Marco Island, Florida, which she calls "the land of Hemingway."

Of "Forty," Sutton writes: "Not long after I wrote that poem, I left my job as an editor for Lippincott, America's oldest publishing company, and began teaching writing at the University of Pennsylvania. I entitled my first class 'Writing as Journey.' It was an unconscious choice that the book to which all the other books in that class were hinged was Elie Wiesel's *Night*. As the years and semesters passed, that book became increasingly difficult to teach even as it grew in importance. I write this as an unorthodox Christian at heart: if anyone ever rose from the dead, physically, spiritually, and psychologically, it was Elie Wiesel. If we're looking for heroes in a disturbing cycle of history, look no further than Elie Wiesel. I never attended one of his lectures while I was a graduate student at Boston University because I was not ready to confront the Holocaust. I was not Jewish, though I absorbed an enormous love of Judaism, having lived in the Netherlands in my twenties. I lived just down the street from the Portuguese Synagogue on Jodensbreestraat, and visited often, always knocked flat by its beauty. And emptiness. Also, as I spelunked into the depths of European history I could only conclude that the Jews shaped Europe into an intellectual and economic powerhouse, and Europe killed them for it. It was a thought I filed away for twenty years until 9/11.

"I became a very different person that day: my English, Irish, and American Indian ancestors rose to the surface and stayed, particularly the latter. On an invisible dimension of time, someone plunged a spear through my back, hurling me off my horse where I landed on the muddy shore of Manhattan. I pulled the spear out of my back, closed my eyes, and drew my bloody fingers down my face, then opened my eyes to a changed world. I am newly dead and newly alive as I attempt to protect my child from Neo-anti-Semitism, while simultaneously teaching her to rejoice in her heritage. She is half-Jewish. Her father is Jewish. I did not think 9/11 could possibly hurt more until Daniel Pearl uttered the words: 'My mother is Jewish,' before terrorists severed his noble and beautiful throat.

"Knowing that his wife was Dutch and expecting their first child multiplied the pain. I wish someone would acknowledge that, as a journalist, he was hot on the trail of bin Laden during an administration that had zero intention of catching bin Laden. Clue: he was not in Iraq.

"I wrote the poem from the steps of Independence Square Park. And

I wrote it almost unconsciously, and in a visceral state of rage. Numbers infuriated me: they can be boring and random, or they can alter history. Like all good journalists, I checked the facts: there are exactly '123 trees in Independence Square Park.' There are 260 colors in the '100 thousand fragments of glass in the Parrish-Tiffany Mosaic'—a hypnotizing mosaic, which is emblematic of the vision quest that transforms the meaning of numbers in the poem. Pointillist details of nature create a hallucinatory state confounding numbers: 'hawk perched on the weathervane'; 'trees, inhaling, exhaling light'; 'carrying my grandmother in my arms and she weighs exactly the same as my child: One beloved child.' I am carrying both history and the future in my arms.

"I refer to America as Rome because, though flawed, America's government is a descendent of Rome. I equate al-Qaeda with Visigoths because their actions have been so hideously barbaric. And I point to the Colossus of Rhodes, because our Statue of Liberty was sculpted by Auguste Bartholdi to resemble the ancient Greek's Colossus. That it is a 'Colossus consecrated to the sun' evokes both the sacred and time itself.

"At the beginning of the poem I am running on a treadmill to pass the time on my lunch hour. At the end of the poem I am desperately running to reverse time."

JAMES TATE was born in Kansas City, Missouri, in 1943. His newest book is *The Ghost Soldiers* (Ecco/HarperCollins, 2008). He teaches in the MFA Program for Poets and Writers at the University of Massachusetts, Amherst. He has won the Pulitzer Prize and the National Book Award.

Tate was the guest editor of *The Best American Poetry 1997*. In his introduction to that volume he wrote, "In my experience, poets are not different from other people. You have your dullards, your maniacs, your mild eccentrics, etc. Except for this one thing they do—write poems. And in this they are singularly strange. They may end up with an audience and a following of some sort, but in truth they write their poems with various degrees of obsessiveness mostly for themselves, for the pleasure and satisfaction it gives them. And for the hunger and need nothing else can abate."

Tate writes: " 'Bounden Duty' is based on a true incident. I had first met President Clinton when he was still in high school. His girlfriend had dragged him to a poetry reading I was giving in Little Rock. I met them and chatted with them briefly at the party afterward. I was struck by the force of his personality: I think her name was Gigi. Years later, I was one of many poets invited to the White House. The president acted as if we were old friends. I was flattered, but also suspicious. Several months later I got the call. He still sends me Christmas cards, but I fear that I let him down in some small way."

NATASHA TRETHEWEY was born in Gulfport, Mississippi, in 1966. She is the author of *Beyond Katrina: A Meditation on the Mississippi Gulf Coast* (University of Georgia Press, 2010) and four collections of poetry, *Domestic Work* (Graywolf Press, 2000), *Bellocq's Ophelia* (Graywolf, 2002), *Native Guard* (Houghton Mifflin Harcourt, 2006), and *Thrall* (Houghton Mifflin, 2012). *Native Guard* was awarded the Pulitzer Prize. She has received National Endowment for the Arts, Guggenheim, Bunting, and Rockefeller Fellowships. She is a professor of English at Emory University and was named United States Poet Laureate in 2012.

Of "Elegy," Trethewey writes: "A few years ago my father and I took a trip to his native Canada to go salmon fishing in New Brunswick on the Miramichi River. He is also a poet, and among the poems he has written about me is one that includes another river we visited when I was a small child in Mississippi."

PAUL VIOLI was born in New York City in 1944 and grew up in Greenlawn, Long Island. He went to Boston University and served in the Peace Corps. He made maps in uncharted regions of northern Nigeria and traveled through Africa, Europe, and Asia. Upon returning to New York he worked for WCBS-TV News and was managing editor of *Architectural Forum*. He met Charles North in a writing class taught by Tony Towle and the three poets became fast friends. Violi's books include *In Baltic Circles* (Kulchur Foundation, 1973; rpt. H_NGM_N BKS, 2012); *Splurge* (Sun, 1982); *Likewise* (Hanging Loose Press, 1988); *Breakers* (Coffee House Press, 2000); *Overnight* (Hanging Loose, 2007); and *Scramble and Glide* (forthcoming from Hanging Loose). *Selected Accidents, Pointless Anecdotes*, a prose collection, was released by Hanging Loose in 2002. His work appears in *The Oxford Book of American Poetry, Great American Prose Poems*, Paul Hoover's *Postmodern American Poetry*, four volumes in *The Best American Poetry* series, and other anthologies. Asked to pick a favorite erotic poem, Violi chose Andrew Marvell's "To His Coy Mistress": "It's so full of life, it reads like a short play, a dramatized syllogism, wildly passionate and irrefutably logical. Witty, allusive, intimate, sexy, playful, serious, intense—the tonal shifts, imagery, and sheer artistry are stunning. Ornithologists are not convinced that mating eagles clutch, tumble, and cannonball down the sky, but I still think Marvell got it right." Violi taught in The New School Writing Program, at Columbia University, and at New York University. He lived with his wife in Putnam Valley, New York. In January 2011 he was diagnosed with pancreatic cancer, and he died on April 2, 2011.

Of "Counterman," Violi wrote: "I can't think of anything to say about the poem itself, so, for what it's worth, I'll resort to recounting what set it off. I'd come across a notebook entry where I'd been playing around with the tempo and diction of a deli counter dialogue. I hadn't read it in about half a year and didn't think I'd make anything more out of it, but then two incidents clicked in. One was recent. I'd walked into an SRO deli on West 3rd Street in Manhattan and heard a customer with a very heavy brogue present the following syllogism to a stolid Mexican counterman: 'So you've never been to Ireland then. So you don't know what you're talking about then. So you should shut your mouth then.' They stared at each other in a very hard way and everyone was tense. Then they both cracked up laughing. Apparently this was a little routine they did every day. The other incident occurred in a Hoboken deli more than twenty years before that. A taciturn, solemn counterman took my order and proceeded to fill it with great care and deliberation that seemed to say that each and every sandwich he made was The Perfect Sandwich. He said not a word and served it with an attitude that was a blend of dignity and disdain. Anyway, even though the poem doesn't retain the tone of either of those recollections, once they came into play I quickly added the second interchange to the notebook dialogue."

ROSANNA WARREN was born in Fairfield, Connecticut, in 1953. She received a BA in painting and comparative literature from Yale University, and an MA in creative writing from The Johns Hopkins University. Her recent books include *Ghost in a Red Hat* (poems, 2011), *Fables of the Self: Studies in Lyric Poetry* (criticism, 2008), and *Departure* (poems, 2003), all from W. W. Norton. With Stephen Scully she published a verse translation of the Euripides play *Suppliant Women* (Oxford University Press, 1995). She has received awards from the Academy of American Poets, the American Academy of Arts and Letters, the Lila Wallace–Reader's Digest Foundation, and the New England Poetry Club. She was a chancellor of the Academy of American Poets from 1999 to 2005.

Of "Necrophiliac," Warren writes: "As the plangencies accumulated in my new manuscript of poems, I became suspicious of my own elegiac impulse. The Shakespearean sonnet (deformed here) came to hand, unpremeditated, as a shape into which rage, love, and writerly anxiety were accustomed to being compressed. 'Collaborate' is meant, of course, to spread its stain throughout the poem."

RACHEL WETZSTEON was born in New York City in 1967. She earned a bachelor's degree from Yale, a master's from Johns Hopkins, and a PhD from Columbia. She taught at the Unterberg Poetry Center of the 92nd Street Y and at William Paterson University. Her books of poetry are *The Other Stars* (Penguin, 1994), *Home and Away* (Penguin, 1998), *Sakura Park* (Persea, 2006), and *Silver Roses* (Persea, 2011). She also wrote a critical study entitled *Influential Ghosts: A Study of Auden's Sources* (Routledge, 2007). Wetzsteon took her life in late December 2009. At the time of her death, she had recently been appointed poetry editor of *The New Republic*. In an obituary, the magazine reprinted her poem "Short Ode to Morningside Heights," which ends with this stanza:

> Ranters, racers, help me remember
> that the moon-faced fountain's the work of many hands,
> that people linger at Toast long after we've left.
> And as two parks frame the neighborhood—
> green framing gray and space calming clamor—
> be for me, well-worn streets, a context
> I can't help carrying home, a night fugue
> streaming over my one-note *how, when, why.*
> Be the rain for my barren indoor cry.

SUSAN WHEELER was born in Pittsburgh, Pennsylvania, in 1955. She grew up mostly in Minnesota and has lived in or near New York since 1985. She is on the faculty of Princeton University, where she directs the creative writing program. The recipient of a Guggenheim Fellowship and the Witter Bynner Prize for Poetry from the American Academy of Arts and Letters, she has taught at Columbia University, the University of Iowa Writers' Workshop, The New School, and New York University. Her poetry collections include *Bag 'o' Diamonds* (University of Georgia Press, 1993), *Smokes* (Four Way Books, 1998), *Source Codes* (Salt Publishing, 2001), *Ledger* (University of Iowa Press, 2005), *Assorted Poems* (Farrar, Straus and Giroux, 2009), and *Meme* (University of Iowa Press, 2012). She is also the author of a novel, *Record Palace* (Graywolf Press, 2005).

Wheeler writes: " 'A Filial Republic' was written during my first visit to the Southwest. The disparate lives of Mexican Catholics (many of them Penitentes) and the white New Age spiritualists around Taos (and the significant economic gaps between the two), as well as an emphasis on isolation and 'the view,' challenged my ideas of personal responsibility and faith, and the poem resulted. It was cast as an echoing response to Alvin Feinman's poem 'November Sunday Morning,' which in an early version ended, 'I sit / And smoke, and linger out desire.' (In the recent Princeton edition of his *Poems,* he adds a final stanza.) 'A Filial Republic' is dedicated to Alvin."

RICHARD WILBUR was born in New York City in 1921 and grew up on a large farm in New Jersey. His father was a portrait painter, and his mother came from a long line of journalists. A graduate of Amherst College (class of '42), he served during World War II with the 36th Infantry Division. Having taught at Harvard, Wellesley, Wesleyan, and Smith, he now co-teaches once a week at Amherst. With his late wife, Charlotte, he lived year-round in Cummington, Massachusetts (which is still his home), and spent many springs in Key West, Florida. His latest book of verse is *Anterooms* (Houghton Mifflin Harcourt, 2010); his *Collected Poems 1943–2004* appeared from Harcourt in 2004. He has won two Pulitzers. He wrote the lyrics for Leonard Bernstein's *Candide,* and his translations from seventeenth-century French drama (Molière, Racine, Corneille) are performed here and abroad. His several books for children have amused some adults.

Of "This Pleasing Anxious Being," Wilbur writes: "I think that people resist as long as they can a full sense of the world's change and of their own aging. At last, when a certain number of irreplaceable people are gone, and the home place has been razed, and one is the only rememberer of certain things, the gut acknowledges what the mind has always thought it knew. That is the source of this poem, which moves both back and forward in time, and considers time in a number of perspectives. The title is taken from the twenty-second stanza of Gray's 'Elegy.'"

C. K. WILLIAMS was born in Newark, New Jersey, in 1936. His most recent book of poems is *Writers Writing Dying* (Farrar, Straus and Giroux, 2012). He is also the author of *Collected Poems* (2006) and *Wait* (2010), from the same publisher. *On Whitman,* a prose study, was published by Princeton University Press in 2010. He has recently published two children's books, *How the Nobble Was Finally Found,* and *A Not Scary Story About Big Scary Things,* both from Houghton Mifflin Harcourt. He won the Pulitzer Prize in 2000 for *Repair.* He teaches at Princeton University.

Of "A Hundred Bones," Williams writes: "I've become fascinated by how many moments of time are in us at once: our own experience, present and past, our imaginings, our reading, our history, our long-gone emotions and thoughts. When I thought that I'd lived through World War II, even though I was very young, I decided to try to account for how much of that period was still within me, and how it had resonated through the rest of my personal and creative life.

"I'd also long loved Bashō's statement about poetry, which is worth quoting in its entirety:

In this mortal frame of mine, which is made of a hundred bones and nine orifices, there is something, and this something can be called, for lack of a better name, a windswept spirit, for it is much like thin drapery that is torn and swept away by the slightest stirring of the wind. This something in me took to writing poetry years ago, merely to amuse itself at first, but finally making it its lifelong business. It must be admitted, however, that there were times when it sank into such dejection that it was almost ready to drop its pursuit, or again times when it was so puffed up with pride that it exulted in vain victories over others. Indeed, ever since it began to write poetry, it has never found peace with itself, always wavering between doubts of one kind or another. At one time it wanted to gain security by entering the service of a court, at another it wished to measure the depth of its ignorance by trying to be a scholar, but it was prevented from either by its unquenchable love of poetry. The fact is, it knows no other art than the art of writing poetry, and therefore it hangs on to it more or less blindly.

"'A Hundred Bones' grew from all this."

ANNE WINTERS was born in St. Paul in 1939. She is the author of *The Key to the City* (University of Chicago Press, 1986) and *The Displaced of Capital* (University of Chicago, 2004), which received the William Carlos Williams Award and the Lenore Marshall Poetry Prize. Her translations from the French include *Salamander: Selected Poems of Robert Marteau* (Princeton University Press, 1979), which won *Poetry* magazine's Glatstein Award. She has traveled widely in Europe and was a resident fellow at the Camargo Foundation in the south of France. She has received grants from the Ingram-Merrill Foundation, the National Endowment for the Arts, a Guggenheim Fellowship, and an award in literature from the American Academy of Arts and Letters. She has taught at Bennington College and most recently at the University of Illinois, Chicago.

Of "The Mill-Race," Winters writes: "When I was about twenty I worked as a typist in an import-export firm on Whitehall Street near the Battery in Manhattan, and recently I went back down there around quitting time. It must be the world's densest concentration of office workers, mainly women, and when they all come down into the streets, ferries, buses, and subways at once, you feel both the force of their numbers, and thousands of signs of individuation that struggle against the deformations of training a life against this work world. Later I was curious about the hundreds of drivers and unmarked cars massed below the skyscrapers; a driver explained they were prepaid by firms to take executives home."

CHARLES WRIGHT was born in Pickwick Dam, Tennessee, in 1935. Educated at Davidson College, he served in the army for four years, then attended the University of Iowa Writers' Workshop. He lectured at the universities of Rome and Padua under the Fulbright program. He has received fellowships from the National Endowment for the Arts and the Guggenheim Foundation and won a PEN award for his translation of Eugenio Montale's *The Storm and Other Things*. From 1966 to 1983 he taught at the University of California, Irvine. A longtime professor of English at the University of Virginia at Charlottesville, he received the Lenore Marshall Poetry Prize for his book *Chickamauga* (1995). *Black Zodiac* (Farrar, Straus and Giroux, 1997) won the *Los Angeles Times* Book Prize, the National Book Critics Circle Award in poetry, and the Pulitzer Prize. *Appalachia* (Farrar, Straus and Giroux) appeared in 1998. *Scar Tissue* won the Griffin International Poetry Prize in 2009. *Bye-and-Bye: Selected Late Poems* appeared from Farrar, Straus and Giroux in 2011.

Wright was the guest editor of *The Best American Poetry 2008*. In his introduction to the volume, he wrote: "Poems are merely foot movements in a larger dance." He also quoted Saisho: "Before I began studying Zen, I saw mountains as mountains, rivers as rivers. When I learned some Zen, mountains ceased to be mountains, rivers to be rivers. But now, when I have understood Zen, I am in accord with myself and again I see mountains as mountains, rivers as rivers."

Wright says: " 'American Twilight' is one of a series of poems leading up to the end of a book—and leading up to the final diminshment of everything. *Appalachia* should have been a Paradiso but it turned out to be a Book of the Dead. The character has come to the end of things, is about to enter the other side of things, and the speaker in the book is trying to help him along by whispering in his ear, as you do in a Book of the Dead."

FRANZ WRIGHT was born in Vienna, Austria, in 1953. He grew up in the Pacific Northwest, the Midwest, and California. He received the 2004 Pulitzer Prize for *Walking to Martha's Vineyard* (Alfred A. Knopf, 2003). Other books include *Ill Lit: Selected & New Poems* (Oberlin College Press,

1998), *God's Silence* (Knopf, 2006), and *Kindertotenwald,* a book of prose poems (Knopf, 2001). He lives in Waltham, Massachusetts.

Wright recalls that he wrote "A Happy Thought" when he was "dying of loneliness in Fayetteville, Arkansas, where I lived for a semester, spring '04. Then I won a certain award, very well known, three weeks before leaving town, and they basically showered me with rose petals as I drove away, everyone's best friend! Strangest thing!" In the note accompanying the poem in *The Best American Poetry 2006,* Wright wrote: "This poem was written very quickly, in a half hour or so (unlike most of my poems, which generally take weeks, months, or years to finish)—perhaps because I noticed right away that the lines were presenting themselves in a more or less iambic manner and that the whole feel of the poem, spatially, in its particular rhymes or off-rhymes and the semi-repetition of lines bore some distant resemblance to the villanelle. So once that was established, and I had a rough sense of how long the poem should be, I was able to proceed in an improvisatory way, and after producing several variants to recognize the one that was most successful in terms of both music and sense."

ROBERT WRIGLEY was born in 1951 in East St. Louis, Illinois, and grew up not far away, in Collinsville, a coal-mining town. Since 1974 he has lived in the West, mostly in northern Idaho, where he directs the graduate writing program at the University of Idaho. He is the author of several books of poems, including *Anatomy of Melancholy and Other Poems* (Penguin, 2013). His previous collections include *Beautiful Country* (2010), *Earthly Meditations: New and Selected Poems* (2006), *Lives of the Animals* (2003), *Reign of Snakes* (1999), and *In the Bank of Beautiful Sins* (1995), all from Penguin. He lives with his wife, the writer Kim Barnes, in the woods near Moscow, Idaho.

Of "Religion," Wrigley writes: "I remember hearing the late William Stafford say, with a wry tone in his voice and a half-smile on his face, that 'the hardest thing in the world to write about is a dead dog,' and although it has taken me too many decades to learn my hard lesson, I am now able to avoid conversations about religion at dinner parties. Which is to say, I'm still extremely fond of dogs, especially those one might refer to as 'faithful.'"

C. DALE YOUNG was born in 1969 and grew up in the Caribbean and South Florida. He was educated at Boston College (BS 1991) and the University of Florida (MFA 1993, MD 1997). He is the author of *The Day Underneath the Day* (Northwestern University Press, 2001), *The Second Person,* and

Torn (Four Way Books, 2007 and 2011). He practices medicine full-time, edits poetry for the *New England Review,* and teaches in the Warren Wilson MFA Program for Writers. A 2012 Poetry Fellow of the John Simon Guggenheim Memorial Foundation, he lives in San Francisco with his spouse, the biologist and classical music composer Jacob Bertrand.

Young writes: " 'Vespers' holds as its genesis a postcard, a photograph I saw at an exhibit on South America, calligraphy, and something I heard my mother say when I was young. The postcard had young girls washing clothes in a river; the photograph, a woman swinging a man's shirt up into the air. The calligraphy was from my sophomore year in high school. My mother's statement: 'There are few things more sobering than the icy water of a river at sunrise.' The poem began the way many of my poems do, with the realization that two things were related (related in my mind at least). And so when I saw that photograph and noticed how the woman's arms resembled the chancery *f*s I had learned in calligraphy, I somehow remembered the postcard, and then there was little I could do to stop the poem. It devoured my Catholic-school guilt, the Crusades, rose-apple blossoms, even the word 'benediction.' Though this may seem odd to some, I have met several poets in the past few years who also give themselves over to this junk shop method of composition."

DEAN YOUNG was born in Columbia, Pennsylvania, in 1955. He has published nine books of poems, including *embryoyo* (Believer Books, 2007) and *Primitive Mentor* (University of Pittsburgh Press, 2008). He has taught at the University of Iowa Writers' Workshop and has received an award in literature from the American Academy of Arts and Letters ("so he tells everyone he got an Academy Award"). He teaches at the University of Texas, Austin, where he occupies the William Livingston Chair of Poetry. A book of outbursts and rambling poetics, *The Art of Recklessness,* appeared from Graywolf Press in 2010. His most recent books are *Fall Higher* and *Bender: New and Selected Poems,* both from Copper Canyon Press.

Of "No Forgiveness Ode," Young writes: "This poem always spooked me a little. Essentially it began as a rhyming list but it seems to develop a more central concern which I'd just as soon know nothing about. Well, as I've said to my students, the imagination is the highest accomplishment of consciousness and empathy is the highest accomplishment of the imagination."

KEVIN YOUNG was born in Lincoln, Nebraska, in 1970, but left before he was one and hasn't made it back. He did root for the Cornhuskers for much of his childhood. His first book, *Most Way Home* (William Morrow, 1995), won a National Poetry Series competition and the Zacharis First Book Award from *Ploughshares;* his third book, *Jelly Roll: A Blues* (Alfred A. Knopf, 2003), won the Paterson Poetry Prize; his most recent book is *Dear Darkness* (Knopf, 2008). Young has edited *The Art of Losing: Poems of Grief and Healing,* an anthology of contemporary elegies (Bloomsbury USA, 2009). He is the Atticus Haygood Professor of Creative Writing and English and curator of Literary Collections and the Raymond Danowski Poetry Library at Emory University.

Young was the guest editor of *The Best American Poetry 2011.* In his introduction he wrote: "Even in the long poem the lyric seems to reign. After the narrative 1990s in which 'reality' became a story to be scripted on television or otherwise, the current writers of the lyric seem to insist on its flexibility, on their ability to take from any source to find their own manifold music." Young also commented on the number of fine elegies ("Our age seems to be an elegiac one") and sonnets he encountered. "The sonnet, like the McRib, is back. As 'little songs,' sonnets prove both compact yet ambitious, which may provide a sense of why many writers have turned to them to evoke our moment."

Young writes: "The poem 'Lime Light Blues' seeks what all good blues seek: laughing to keep from crying. And maybe even to get you to dance a little. Or at least sway some."

ACKNOWLEDGMENTS

The series editor thanks Mark Bibbins and Stephanie Paterik for their invaluable assistance. Warm thanks go also to John Ashbery, Donald Hall, Stacey Harwood, and Ron Horning; to Glen Hartley and Lynn Chu of Writers' Representatives; and to my editor, Alexis Gargagliano, and her colleagues at Scribner, including Susan Moldow, Nan Graham, Daniel Cuddy, Erich Hobbing, Kelsey Smith, Gwyneth Stansfield, and David Stanford Burr.

Grateful acknowledgment is made of the publications in which these poems first appeared. A sincere attempt has been made to locate all copyright holders. Unless otherwise noted, copyright to the poems is held by the individual poets.

Sherman Alexie, "Terminal Nostalgia." Reprinted with the permission of the poet.

A. R. Ammons, "Garbage" (Sections I–V) from *Garbage*. Copyright © 1993 by A. R. Ammons. Used by permission of W. W. Norton & Co.

Rae Armantrout, "Soft Money" from *Money Shot*. Copyright © 2011 by Rae Armantrout. Reprinted by permission of Wesleyan University Press.

John Ashbery, "Wakefulness." Copyright © 1997 by John Ashbery. Reprinted by arrangement with Georges Borchardt, Inc., for the author.

Margaret Atwood, "Bored" from *Morning in the Burned House*. Copyright © 1995 by Margaret Atwood. Reprinted by permission of Houghton Mifflin Harcourt Publishing Company. All rights reserved.

Frank Bidart, "Injunction" from *Star Dust*. Copyright © 2005 by Frank Bidart. Reprinted by permission of Farrar, Straus and Giroux.

Stephanie Brown, "Feminine Intuition." Reprinted with the permission of the poet.

Charles Bukowski, "Three Oranges" from *OnTheBus* (1992). Reprinted with the permission of Linda Lee Bukowski.

Anne Carson, "The Life of Towns" from *Plainwater*. Copyright © 1995 by Anne Carson. Used by permission of Alfred A. Knopf, a division of Random House, Inc.

Henri Cole, "Self-Portrait as Four Styles of Pompeian Wall Painting"